A mon cher
Haskell —
compagne et fréret
Bee
16 juillet 78

COMPARATIVE LITERATURE AS ACADEMIC DISCIPLINE

A Statement of Principles,
Praxis, Standards

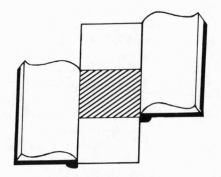

This volume was written with the assistance of a grant from
the Humanities Council of New York University

Previous Books by the Author

Critical Theory and Practice of the Pléiade
Cambridge: Harvard University Press, 1942
Revised edition, New York: Octagon Books, 1968
The Teaching of French and Spanish
University Park: Pennsylvania State University, Extension Division, 1954
Platonism in French Renaissance Poetry, with R. V. Merrill
New York: New York University Press, 1957
Revised edition, New York: Octagon Books, 1970
The Peregrine Muse: Studies in Comparative Renaissance Literature
Chapel Hill: University of North Carolina Press, 1969
Enlarged revision, 1969
Picta Poesis: Humanistic and Literary Theory in Renaissance Emblem Books
Rome: Edizioni di Storia e Letteratura, 1960
Michelangelo's Theory of Art
New York: New York University Press, 1961
Zurich: Buehler Buchdruck, 1961
London: Routledge and Kegan Paul, 1962
New York: Gramercy Press, 1963
Michelangelo: A Self-Portrait
New York: Prentice-Hall, 1963
Michelangelo Scultore, with Eugenio Battisti
Rome: Curcio, 1963
American Critical Essays on the Divine Comedy
New York: New York University Press, 1966
London: University of London Press, 1967
The Poetry of Michelangelo
New York: New York University Press, 1965
London: Peter Owen, 1966
Italian version contracted by Mondadori
The National Book Award Reader, editor
New York: Popular Library, 1966
Michelangelo: Le Idee sull'arte
Milan: Alberto Mondadori, 1967
Michelangelo: A Self-Portrait, revised, annotated edition with plates
New York: New York University Press, 1968
London: University of London Press, 1968
Directions of Literary Criticism in the 1970s (colloquium)
Cincinnati: University of Cincinnati Press, 1971
Renaissance Letters: Revelations of a World Reborn,
edited with Introductions, Commentaries, Notes, and Translations;
with Lorna Levant Clements
New York: New York University Press, 1976
*Anatomy of the Novella: The European Tale Collection from
Boccaccio and Chaucer to Cervantes*, with Joseph Gibaldi
New York: New York University Press, 1977

COMPARATIVE LITERATURE AS ACADEMIC DISCIPLINE

A Statement of Principles,

Praxis, Standards

ROBERT J. CLEMENTS

Chairman, Comparative Literature Department
New York University

The Modern Language Association of America

New York

ACKNOWLEDGMENTS

Educational Testing Service. Sample Questions: French, German, Spanish. Reprinted by permission of the Educational Testing Service from *A Description of the Graduate School Foreign Language Testing Program, 1976–77.* Copyright 1976. All rights reserved.

Review of the International Organization for Ancient Languages by Computer. "A Method of Structural Analysis with an Application to *Les Liaisons dangereuses,*" by Christiane and Claude Allais. Reprinted by permission of the publisher.

Albert Sonnenfeld. "A Comparative Poem." Reprinted by permission of the author from the *MLA Newsletter* (December 1975).

Alfred A. Knopf, Inc. "The River Back Home," by Te Hanh. Reprinted by permission of the publisher from *A Thousand Years of Vietnamese Poetry,* ed. and trans. Nguyen Ngoc Bich, with Burton Raffel and W. S. Merwin. Copyright 1967 by Asia Society, Inc.

New Yorker Magazine, Inc. "A Salute to the Modern Language Association Convening in the Hotel Pennsylvania, December 28th–30th," by Morris Bishop. Reprinted by permission of the publisher.

PEN American Center. *The Rights of the Translator* (1977 ed.). Reprinted by permission of PEN American Center.

Thomas Y. Crowell Co., Inc. Excerpt from Leo Tolstoy, *War and Peace,* trans. Constance Garnett. Reprinted by permission of the publisher.

Published by The Modern Language Association of America
62 Fifth Avenue, New York, New York 10011

DEDICATION

This volume is dedicated to the first generation of philosophiae
doctores *to emerge as comparatists at New York University and
who had a hand in working out the principles and practices advanced in this volume.*

1962–69: Joseph B. Cary, Arthur Kahn, Michael Anthonakes, Angela Belli, Kathleen McHugh, Frederick Benson, Yvonne
Rodax, Rose Maria Ferraro, Thomas Paruvanani, David Gershator, Fred Nichols, Ronald Christ, Nancy Cirillo, Richard
Neuville, Leslie Shepard, Sharon Spencer, Josephine Grieder

1970–74: Kenneth Harrow, Alice M. Farrell, Eugenie Harris,
David Leeming, Christopher Nash, Renata Weiss, Gloria
Orenstein, Marilyn Rosenthal, Ivan Sanders, Maria Crawford,
Haim Finkelstein, Michel Fougères, Paul Reisch, Joseph Gibaldi, Alfred Wolkowitz, Richard Fabrizio, Fred Heuman,
Madeleine Marshall, Carole Slade, John Friedman, Sung-Won
Ko, Eleanor Rowe, Roberta Bayer

1975–77: Sondra Heller, Milena Ebanks, Walter Eden, Flora Edwards, Theodore Hoen, Suzanne Killeen, Sonia Lee, Philip
Linker, Catherine Temerson, Patricia Kellogg, Rina Indictor,
Helen Pushchin, Berthold Ringeisen, Nomi Tamir, Adele
Barker, Gastone Cuffaro, Sheena Gillespie, Maria Anita Tannenbaum, Nicholas Carbo, Linda Stanley, John J. Lynch, Ana
María Hernández, Barbara Kaplan, Pearl Brandwein, Samuel
D. Wallace, Nora Glickman, Silvia Genske, Dorothy von
Huene, Wendy Deutelbaum, Nehama Aschkenazy

Contents

Figures:
Tables, Syllabi, Samples

Common Abbreviations

The following list includes several widely used abbreviations in the discipline of comparative literature. They will be adopted sparingly in this volume but should be familiar in any case to comparatists.

ACLA	American Comparative Literature Association
ACLS	American Council of Learned Societies
ASTP	Army Specialized Training Program
CATP	Civil Affairs Training Program
ETS	Educational Testing Service
FILLM	Fédération Internationale des Langues et Littératures Modernes
GSFLT	Graduate School Foreign Language Tests
ICLA	International Comparative Literature Association
MLA	Modern Language Association of America
NEH	National Endowment for the Humanities
PEN CLUB	Poets, Playwrights, Editors, Essayists, and Novelists Club
YCGL	*Yearbook of Comparative and General Literature*

Foreword to Teachers, Administrators, and Students

Grande serait l'erreur de juger de la littérature comparée par les inévitables défauts pratiques de son enseignement.
Claude Pichois and André Rousseau, *La Littérature comparée*

One warm evening during the reception of the 1976 meeting of the International Association of Italian Language and Letters (AISLLI) in Palermo, I was enjoying an after-dinner brandy with a new acquaintance, a British professor of English at the University of Zurich. At a certain point he posed the familiar question. "I say, you're in comparative literature, aren't you? Just what do you do? I judge it means studying the influence of French authors on the English and vice versa—English authors on the French. Right?"

I gazed for a moment at my inquisitive British colleague, brandy snifter in his hand, and began an informal clarification on just what comparative literature is, if not the influence of French and English writers on one another. I had to answer in as informal a manner as possible. Since Englishmen are notoriously modest, I had to avoid any suggestion of the elitist view expressed in an ACLA report that our discipline "required harder work and longer study than those of neighboring departments." I began, "Let me assure you at the outset that we comparatists do not pretend a knowledge of what the French call *littérature universelle*. We don't know everything about everything. What we do know are a few approaches to literature in the Western tradition—mainly through theme, form, or movement, and a couple of interrelations—and the books that best illustrate these.

As it turns out, these works tend almost of necessity to be major works of major writers. If the theme is Faustus, then we are dealing with major writers from Marlowe to Mann. If the form is comedy, then we're limited to the major comedians from Aristophanes, Plautus, Machiavelli, Shakespeare, Lope, to Wilde, Shaw, or Ionesco."

"I see," said my new friend. "Then if it's romanticism, you chaps give them Rousseau, Goethe, Shelley, Pushkin, and so on."

"Exactly. Happily our syllabi are restricted to what are sometimes called the Great Books. It's not like the old traditional Ph.D. in—let us say—French, which required that you know Vauvenargues, Loti, Sardou, and the like. Despite the overwhelming title of our discipline, the number of books our candidates must read is not out of line with the number students must read for degrees in your English or French department."

"You're telling me, I take it, that you don't learn less and less about more and more, although I suppose you might accuse our students of learning more and more about less and less."

"Maybe so. I suppose that your monographic courses could be so defined. Yet we wish our students to have the special training and experience offered by the monographic courses the English or French or German departments offer. That is why we legislate in our department that every M.A. candidate must take two or three of his eight required courses for the M.A. in a national literature department or departments. Of the eighteen courses required for our Ph.D., candidates must take seven or eight in other literature or thesis-related courses. We even suggest that our candidates take one or two of the narrowest monographic courses—even on single authors or single works, like those on Vergil, Cervantes, Dante, Shakespeare, Mann, or Proust."

"The question occurs to me: if the monographic courses are so useful to your students, why don't you offer a few in your comparative literature department?"

"The question seems logical. Obviously, some of the older generation of comparative literature professors who obtained their doctorates in a single-literature department before retooling and branching out for comparative literature did write and defend narrow, monoglottal theses and were originally specialists in Shakespeare or James or Mallarmé—to recall the first books of several now distinguished comparatists. The fact remains that so much coverage of periods and areas is required of the small number of actual courses budgeted under comparative literature that no financial provision is left for the monographic courses. In any case, the monographic course has its logical *droit de séjour* in the single-literature department, and its best practitioners are usually found therein."

Either satisfied with my summary reply, or perhaps wearied by it, my new British friend nodded politely and thanked me. If he had learned anything, it was that discussing comparative literature in vacuo, if that is the way to characterize a nonacademic or theoretical context, is easier for a literary historian or theoretician than for those comparative literature chairmen plunging their *mains sales* into the day-by-day administration, budgeting, and politicking required by literature departments.

Such summary and informal clarifications of comparative literature on my part, offered in discussions and conversations in which I have participated over the past few decades, have formed in large part the motivation behind the writing of this book.

The aphorism *habent sua fata libelli* implied among other things that certain books could wait no longer to be written. Comparative literature as an ideal has by now won over most of the doubters and become a permanent fixture of many college and university curricula. As is obvious from the several bibliographies now available, keen minds have devoted over a century to analyzing what Baldensperger called "le nom et la chose." But like any broad intercultural, interdisciplinary subject in the university curriculum, it has not found its universally accepted norms. In neighboring universities there will be honest divergences of opinion about the conduct of this discipline. Some will even state that one could never bridle Pegasus, let alone saddle him. They sense a difficulty in trying to establish fixed principles, policies, and practices. They quote Harry Levin's presidential remark after his American Comparative Literature Association (ACLA) Committee on Professional Standards had issued its first report, to the effect that it was henceforth time to get on with the comparing of literature. Yet the two reports of that committee (1965, 1976), which competently defined the academic parameters of comparative literature, the relations of comparative literature with its cooperating departments of literature, the setting of objectives, the importance of foreign languages, and so on, aimed at establishing standards rather than providing optimum procedures for organizing, administering, and teaching in a department of comparative literature. The reports stress the need of harmony and cooperation between comparative literature and the national literature departments without specifying in detail the potentials for harmony or disharmony.

After over a quarter century of administrative experience in comparative literature, this writer believes that there are now identifiable principles and practices that have worked well and have led to efficient and qualitative operation, which everyone, including critics, expects of our discipline. The reader will understand that I am setting up an optimum set of principles and practices; these need not be prescriptive and may not be always feasible, but they have grown out of experience in three universities. In the revival of comparative literature at Harvard Harry Levin invited me to play a modest role in the planning and to teach a graduate course during the first year of that revival. While chairman of Romance languages at Pennsylvania State University, I cooperated with Philip Shelley in creating a doctoral program in comparative literature. In 1954 I became the first (and thus far only) chairman of the discipline at New York University. Thus I have had three decades of trial and error out of which the suggested principles and praxis in the following pages have evolved.

This book, therefore, is intended to be what has long been needed in the field but has not as yet been available: a sustained exposition of the principles, practices, and standards of comparative literature. The volume's first two chapters on the origins, definitions, and dimensions of the discipline provide the necessary background to the ensuing discussion. The third, fourth, and fifth chapters address some of the more important questions of establishing and maintaining a department of comparative literature: staffing, budgeting, selecting students, setting up a curriculum, and instituting the foreign language requirement. The next six chapters are devoted specifically to the teaching of comparative literature. Chapters vi through x deal with the major comparative approaches—genres and forms, periods and movements, themes, interrelations of literature, and literary history and criticism—and discuss courses appropriate to each. These are followed by a general chapter on teaching, textbooks, and examinations. Chapter xii treats the subject of the thesis. The sensitive issue of the evaluation of comparative literature departments and programs is presented in Chapter xiii. A chapter on academic diplomacy and politics is followed by our concluding chapter on the future of the discipline. An appendix on the organizational structure of the discipline, a bibliography, and an index round out the book.

The volume is making an appearance at a time when a few comparative literature departments have foundered for lack of guiding principles and dedication to them, one such disappearance having occurred on the home campus of a major state university in the East. With the resurgence of the state, city, or professional evaluation committees, principles and procedures are being examined more critically from inside as well as outside. There have been many new recent converts and transfers to the burgeoning comparative literature departments and programs who have not had specific preparation or indoctrination in our field. Even in 1976 the ACLA Committee on Professional Standards decried in print the widespread "confusion about the nature of our discipline." There has been discussion in the upper echelons of the ACLA about setting up NEH-subsidized seminars to help the new recruits adapt to the specific methods and administrative routines of comparative literature. It is for this new group as well as for specifically trained teachers and students that this volume is intended. Since there is at present much concern over the evaluation of comparative literature programs and variance concerning the standards and criteria of judgment (see Ch. xiii), it is hoped that this volume will contribute largely to the resolution of the problem. It is even to be hoped that university administrators might leaf through these pages and understand better the necessary autonomy and financial needs of our discipline. Without adequate subsidy a principled, uncompromising administration of comparative literature is not possible.

Administrators will doubtless find interest in those sections of the book that deal with establishing program standards, creating courses, and avoiding interdepartmental rivalry, not to mention those concerning the staffing, budgeting, and evaluating of comparative literature departments. Teachers may find useful not only the chapter on teaching (Ch. xi) but also the various syllabi, checklists, and surveys of textbooks that are scattered throughout the volume. The book is also intended for the future comparatist: the present student of comparative literature.

As perhaps too amply shown below, it is difficult for a student of the humanities during this late century to count many blessings. Yet we may unashamedly repeat to the student of literature what Gargantua said to his son Pantagruel: "Le temps n'estoit tant idoine ne commode ès lettres comme est de présent." For students now have the option of studying literature in its broadest dimensions, both in its thrust across the multicolored patches of our *mappa mundi* and in its extensions into other disciplines already sampled in school. Indeed the present generation can study literature as an intercultural, interdisciplinary program in which finally, as the scientists would say, the kinks are being hammered out. Still flexible enough to allow for further experimentation or perfection, comparative literature is now settling into its final method and structure.

Students of comparative literature will probably find particular interest in the sections on the selection and evaluation of students (in Ch. iii), the foreign language requirement (Ch. v), examinations (Ch. xi), the term paper and the thesis (Ch. xii), the choice of a program (Ch. xiii), student participation in departmental decision making (Ch. xiv), and postdoctoral concerns: scholarly publishing and vocational opportunities (Ch. xv). Finally, those students "on the brink," who are still debating over the celestial manna and worthy learning (as Rabelais put it) that awaits them, would do well to read all the following chapters, which should provide some objective answers needed for their important decision.

Pedagogical writing incubates and encourages a certain dryness and stolidity of style. Because of a sense of collegiality that I feel between myself and the reader, whether professor or student, I shall try to avoid such a style. I have written my share of books, but this one for the first time will carry almost no footnotes. (Most books or authors that I refer to are listed in the Bibliography.) This decision is made in a further endeavor to avoid a pedantic tone.

Although the suggestions below are largely based on my own observations and experiences, many colleagues have helped shape this book. I wish to thank Haskell Block and Frederick Garber of ACLA for providing me with materials, reports, and statistics, as well as colleagues in other universities who have provided me with information, syllabi, and catalog materials. My colleagues Owen Aldridge, Leland Chambers, W. Bernard Fleischmann, Frederick Garber, Fred Nichols, Stephen Nichols, and Carol Slade have generously read the book script and suggested useful additions and revisions. Foremost among my colleagues during months of composition, rewriting, and preparing the book script for printing has been Professor Joseph Gibaldi of the MLA, always encouraging and helpful, whose many counsels helped to shape the final version of this volume. I am most grateful to the editors of the *Yearbook of Comparative and General Literature*, Werner Friederich and Horst Frenz, for the useful information it has provided. Equally informative have been the following five committee reports of considerable importance, often quoted throughout the present volume:

ACLA Committee on Professional Standards, Report I (1965): Harry Levin (Harvard), chairman; A. O. Aldridge (Illinois), Chandler Beall (Oregon), Haskell Block (Delaware), Ralph Freedman (Princeton), Frederick Garber (SUNY-Binghamton), Horst Frenz (Indiana), J. C. La Drière (Harvard), Alain Renoir (California-Berkeley), and René Wellek (Yale).

ACLA Committee on Professional Standards, Report II (1976–77): Thomas Greene (Yale), chairman; Haskell Block (Delaware), Nan Carpenter (Georgia), François Jost (Illinois), Walter Kaiser (Harvard), Elizabeth Trahan (Monterey Institute, California), and Herbert Weisinger (SUNY-Stony Brook).

ACLA Committee on Graduate Programs, Report I (1974): Eugene H. Falk (North Carolina), chairman; Konrad Bieber (Connecticut College), Phillip Damon (Stanford), A. Bartlett Giamatti (Yale), Gayatri Spivak (Iowa), Ulrich Weisstein (Indiana).

ACLA Committee on the Undergraduate Curriculum (1974): Stephen Nichols (Dartmouth), chairman; Cyrus Hamlin (Toronto), Ulrich Goldsmith (Colorado), Eva Maria Stadler (Fordham), Rose Migliaccio (Wisconsin).

ACLA Committee on Professional Opportunities, Interim Report (1974): Leland H. Chambers (Denver), coordinator.

In addition to the distinguished colleagues who have kindly examined this book script, I thank my fellow NYU chairmen

James Tuttleton, Doris Guilloton, John A. Coleman, Lionel Casson, Robert Fowkes, and the many others for their generous and patient cooperation over the years with an underbudgeted comparative literature department. I add gratitude to my friend and colleague Anna Balakian, who has served as chairman during my semester sabbatical during which most of these pages were written. And I cannot forget Margaret E. Foley, our department's administrative secretary and Ph.D. candidate comparatist herself, who will one day administer a department better than any of us. She and Maria Gawrilowa have proposed many useful suggestions and additions in these pages from the graduate student's viewpoint. I am grateful to the Humanities Council of New York University and the Mellon Fund for a grant-in-aid in support of this book. Finally, the many names in the Index—not only of individuals but even of universities whose bulletins have taught me much—are evidence that my original purpose of leaving in these pages a personal testament was, fortunately, impossible of achievement.

And to my wife Lorna, an English scholar who gently corrects my Shakespeare quotations, I echo the sentiments of *Twelfth Night* III.iii.14–15.

R. J. C.
Teakettle Spout Lake, Mahopac, New York

COMPARATIVE LITERATURE AS ACADEMIC DISCIPLINE

A Statement of Principles, Praxis, Standards

I

Origins and Definitions of Comparative Literature

Comparative Literature sometimes figures in university curricula, but very few people know what they mean by the term or approach it with a considered, conscious method.

EZRA POUND, *Literary Essays* (1954)

Introduction

Comparative literature as an academic discipline, which is our chief interest in the present volume, has been distinguished by various manifestations of literary cosmopolitanism in diverse ages of the past. The eventual, meaningful status of comparatism in the schools of America and Europe has been achieved only recently after the mid-century. Of the period during the first half century, when comparative literature was seeking a method and an identity, Urban T. Holmes once observed: "The primroses along the path have been rather bright and distracting." The present writer contributed to the issue of the *Proceedings of the ICLA Congress* at Chapel Hill in 1958 the article "Pegasus or Clavileño," in which he worried that "administrative experience shows us comparative literature all too willing to wend its quixotic way and to take its own shortcuts once embarked on the royal road. The one advantage Clavileño had over Pegasus was a greater propensity for keeping its feet on the ground." Both then and now, newly constituted and reconstituted programs have needed to be not only founded on principle, but constantly checked to see if they continue to conform with principle.

Others besides Ezra Pound have questioned our definitions and methods.[1] Indeed, misconceptions and honest confusions about our discipline exist even among our most learned colleagues. Whereas it is not surprising when someone outside the field cannot grasp the nature—and demands—of comparative literature, it does surprise when our own partisans refuse to grasp it. One thinks of Henry Gifford in England, whose *Comparative Literature* (see Bibliography) states, "Comparative Literature cannot pretend to be a discipline on its own. . . . Rather, it is an area of interest." Or Herbert Weisinger, in his preface to Étiemble's *Crisis in Comparative Literature*: "There is no agreement as to what it is, except that it is a good thing. . . . Its tutelary gods then are Procrustes, the divinity of narrow definition, and Proteus, the ruler of amorphous shapes." Yet before we respond to such voices by attempting to define and describe comparative literature, it is essential for us first to consider in brief, summary fashion the historical development of the discipline to our age.

The Historical Rise of Comparative Literature

The act of comparing national literatures originated long before it became a science or discipline governed by principle and method. There were for example Babylonian-Hellenistic specialists like Berossos and Phoenician-Hellenists like Philon of Byblos who were versed in two literatures and wrote about them. Myths paired literatures, and the same fictional world inundation appeared in the literatures of Babylonia, Greece, and Judea. The mythographers were busily comparing texts from various areas and creating their own tribal mythic heroes out of earlier tales: Sargon breeds Moses, Moses breeds Karna, Karna makes Oedipus

---

[1] There is no lack of bromides about comparative literature. When Herbert West taught at Dartmouth, the story goes, he was approached by Dylan Thomas, who asked him aggressively, "And what do you teach?" To the answer "comparative literature," Dylan rejoined as if in triumph, "Ah! And to what do you compare it?" In Harry Levin's ACLA Presidential Address of 1968, Dylan is quoted as responding with a blunt "monosyllabic suggestion." Many of us have also heard of the story reported by Antonio Regalado of NYU. Regalado dreamed that Professors Levin and Poggioli came to visit him but were stopped in the lobby by a suspicious superintendent. Regalado went down and, noting that the two professors were in overalls, reassured the super that these were indeed the men who had come to "compare the literature." Finally, to show that pioneers everywhere are the object of irony or skepticism, Pichois and Rousseau note in their lively manual of comparative literature that since some French *facultés* still use the plural form of the discipline, wags often inquire derisively of its registrants, "Quelles littératures comparez-vous?"

possible, and so on through the concatenation that Otto Rank established for us. Perseus and Andromeda evolve into Saint George and his rescued maiden. Horace, "the little Greek pig," bade Roman writers to leaf through Greek manuscripts by day and by night, urging those who liked Vergil to compare him to Homer, those who liked Plautus to measure him against Aristophanes. As Frank Chandler reminds us in the 1966 *Yearbook of Comparative and General Literature* (*YCGL*), Macrobius and Aulus Gellius were early comparatists, evaluating Roman poets with their Greek prototypes or analogues. Each European *Sprachraum* rivaled the others with its own Tristan and its own Parsifal. Comparatism was thrust upon the scholars and poets of Europe, for example, by the Greco-Roman doctrine of imitation (including plagiarism), imposing comparisons and influence studies. Later, the comparison of classical and modern works of literature exploded in a vigorous if prejudiced campaign culminating in the Querelle des Anciens et des Modernes. Whereas Ronsard in a preface had once commanded his epic poem to acknowledge the superiority of the *Iliad* ("A genoux, Franciade, adore l'Iliade!"), exactly one hundred years later the French Academy applauded the contrary decision:

> Je peux lire les Anciens sans plier les genoux,
> Ils sont grands, il est vrai, mais hommes comme nous.

Afterward comparative studies could not always award the palm to antiquity, and the French kings' control of literature brought chauvinism with it. Fortunately in 1832, well after the fall of the Ancien Régime, Jean-Jacques Ampère condemned chauvinism as incompatible with literary cosmopolitanism, although it remained a hydra difficult to dispatch, as French historians of comparative literature acknowledge.

Many were the isolated Europeans who pioneered in amateurish fashion the challenging game of cosmopolitanism, confronting authors, works, or literatures. Chief among these were Herder, Goethe, Lessing, Mme de Staël, the Schlegels, Henry Hallam, and Sismondi. Between 1828 and 1840 the Sorbonne professor Abel-François Villemain not only employed the term "comparative literature" in his writings, but led the pack by offering course work in this discipline. The influential Sainte-Beuve legitimized the term in the *Revue des deux mondes* (itself a comparative title) and his *Nouveaux lundis*, to be followed by an international company including Louis Betz, Max Koch, Joseph Texte, Longfellow, Georg Brandes, and others. In Italy Mazzini's *Scritti* (1865–67) declared that no literature could be nurtured by itself or could escape the influence of alien literatures.

René Wellek believes that the first occurrence of the coinage "vergleichende Literaturgeschichte" was in Moriz Carrière's book of 1854, *Das Wesen und die Formen der Poesie*. By 1886 Hutcheson Posnett, a professor of English at Auckland, New Zealand, wrote a book bearing the title *Comparative Literature*. As Ulrich Weisstein writes, it was the first comprehensive methodological survey of the field so labeled, in any language. His approach was that of a specialist in the history of science or even sociology, and he "confessed a desire to see the study less exclusively in the hands of literary men." Again he writes, "We therefore adopt, with a modification hereafter to be noticed, the gradual expansion of social life, from clan to city, from city to nation, from both of these to cosmopolitan humanity, as the proper order of our studies in comparative literature" (Weisstein, pp. 222–25). Surely, a critical date for our study was 1897, the year that marked the major bibliography compiled by the zealous Louis Betz. Its 1904 edition contained 6,000 entries. This pioneer work, which contributed much to the evolving definition of comparative literature, formed the basis for a sequel, the *Bibliography of Comparative Literature* by Fernand Baldensperger and Werner Friederich (1950), the work that inaugurated the modern age of comparative literature bibliography.

Comparative Literature Defined and Described

With some history behind us, we are able to address ourselves to a series of formal definitions of comparative literature articulated by some of its major proponents in America and Europe.

After the maturation of comparative literature during the first half of the present century, a new intensified effort was made to define in simple terms the nature and significance of our discipline. Some contemporary definitions of recent gestation follow from five works of wide circulation.

Comparative Literature is the history of international literary relations. The comparatist stands at the frontiers, linguistic or national, and surveys the exchanges of themes, ideas, books, or feelings between two or several literatures. His working method will adapt itself to the diversity of his researches. A certain equipment is indispensable to him. He must be informed of the literatures of several countries. He must read several languages. He must know where to find the indispensable bibliographies.

> MARIUS-FRANÇOIS GUYARD, *La Littérature comparée*, pp. 12–13 (slightly condensed in translation)

It is now generally agreed that comparative literature does not compare national literatures in the sense of setting one against the other. Instead, it provides a method of broadening one's perspective in the approach to single works of literature—a way of looking beyond the narrow boundaries of national frontiers in order to discern trends and movements in various national cultures and to see the relations between literature and other spheres of human activity. . . . Briefly defined, comparative literature can be considered the study of any literary phenomenon from the perspective of more than one national literature or in conjunction with another intellectual discipline or even several.

> A. OWEN ALDRIDGE, in *Comparative Literature: Matter and Method*, p. 1

Comparative Literature is the study of literature beyond the confines of one particular country and the study of the relationships between literature on one hand and other areas of knowledge and belief, such as the (fine) arts, philosophy, history, the social sciences, the sciences, religion, etc. on the other. In brief it is the comparison of one literature with another or others, and the comparison of literature with other spheres of human expression.

> HENRY REMAK, in *Comparative Literature: Method and Perspective*, p. 1

Western Literature forms a historical community of national literatures, which manifests itself in each of them. Each lyrical, epic, or dramatic text, no matter what its individual features, was drawn in part from common material, and in that way both confirms this community and perpetuates it. For the creator of works of literary art, literature from both the past and the present forms the main ideational and formal context within which he works. Literary movements and literary criticism also document this basic unity of Western Literature. Comparative Literature is based on this view of Western Literature. It is by viewing objects of literary research—texts, genres, movements, criticism—in their international perspectives that it contributes to the knowledge of literature.

> JAN BRANDT CORSTIUS, *Introduction to the Study of Literature*, p. v

Professors Pichois of Basel and Rousseau of Aix admit in *La Littérature comparée* a penchant, one toward philosophy and the other toward history, which infuses their definition "so lapidary as to figure in a repertory."

> Comparative literature: analytical description, methodic and differential comparison; synthetic interpretation of interlinguistic or intercultural literary phenomena, through history, criticism, and philosophy, in order to understand better literature as a specific function of the human spirit. (p. 197)

Not as a definition of comparative literature, but as an incremental view of the dual nature of literary study (viz., the work itself and the principles and criteria that envelop it), we add an often quoted passage from Wellek and Warren's *Theory of Literature*:

> Within our "proper study," the distinctions between literary theory, criticism, and history are clearly the most important. There is, first, the distinction between a view of literature which sees it primarily as a series of works arranged in chronological order and as integral parts of the historical process. There is, then, the further distinction between the study of the principles and criteria of literature and the study of the concrete literary works of art, whether we study them in isolation or in a chronological series. It seems best to draw attention to these distinctions by describing as "literary theory" the study of the principles of literature, its categories, criteria, and the like, and differentiating studies of concrete works of art as either "literary criticism" (primarily static in approach) or "literary history."

These six recent quotations represent a whole catalog of similar statements concerning comparative literature as an art or a science. Although Guyard limits his remarks to the European heritage of literature, they tend to agree on the principles and methods of comparative literature and its involvement as a field of study and research with literary theory and criticism. There is little that anyone at this late date can contribute in the realm of definition.

I should like, however, to sum up and describe (not define) comparative literature as an academic discipline. Throughout the following pages this description will come into contact with definitions, of course, but the premises behind this volume must be stated in minimal form, to be explained and developed below. In the manner of the Renaissance philosophical tables, I shall describe the divisions and dimensions of our discipline—an area in which there is still something to contribute as more and more colleges and universities initiate comparative literature.

The basic premises of Guyard, Corstius, Remak, and Aldridge are all acceptable. Within these definitions five approaches to literature impose themselves: the study of (1) themes/myths, (2) genres/forms, (3) movements/eras, (4) interrelations of literature with other arts and disciplines, and (5) the involvement of literature as illustrative of evolving literary theory and criticism. The reading of literature must be in the original language, in conformity with, and to the extent of, the language requirement. A seminar on the nature and methods of comparative literature and another on the history of literary theory and criticism must be incorporated into the curriculum.

The three major dimensions of comparative literature as presently practiced must be firmly understood and will occupy Chapter ii. The narrowest dimension is the Western Heritage and its traditional minimal components French-English, German-French, Latin-English, etc. This narrowest dimension, when restricted to only two authors or literatures within the Western Heritage, is to be discouraged at the level of academic discipline. The second dimension is East-West, an area in which some exploration has been undertaken. The third dimension is World Literature, a much abused term in America. These three dimensions are not static terms, not passively conjoined, but they must, as fiefs of comparative literature, follow the methodology of

Western Heritage comparative literature, utilizing the five approaches whenever possible to achieve meaningful comparison. It is of course logical to predict a future development of other dimensions than these three—conceivably Asian-African (Asian poets are now aware of the freedom movements in Africa, as demonstrated on p. 47), Western Heritage–African, or even an Eastern Heritage dimension within the vast continent of Asia itself, a development hindered by the particular language problems in Asia (see p. 33). As Pichois and Rousseau remind us, if our approaches and dimensions seem rigorously defined, our researches themselves offer great freedom.

All comparatists must surely be grateful to UNESCO for its effort to present a viable description of what goes on, or should go on, within comparative departments. Since UNESCO's *International Standard Classification of Education* (*ISCED*) (Paris, 1976) endeavors to summarize in three paragraphs the "Levels and Programs of Study" of our discipline—reducing the *Iliad ad nucem* as it were—it may be useful to quote them before embarking on a large and detailed volume on the subject. This statement in somewhat simplified form reads:

Programs in comparative literature generally require as a minimum prerequisite a secondary-level education and lead to the following degrees: Bachelor of Arts, Master of Arts, and the doctorate, or their equivalents. Programs consist primarily of classroom sessions, seminar, or group discussions, and research.

Programs that lead to a first university degree deal with the study of international literary and cultural relationships. Principal course content usually includes some of the following: the currency, reception, and influence of writers and their works in countries other than those of their origin; the transmission and evolution of international literary movements; the characteristics of and relationships between genres, themes, and motifs; folk literature and folklore; criticism; esthetics; intermediaries, and the relations between literatures, as well as those between literatures and the other disciplines. Background sources usually include history, the social and behavioral sciences, philosophy, religion and theology, and the natural sciences.

Programs that lead to a postgraduate university degree deal with the advanced study of international and cultural relations. Emphasis is given to research work as substantiated by the presentation of a scholarly thesis or dissertation. Principal subject matter areas into which courses and research projects tend to fall include the origin and evolution of international literary movements, folk literature and folklore, criticism, esthetics, intermediaries, epics and sagas, tragedy, comedy, modern dramas, the contemporary novel, problems of comparative literature, the comparative method in literary studies, the forces in contemporary literature, and research techniques in comparative literature.

This composite description of comparative literature as an academic discipline will do very well as a start. Since it is applicable to Europe as well as America, one notes a few points on which American practice may differ. The basic foreign language requirements are bypassed. The early French, Dutch, and Finnish stress on folklore study is reflected. The various dimensions (Western Heritage, East-West, World) of comparative literature are not specified. The fairly common American honors thesis for the B.A. is not mentioned. Yet all these matters will be dealt with at length in the pages to follow.

The Names of Comparative Literature

The importance of Betz's bibliography of 1896–97 was considerable, for it did much to establish the terminology of our discipline. Wellek's researches into the origins of this terminology have revealed the number of rival terms that persisted during the eighteenth and early nineteenth centuries: universal literature, international literature, general literature, world literature, comparative literature science, and so on. At least in French and English the term we use was eventually fixed once and for all. The European origins of comparative literature have been traced diligently by several European and American scholars, notably Baldensperger, Weisstein, and Wellek. The evolution toward a terminology satisfactory to all nationalities has understandably been a slow one.

As is further demonstrated in Chapter iii, the name of comparative literature has been elastic in its application. It is used for the study of one or more authors of one *Sprachraum* with one or more authors of another speech area, or one national literature with another. It is used for the study of individuals or literatures within a more encompassing Western Heritage dimension. It is used for authors or literatures within the East-West or, finally, global dimension. Other dimensions, as yet largely unexploited, are mentioned in the following chapter. As we know from some commercial anthologies, these terms may be rendered static by the mere chronological juxtaposing of texts, making no commitment to method as comparative literature does. To be truly precise, one should in our profession refer to Comparative Western Literature, Comparative East-West Literature, and so on. However, in an academic context these terms in their simpler form imply a methodology and thus meet reservations of Bataillon, Frye, and others (see p. 13) about the exact meaning or *engagement* implied in the word "comparative."

Let us pause over this nomenclature, which seems to trouble many or did so at least until the recent past. In Latin the word *comparativus* was used by Cicero, Quintilian, Gellius, and others as "pertaining to or depending on comparison," or denoting degree or the ablative case. The *Oxford English Dictionary* offers seven traditional meanings of this crucial adjective, other than the common and here irrelevant occurrence as the "comparative" degree of adjectives and adverbs. These include: of or pertaining to comparison; involving different branches of a study; estimated by comparison; quick at comparisons (cf. *Henry IV*: "Thou art indeed the most comparative rascalliest sweet young prince"); serving as a means of comparison; comparable or worthy to be compared; in competition or rivalry. As we mention elsewhere, eighteenth-century chauvinism seized upon this last meaning of the adjective. The old Hatzfeld-Darmsteter lexicon shows us that the adjective *comparé* in French was not recognized until the Academy accepted it in 1835, qualifying it then as a neologism. On the other hand the word *comparatif* was used as early as the fourteenth century, contrasted with *absolu*. We learn from Gregory Smith that by 1598 the adjective carried our modern meaning in a "Comparative Discourse of our English Poets with the Greek, Latin, and Italian Poets." The use of the past participle, indicating in European usage the study of literatures either already compared or being compared, was probably derived from the early use of *anatomie* or *philologie comparée*. The preference in English for *comparative* was obviously borrowed from the

Latin. The German adjective *vergleichend*, a present participle, beckons one to compare, collate, or even reconcile literature. It carries the strong suggestion of likening absent in other forms. The terms *sravnitelnoe literaturovedenie* in Russian and *srovna-vaci literatura* in Czech contain the several meanings in *vergleichende Literatur* of comparing, leveling, and equalizing.

Importantly, these verbal etyma, present or past participles, do imply an operation or process inherent in our discipline. This operation of comparing, leveling, equalizing, or contrasting by the juxtaposing of literatures is accomplished through the avenues of genres, movements, and themes particularly, as explained in Chapters vi, vii, and viii.

The East Asian terms are a compound essentially of two substantives. The Chinese *pi-chiao wên-hsüeh*, the Japanese *hikaku bungaku*, and the Korean *pigyo munhak* consist of "comparison" plus "literature." The terms thus denote, as Professor Won Ko informs me, the scientific comparison of two or more literatures without inclusion of adjectival modifiers. Perhaps if we followed suit and adopted the simple "literature comparison" we might eliminate a great deal of discussion.

In any case, now late in the twentieth century it is a fact of life that the often maligned term "comparative literature" is here to stay and that we must live with it. Indeed it has achieved a rank of distinction in many quarters—in the titles of many important literary journals and books (see Bibliography), a plethora of articles on every continent, and most college catalogs. (We leave for, respectively, Chapters ii and iv the subject of the often misused term "world literature," which is merely a dimension of the generic term "comparative literature" itself, and that of the term "comparative literature" applied to the undergraduate, as well as graduate, program.) We are further reassured by the fact that the National Endowment for the Humanities now makes specific provision for grants and seminars under the rubric of Comparative Literature.

Comparative and General Literature

A particular problem concerns the real or imagined distinctions between comparative literature and general literature. General literature had become a term current in England and Germany (as *allgemeine Literatur*) during the late eighteenth and early nineteenth centuries. Even today Oxford offers a B.Phil. in General and Comparative Literature, the compound name of our discipline also at the Sorbonne. General literature at the Sorbonne seems to feature forms, genres, techniques, and themes, while comparative literature stresses relationships of national literatures, evolutions, interpretations, parallels, ideological movements, and so on. Yet just as Lane Cooper had felt more comfortable with the amplitude of "the Comparative Study of Literature," the word "general," like "comparative," seemed to demand the further identification of study, history, research, or science. Wellek records that the German scholars Eichorn, Hartmann, Wachler, and Grässe entitled their studies *Allgemeine Geschichte der Literatur, Versuch einer allgemeinen Geschichte der Poesie, Lehrbuch einer allgemeinen Literargeschichte*. Wellek cites also the "Lectures on General Literature" (1833) of James Montgomery.

The required additional word to amplify the bare concept of comparative literature, as chosen by the German literary review *Arcadia*, is *Wissenschaft*, with its variant meanings of science, knowledge, learning, or scholarship, perhaps even "study" as used by Professor Cooper. This augmentative that seemed to be needed for its semantic breadth is still commonly used, and is incorporated into two of the leading European literary associations, the Deutsche Gesellschaft für Allgemeine und Vergleichende Literaturwissenschaft (Bonn) and the Nederlandse Vereniging voor Algemene Literatuurwetenschap (Utrecht). *Vergleichende Literaturwissenschaft* is offered in various ways at the University of Vienna, University of Innsbruck, Leopold-Franzens University, Westfälische Wilhelms University, and elsewhere. Similarly, the Japanese often add *kenyu* (research) to their standard name for our discipline, *hikaku bungaku*.

Actually, the discipline of comparative literature is all these things: a study, a history, a research, and if not indeed a science, surely unified by a method. If one will accept the meaning of "comparable; worthy or useful to be compared," a seventeenth-century usage mentioned by the *OED*, the need for augmentative terminology need not be felt necessary.

In a thoughtful 1976 presidential statement on the subject Haskell Block wrote:

> The distinctions of language and geography have needlessly complicated the problem of terminology. We do not speak of comparative music or comparative art, for in these instances the art addresses us in a universal language. Perhaps in time we shall speak of literature in the same broad and universal sense. The term "comparative"—in many ways a most ambiguous term—has the merit of drawing attention to the necessity of a broad perspective as a condition of literary study.

After reading an essay of Simon Jeune, he notes that while there is "no essential difference between 'general literature' and 'comparative literature,'" the adjective "general" might encourage the student "to move toward fresh critical interpretations," take fuller account of literary theory, and attempt to define the groundwork of literature and its essential characteristics:

> The separation of fact and value in literary scholarship has led to the expenditure of considerable energy for marginal or trivial results. . . . We must give over the vain hope of rigorous systemization of literary study and of the separation of the uniquely comparative or international aspects of our subject. Let us instead turn our attention to the literary; if we do our job well, the comparative will take care of itself.

Considering the importance of the need for method in our discipline and the prominent role of the history of literary theory and criticism that we have built into our curricula, we might on first reading assume these thoughts unusual coming from the president of ACLA.

Such doubts and concerns were common enough in the forties and fifties—even in the sixties. Marcel Bataillon, one of the first presidents of ICLA, felt this restrictive nature of the term when he stated that comparison was only one of the *moyens* of what we call—"by a name which expresses badly what it means— comparative literature." Back in the fifties Northrop Frye declared at the ICLA Congress in Chapel Hill, "Every problem in literary criticism is a problem in comparative literature, or simply of literature itself." The relations between comparative and general literature seemed in those days to be confused, as indeed they remain today. The editor of the *Yearbook of Comparative and General Literature*, Werner Friederich, confessed, "I don't quite know what 'General Literature' is, and for some years now I have been trying to find a learned article which could unscramble the various definitions . . . so that, *post facto*, we shall know at last exactly what our *Yearbook* is supposed to do." A demurrer less revolutionary than one might expect from Étiemble in his *Comparaison n'est pas raison* reads: "Dans la littérature comparée je n'oublie jamais qu'il y a comparée; on oublie trop souvent qu'il y a littérature."

Much ink has been shed in our profession over the meaning, if any, of general literature. Van Tieghem's definition of general literature reads specifically: "un ordre de recherches qui porte sur les faits communs à plusieurs littératures, considérées comme tels, soit dans leurs dépendances réciproques, soit dans leur coincidence." Since Van Tieghem was an early proponent of this term, let us note the two traditional meanings of *général* (in Hatzfeld) that might apply here: "qui se rapporte à un ensemble de choses" or "qui convient au genre tout entier." We thus seem to be debating whether to characterize our subject as "collective" or comparative literature. It is obvious that the concept collective/ general in no way implies the methodology inherent in the present stage of our discipline.

Most recent reflection on the term "general literature" has found it unsatisfactory. As Remak explains in *Comparative Literature*, Van Tieghem claimed for general literature a broader geographical dimension than for national or comparative literature, embracing a continental, pan-European, or even bicontinental span. Remak concludes, "It is to be hoped that the term general literature will be avoided, whenever possible. It means too many different things to too many people." Wellek, too, objects to Van Tieghem's propagation of general literature as meaning "those movements and fashions of literature which transcend national lines . . . Comparative and General Literature merge inevitably." Owen Aldridge, on the other hand, recalls the German background of this term, which differs conceptually from that of Van Tieghem:

In this [German] sense, general literature would comprise themes, genres, and masterpieces without explicit reference to time or period. Comparative Literature would comprise both social history (including movements, periods, and influences) and the relations of literature to the social, political, and philosophical background. . . . So much for the distinction. In practice, the two tendencies usually merge, and even when they do not, the term Comparative Literature is widely used for both.

Guyard, too, is forced to the conclusion that any meaning assigned to *littérature générale* applies to comparative literature itself. In Weisstein's excellent *Comparative Literature and Literary Theory* (p. 17) the basic inconsistency underlying Van Tieghem's view is demonstrated. Beyond the basic inconsistency, beyond his confusion of dimension and definition, Van Tieghem's problem was an inability to see the methodological imperative contained in the adjective *comparée*. Indeed, the fact surprises that both Étiemble and Block seem to conclude that the term *littérature générale* liberates a scholar for even deeper probing.

The praxis of comparative literature by the 1970s has become recognizable and productive. As mentioned above, it consists of comparing and contrasting literatures through the approaches of theme, form, movement, interrelation, and an evolving confrontation with critical theory. The commitment to analysis is the same as presented by the terms "comparative anatomy" and "comparative linguistics." Actually the German adjectival form with its more cogent meaning beckons one, as mentioned elsewhere, to compare, collate, liken, or even reconcile authors and literatures. Although comparative literature operates in three recognizable dimensions so far—Western Heritage and its individual national components; East-West; and World Literature, a term abused by college textbook editors and publishers (see p. 42) but one promising a *Krönung* of Goethe's ideal dimension—none of the three commits itself to a method unless it is recognized as a dimension of the host discipline comparative literature and subject to the host's method. To ensure that there is an emphasis on "fresh critical interpretations and an avoidance of marginal or trivial results" (Haskell Block), comparatists throughout the country, as Stephen Nichols has certified even at the undergraduate level, insist on at least one course on the history of literary theory as a requirement for majors.

Comparative Literature as an Academic Discipline

Deviation is still permitted when one theorizes upon the nature of comparative literature. However, when one is forced to confront comparative literature as a consistent academic discipline under constant scrutiny by administrators and colleagues, practice may dictate which of the theorizing is helpful and which is mere luxury. More will be written on this issue throughout the following pages. Suffice it to say here that by 1900 there was finally unanimity enough on principles to permit the establishment of comparative literature as an academic discipline. Since it is this practical side of comparative literature that will so often occupy us herein, we must turn now to a summary review of the discipline within the academy.

We have recorded the chair of comparative literature occupied at the Sorbonne by Villemain, apparently the pioneer in the field. Although comparative literature has been slow to develop in contemporary Italian faculties, Francesco de Sanctis created the chair of comparative literature at Naples University in 1871 and Arturo Graf occupied the chair at Turin in the same year. In 1886 Max Koch brought comparative literature to the University of Breslau. Lyon created its chair for Joseph Texte in 1897. The nineteenth-century pattern was thus obviously to create one single teaching post or chair in comparative literature and not to create a program or department.

The pattern in America was similar. In 1897 Harvard created a professorship for A. R. Marsh (actually an assistant professorship) to teach at both the undergraduate and graduate levels. The undergraduate courses were "Comparative European Literature in the Middle Ages with Especial Reference to the Influence of French and Provençal" and "Classical Learning from the Fifth to the Fifteenth Centuries." The graduate offerings were "Origin and Development of Epic Poetry in Mediaeval Europe" and "Legendary and Poetic Material of Celtic Origin and Its Treatment in Narrative Poetry of the Middle Ages." These courses are excellent examples of what we shall later call "touching all geographic bases." Unfortunately in 1889, as Urban T. Holmes has chronicled, Marsh resigned his chair to become vice-president of Planter's Compress Company.

Columbia University granted a similar chair to George Woodberry in 1899. The most famous activist on Morningside Heights, however, was Joel Elias Spingarn, author of an early basic study on Renaissance literary criticism in Italy, France, and England. Spingarn initiated comparative literature courses within the English department, where they are lodged even at this writing, and created a short-lived journal in the field. Almost two decades later he resigned from Columbia to protest the suicide of Harry Thurston Peck (dismissed for an amorous misadventure) as well as Nicholas Murray Butler's attitudes about the First World War.

Europe kept pace in the early century, as comparative literature chairs were created in Paris (1910), Strasbourg (1918), the Collège de France (1925), and Leipzig (1927). Although Baldensperger and Carré made lasting contributions, they have been charged with fostering a "cumbersome and restricted methodology" that brought on a "crisis" in comparatism. In the twenties, as Wellek has noted, the Cornell classicist Lane Cooper chaired not a comparative literature department, but one of "The Comparative Study of Literature," as illustrating better sense and syntax. ("You might as well permit yourself to say 'comparative potatoes' or 'comparative husks.'") His nicety did not prevail, even in his own university, as we observe from recent Cornell bulletins. Yet the Chicago program even today is called "Comparative Studies in Literature." Similarly Northwestern's course in our discipline is called "Studies in Comparative Literature." In 1900 Joseph Texte had written in a preface to Betz's *La Littérature comparée: Essai bibliographique*: "Le dix-neuvième siècle aura vu se développer et se constituer l'histoire nationale des lettres. Ce sera sans doute la tâche du vingtième siècle d'en écrire l'histoire comparative." This optimistic prediction is slowly proving true, but curious doldrums occurred between the beginning of the First World War and the end of the Second. Although this interregnum witnessed the creation of comparative literature as a discipline in North Carolina (1923), University of Southern California (1925), and Wisconsin (1927), it was not until after World War II—during which systematic governmental and foundation sponsorship of teaching foreign languages gave our discipline its broad linguistic base—that it found a permanent place in the curricula of our colleges.

Harvard started the revival under the initiative of Harry Levin,

Baldensperger having shortly before left Cambridge. This movement was quickly joined by Berkeley, Indiana, Yale, New York University, Oregon, and others. David Malone has reported in *YCGL* that the decade 1957–67 witnessed a 600 percent increase of comparative literature students, and even this rate eventually accelerated. As reports prepared for ACLA by the Nichols Committee and by Leland Chambers will attest (see especially Chs. iv, v, and xv), there has been a ground swell of interest and planning leading to expansion of comparative literature at both graduate and undergraduate levels despite the current decline of language study in our institutions. Although there is in Europe an occasional conspicuous university without professorships in comparative literature at this writing (Vienna, Oxford, and Cambridge), the same can scarcely be said of the United States and Canada. Rare indeed are universities without graduate work in this area. Both the United States and Canada have national associations of comparatists, and there are eleven others in Asia and Europe (see Appendix for a descriptive listing of associations and research institutes concerned with the discipline).

That comparative literature had come of age in the United States was heralded in 1974 when the American Council of Learned Societies (ACLS) elevated the American Comparative Literature Association (ACLA) to the full status of constituent society.

The 1976 Report of the ACLA's Committee on Professional Standards recalled the elitism of the 1965 Report: "It did not of course minimize the strenuous sweep of its aspirations and it did not perceive itself to be available to all students or even universities. It defined itself as a discipline appropriate only to institutions endowed with excellent libraries, with consistently strong foreign language departments, and with gifted students." The Report isolated six salient facts concerning the present state of the discipline. As the Committee viewed them, they were not encouraging.

1. The fact of rapid growth. There were by then entities (departments, programs, committees) administering comparative literature at 150 institutions in this country, a figure twice that when the Levin Report was submitted, and rising every year.
2. There was a heavy swing toward undergraduate teaching and indeed toward colleges with no graduate training.

3. There was a growth of comparative literature programs whose staff included no Ph.D. trained in the subject, programs depending on libraries whose holdings were modest, and supported by language departments not fully equipped for comparative purposes.

4. There was a growth of the large lecture course teaching literature in translation and making no linguistic demands on its undergraduate audiences and seeming to establish an equation between world literature and comparative literature. (This criticism will be elucidated in Ch. ii below.)

5. There was admission into graduate school of larger numbers of matriculants than ever before, even despite a deteriorating job market. A few graduate departments now numbered over a hundred registrants.

6. The Committee noted an erosion, if not withering, of foreign language departments in the wake of abolished requirements, an erosion that in some places seemed to stem in part from the growing popularity of comparative literature courses. This trend it found deeply ironic, since comparative literature needs the continuing support of neighboring disciplines and depends on them.

These features of the development of comparative literature constitute a mixed bag of welcome and unwelcome developments. The fact that the earliest professors of comparative literature in the forties were not Ph.D.'s trained in the subject was inevitable, since there was almost no place where they could have been so trained, unless perhaps in schools offering comparative Romance studies. At this stage comparatists were born, not made. True, libraries in the forties and fifties were only modestly stocked, but so were those back when Harvard, Lyon, Columbia, Strasbourg, and Paris were pioneering in comparative literature. Furthermore, most libraries contained the "great books" of Greek, Roman, French, English, and German literature, among others— precisely the languages that Dean Weisinger identifies with the Western tradition. As for the situation by the bicentennial year 1976, the holdings of the American libraries and their ability to acquire microcards and microfilms to complement their basic collections were considerable. Techniques of bibliographies improved. And geography did not enter into the matter. Illinois,

Indiana, and California were now the major university libraries, after Harvard's Widener. Many of ACLA Report II's concerns were valid ones, but by now the ACLS had, by its confidence and vision, foreseen an end to our growing pains and uncertainties. Comparatists are assured by the above-mentioned fact that the National Endowment for the Humanities (NEH) now makes specific provision for seminars and grants under the rubric of comparative literature. Moreover, an examination of college catalogs from Europe and Asia shows that the planning and innovating pioneered by our European colleagues have now been taken over by the American universities.

II

The Dimensions of Comparative Literature

Avant la fin de ce siècle on ne pourra plus analyser des grands
processus historiques, en littérature grecque, française, ou améri-
caine, sans puiser des éléments de comparaison dans les séries
orientales.

RAYMOND SCHWAB, *La Littérature orientale*

The Western Heritage

There are of course many different dimensions to the study of
comparative literature. One could conjecture so many that could
be practiced, but are most infrequent—African-Asian, African-
European, American–Asian–South American, and so on—as to
sound like the zany tragical-comical-historical-pastoral divisions
of Polonius. Three dimensions are particularly applicable to the
curricula of the American or European comparative literature
department—Western Heritage (or Western Literature), East-
West, and World Literature. These juxtapositions of bodies of
literature could of course be called divisions, but the term dimensions is more suitable to our purpose.

It is true that the slightest exercises in bringing together two
literatures, two authors, or two documents of literature (perhaps
even two passages, such as Gonzalo's pillaged lines from Montaigne's essays in *The Tempest*) demand acceptance as comparatism. As we learn elsewhere in this volume, the comparison or
contrast of two individuals writing in differing languages is the
minimal demonstration of our profession. The early French
school of comparatism left us several classics of this binational
dimension: Baldensperger's *Goethe en France*, Carré's *Goethe en
Angleterre*, Bataillon's *Erasme en Espagne*, Lesage's *Giraudoux et*

21

l'Allemagne, Lindstrom's *Tolstoï en France*, etc. The last two books were theses.

Yet in the fifties some of the new American departments of comparative literature were still offering one-author theses. From four different universities one notes these topics: "The Fiction of Ivan Bunin," "The Prose Fiction of Charles Williams," "Bossuet on Politics," and "André Gide's Ideas on Drama." By the late seventies things had not improved. A census of American Ph.D. theses in our discipline in the 1976 *ACLA Newsletter* shows that too many departments still cling to the one-author dissertation.

A gray area of definition is raised by a fifth comparative literature thesis accepted by a major university: "The Literary Criticism of Virginia Woolf." One can of course reason that this inventive author was a cosmopolite familiar with other literature and authors (Dostoevsky and Tolstoy especially) and voiced opinions on them; this would justify the thesis as comparative. If the authors commented upon were the many habitués of the Bloomsbury group, then of course the thesis would be proper for the English department. Some of the theses in the 1976 *Newsletter* mentioned above surely trespass on the domain of the individual literature department, which need not forfeit all its comparative interests in theses or classroom teaching owing to the presence of a more organic and extensive department or program of comparative literature. To cite a specific example, the NYU English department processed a thesis on Edmund Gosse and André Gide with readers from the English and French departments. The comparative literature staff was not officially involved or needed for this minimal exercise.

It would seem that there is no need to endanger cordial relations with the cooperating literature departments by comparative literature's sponsoring either single-author or perhaps even binational authors theses. Our discipline is still new enough that we remain somewhat on display. The English professor John Fisher, while executive secretary of MLA, severely criticized in 1965 the two-literature limitation to which the new Comparative Literature Groups at the annual conventions were addicted. He wrote, "The Executive Council is concerned that Comparative Literature Groups should be comparative and not just the extension, limited to one country or one genre, of a literature already provided for in another Group or Section." Even the pioneer comparatist Van Tieghem had long before deplored narrowness of dimension, writing his section (III, 1) on "L'insuffisance de la Littérature Comparée bornée aux rapports binaires." We shall return to this matter in our chapter on the thesis (see p. 237), as well as in our discussion of academic diplomacy (p. 269).

What can be concluded herewith as we contemplate the narrowest dimensions of our potentially vast discipline is that courses on two authors or even two literatures can scarcely be compounded to constitute a satisfactory curriculum in comparative literature. An amalgam of courses on Hemingway and Baroja, Opitz and Boileau, or Theocritus and Sannazaro cannot add up to such a curriculum. Furthermore the methodological limitations of binary studies of authors have been well voiced by René Wellek in his *Theory of Literature*: "No distinct system can emerge from the accumulation of such studies. There is no methodological distinction between a study of Poe's influence on Baudelaire and one on Dryden's influence on Pope." Furthermore, our commitment to geographical extension is already implicit in the requirement of three foreign languages that most universities impose on their Ph.D. candidates in our field. What we should call the inclusive dimension just beyond the binational dimension is commonly known as the Western Heritage. It is the inevitable coalition of those literatures commonly taught in the American or English universities: ancient Greek and Latin, English, American, French, Spanish, Portuguese, Italian, German, and Russian. The tradition includes naturally the mediaeval and Renaissance stages of these latter literatures. Arabic, Norwegian, or Polish is commonly omitted merely through the accident not of the ethnic immigrations into America, but of the largely European component literatures in the college and university curricula. The confines of cosmopolitanism or internationalism were predestined. ACLA Report II says of comparative literature:

> It wanted to stand, and in large part did stand, for a new internationalism: for broader perspectives on works and authors, for a European grasp of historical movements, for larger contexts in the tracking of motifs, themes, and types as well as larger understandings of genres and modes. It aimed also at the clarification of the great theoretical issues of literary criticism from a cosmopolitan vantage point. Within the academy, it wanted to bring together

the respective European language departments in a new cooperation, reawakening them to the unity of their common endeavor, and embodying that unity in various ways, both customary and creative, which could transport faculty and students across disciplinary boundaries. Beyond even these boundaries, the Comparative Literature movement wanted to explore the relationships of literature with the other arts and humanities (these essentially European as well): with philosophy, history, history of ideas, linguistics, music, art, and folklore among others.

It is obvious that the linking of Western Heritage literature could be effected most easily with Western Heritage philosophy, history, art, and other disciplines represented by university departments working mainly in this same cultural area.

Most of the Ph.D. programs aim then at presenting the major literary works of the Western Heritage, the most common dimension of comparative literature today. A glance at an atlas reveals that the Western Heritage could by definition cover scores of countries in Europe and the Americas. Obviously this term must be accepted as meaning only the major authors in this vast area, and we are grateful to Fritz Strich for reminding us that the term must be accepted in a rigidly qualitative sense.

However, it is obviously true that the Western Heritage implies an obligation to extensive coverage. Every executor of a comparative literature department has had the thankless obligation of having to decline a colleague's offer to present a course on, let us say, Dickens, Balzac, and Zola—that is, a course that embraces two or three authors from one, or two, or even three *Sprachräume*. The value of such a course is undeniable, especially when one remembers the successful course on Proust, Mann, and Joyce taught by Professor Levin. When one of his distinguished students, later at Princeton, wished to give the course at NYU, we requested, feeling like ungrateful curmudgeons, that he add Dostoevsky to add breadth. Fortunately, he understood and accepted.

This problem of breadth is at the very core of our comparative literature curricula. It is easy to criticize as superficial a course that will include authors from seven or eight countries. However, the critic must pause and consider that a course that will cover

Homer, Vergil, Petrarch, Tasso, Camoëns, Ercilla, Milton, and Voltaire is not centrally about their literatures. It is a course about epic poetry. It is about the motivation behind and definition of epic during its bi-millenary existence. It must be stressed again that comparative literature is inevitably organized about the themes, forms, movements, and interrelations that bind the literatures of both similar and disparate areas. In order to attain this breadth, almost all universities (see p. 100) have required that doctoral candidates read three foreign languages and master's candidates two. Incidentally, all official writing about comparative literature, including what one reads in publications of ICLA or ACLA, stresses knowing three foreign languages but never mentions that in many universities comparative literature students command more than three. This is especially true of the universities in large metropolitan centers, which admit many foreign-born, foreign-educated, or foreign-resident candidates. At the present writing students matriculated in the department at NYU possess, by a hasty and probably incomplete census, a native command of the following languages: Arabic, Bengali, Brazilian, Chinese, Danish, Dutch, Estonian, French, Gaelic, German, Greek, Modern Hebrew, Hindi, Hungarian, Italian, Japanese, Korean, Latvian, Norwegian, Polish, Luso-Portuguese, Romanian, Russian, Spanish, Swahili, Swedish, Ukrainian, and Yiddish.

Several of these students have come to complete doctoral work here and then institute programs of comparative literature at home. Two such programs have started at this date in India and Portugal, and one is projected in Damascus. New York is not unique as an "unmelting pot." Other comparative literature departments in urban areas, including state university campuses, will have comparable language resources to be tapped among their graduate students.

This cosmopolitan group of students is a tremendous resource. Its presence is an incentive to plan for extensive geographic coverage in our Western Heritage courses. In a course on romanticism embracing six major European areas, one may use foreign-born students to extend even further the coverage by class reports on romantic writers of their native countries, such as Greece or Portugal. In a course on epic a class report on an Estonian epic becomes thus possible and will be meaningful to students (because of an interest in the emergence of epic poetry in the Baltic area rather than a preoccupation with Estonian literature, as we stress once more).

Of course a theme can be extended so taut as to lose all depth whatsoever. A West Coast university has offered a course, "The Short Story in World Literature," which would apparently have to embrace so much and resist unifying principles so consistently as to be of doubtful value in exemplifying comparatism. In any case, the vaster dimensions of World Literature will be examined directly.

East-West and World Literature

We have defined World Literature as one of the three major dimensions of comparative literature as commonly practiced today. In his excellent third chapter (see Bibliography) François Jost views this relationship differently:

> "World Literature" and "Comparative Literature" are not identical notions. The former is a prerequisite for the latter, and it provides the scholar with raw materials and information, which he groups according to critical and historical principles. Comparative Literature may therefore be defined as Weltliteratur; it is an articulated account, historical and critical, of the literary phenomenon considered as a whole.

Several readings of these lines leave me with the impression that they contain a basic contradiction, holding that two concepts not identical may yet be each defined as equating the other. In any case, I am more comfortable with the definition of World Literature or *Weltliteratur* as the maximum geographical dimension of comparative literature. Even as I agree that the adjective "comparative" explains what is to be done about literature, the "raw material" of literature that we compare in our classes and research is most commonly from the Western Heritage dimension. Thus I find the three major dimensions of Western, East-West, and World (including their lesser components) as more easily chartable and more precisely articulated. If one conceded that the global phase is at hand, as Goethe seemed to predict, one might concede François Jost's absolute equation of *Weltliteratur* and comparative literature. But we are still working toward that ultimate global dimension, which presents various orders of difficulty to be analyzed in the present chapter.

The term "East-West" has become widely and permanently accepted, even though it too presents problems of definition. In the preface to his anthology *Masterpieces of the Orient*, George L. Anderson poses the question:

> The word "Orient" itself is a vague term, of use only for convenience. "East" would not be better: there is an Arab literature in Morocco, which ·; 1500 miles west of Athens, and there is a Western literature in Vladivostok, almost a thousand miles east of Peking. "Asiatic"—a term frowned upon by Asians as reflecting nineteenth-century Western attitudes toward the Orient—and "Asian" will not do. The literature of the Arabs has largely been produced in Africa, but for many centuries in Europe the Near East is the "Orient."

One must take a stand nevertheless. So East-West literature must include Arab as Eastern and one must include Vladivostok as part of the great Russian land mass included in the Western Heritage.

Asian universities are well embarked on East-West programs. In addition to the University of Tokyo mentioned elsewhere in this chapter, the University of Hong Kong offers such courses as European Sources of Modern Chinese Literature and Chinese Literature in the West. Hong Kong–Chung Chi College offers a basic seminar on comparative literature and a history of comparative criticism. These same two courses are taught at the National University of Taiwan. In Japan, Nagoya University offers eight courses in comparative literature. In the Philippines it is the English department that offers comparative literature at the University of St. Augustin and world literature at the Central Philippine University. In the Asian Middle East, Hebrew University of Jerusalem offers nine varied courses in comparative literature (especially genre and criticism) and Bar Ilan University offers eleven. The University of Mosul in Iraq and the Middle East Technical University in Turkey list two or more courses (among the latter a course in world literature). Comparatism in these "Eastern" institutions is inevitably of an "East-West" dimension.

Although the ACLA has not at this writing come to grips with the possibility of global literature as an academic discipline, the challenge of its realization is receiving more and more attention by ACLA and FILLM. ACLA Report I misunderstood the challenge and curiously equated this supreme discipline with the undergraduate literature-in-English survey: "A distinction might conceivably be drawn between the Humanities or World Literature or Great Books at the undergraduate level and Comparative Literature as a graduate discipline." This sanction to a misnomer invented largely by the textbook publishers did little service to lexical coherence in our profession. ACLA Report II, on the other hand, made the necessary correction, stating: "We must beware of ever again confusing 'world literature' with the literature of our inherited culture, however rich." Report II viewed it as the most challenging, advanced dimension of comparative literature, a veritable Ultima Thule beckoning to the most advanced professors and graduate students:

> There has also arisen widespread and growing interest in the non-European literatures—Chinese, Japanese, Sanskrit, Arabic, and many others less familiar, as well as those oral "literatures" of illiterate communities which are not properly described by our most basic term but for which we have no alternative. A new vision of global literature is emerging, embracing all the verbal creativity during the history of our planet, a vision which will soon begin to make our comfortable European perspectives parochial. Few comparatists, few scholars anywhere, are prepared for the dizzying implications of this widening of horizons, but they cannot be ignored.

This recognition of the imminence of World Literature as a well-defined, carefully constructed discipline is welcome. It is a statement of faith that a long-dreamed goal is drawing ever closer and that there is an immediate need to discuss its feasibility, consistently defined and ethically presented as a graduate school curriculum. Current recognition of global literature in our discipline is firmly expressed in Pichois and Rousseau's recent study: "Sans nulle contestation tel est aujourd'hui son fief naturel."

For World Literature is the logical third step of comparative literature. The first dimensional stage was of course the Western Heritage, which Dean Weisinger too severely branded as "a confining concept" to which "many comparatists enslave themselves." In its narrowest (Western) exercise, of course, the somewhat overworked French-English comparatism (chosen by many American students because it requires only their native language and their most commonly studied foreign language), it might become confining. The second step is East-West Literature, in which tentative courses are being tried. I shall return to this step below. Finally, there remains the goal of World Literature, encompassing the two previous categories. This *littérature universelle*, it is hoped, is becoming an academic reality to which we may legitimately, if cautiously, aspire, but one on whose demands even Goethe probably never reflected when making his titillating remark about *Weltliteratur*. Indeed, as François Jost has made clear, Goethe's call was actually for an East-West (West-östlicher) dimension to literature. *Weltliteratur* is something even further, the *Krönung* (another favorite word of Goethe) and utmost demonstration of comparatism.

To pause momentarily for an interesting digression, we quote Professor Wellek's *Theory of Literature*: "Goethe himself saw that this [*Weltliteratur*] is a very distant ideal, that no single nation is willing to give up its individuality. Today we are possibly even further removed from such a state of amalgamation, and we would argue that we cannot even wish that the diversities of national literatures should be obliterated." Obviously, comparative literature often departs from similarities to the examination of meaningful diversities. The real excitement of our discipline, however, and indeed its challenge, remains in the mythic, generic, and other homogeneities inexplicably occurring over two millennia on our five continents. It is more exciting to discover that a great number of folk epics include a trip to the afterworld/underworld than to observe that a lesser number do not. Little is to be gained by proving that there are exceptions to Otto Rank's unifying observation about the birth and death of the epic hero. It is intriguing to discover that epic heroes even among the Araucanian pagans must have twelve paladins (i.e., disciples), even at the cost of their individuality.

Let us now dwell on the remaining problems in achieving World Literature, and then proceed to some of the resources that will help us to resolve these problems. The first difficulty to be eliminated is the misuse of the phrase "world literature" in academia itself. I can find no more striking example of this than in a recent report circulated by the South Central Comparative Literature Association (SCCLA) bearing the incredible statistic that ninety-one percent of college departments surveyed in that region offer world literature courses, usually at the junior rather than senior level, whereas few comparative literature courses exist. A state university in the Northeast once boasted a Department of Comparative and World Literature, with no world literature courses listed. Indeed the department has since folded. We know from *The Teacher's Guide to World Literature*, prepared for the National Council of Teachers of English, that the term is applied at best, as in the SCCLA survey, to Western classics in translation.

Even Robert Neal, author of the *Teacher's Guide*, in discussing "world lit" in American high schools, has deplored in *YCGL* (1963) the lack of philosophy, vague aims, methodological deficiency, poverty of course planning, poor anthologies, superficial teaching, and lack of any world scope in such mislabeled courses. Nor does he forget the unpreparedness of high school teachers for this task. I am informed by Bonnie Crown of the Asian Literature Committee that the latest revision of this *Guide* will include some Asian works.

The fraudulent claims of American "world literature" textbooks have been recently exposed by Mrs. Crown, who sampled sixteen such texts and found that pages devoted to Asian literature ranged from .02 percent to 14.7 percent; these percentages included such Asians as Rudyard Kipling and Pearl Buck!

When I was preparing for a major publisher a Western Heritage undergraduate anthology in English, I was informed that the book was to be advertised as "world literature" to increase sales. We must not accept easy outs. World Literature as a discipline means the study of literature from the maximum geographical extent where major authors are found, taught as often as possible by teams of teachers who read most authors in the original language. Its method must be that of comparatism rather than of random samplings.

World Literature, our third phase, must establish in its wide area meaningful points of contact and assimilation, most conveniently through the familiar approaches of theme, form, and movement. We may have to adjust our definitions and critical vocabulary. Some years ago, while planning with R. K. DasGupta three East-West courses to be given alternately at NYU and University of Delhi, I proposed a course on five Western and five Asian tragedies. He reminded me that whereas Aristotle's generic approach might have some value for epic poetry, it was irrelevant to Indian theater. The course would have to deal instead with "drama." The first World (like the first East-West) Literature courses will have to sift out common denominators that may best bring differing literatures into juxtaposition.

African Literature

The greatest deterrent to World Literature is of course the language problem, already a challenge to any comparatist, especially if we are to sample the major literary works of the five continents. Africa, which would seem at first to present the major language problem, presents fortuitously little difficulty, for the literary vehicles will remain French and English. Portuguese will surely decline, especially as the chief theme of its poetry, liberation, has been achieved. The same fate awaits Afrikaans. Although the Negro poet Samuel Allen defines the negritude movement as "representative of the Negro African poet's endeavor for his race a normal self-pride," the leaders, with their European schooling and syncretic tendencies, do not espouse black native languages. Their writing and their editing of *Présence Africaine* is in French or English. Some Africans wrote in English as early as the eighteenth century. The common native languages—Bantu, Swahili, and Yoruba—have a small literate audience. Yet their themes and concerns are of course based on what Langston Hughes calls the African heritage. Thus, when Patrice Lumumba stirred the Congolese natives with his verses on the white man's savagery and rapine, he wrote in the white man's language. In her anthology *Black Poets in French* Marie Collins explains simply: "More than 400 different tribal languages are spoken in Africa. . . . For the time being at least, French and English are a unifying means of communication." The languages of Alan Paton in the South and the francophone Kateb Yacine in the North are preferred to a continent-wide Babel.

Black African literature is of course the most visibly lacking component in the plans for World Literature. Its major oral tradition of myths, poetry, and folktales—with its novels, derivative in form but local in character—could play a modest but useful role in World Literature classes. Any course on myths or oral literature could hardly exclude Africa. In the area of oral poetry Africa contributes odes of praise, oracles, incantations, dialogues, and of course political polemic. Prose forms to consider would vary from the sociopolitical novel and autobiography to folktales, bestiaries, picaresque narratives, and dilemma tales, where the hearers are invited to supply a conclusion.

Since Africa has contributed fewer literary works that satisfy the first of the dual criteria established by Fritz Strich (international acclaim and enduring values), African authors will play a minor role in the new universal literature curricula. Similar massive areas, like Indonesia with a population of 100 million, would be minimally represented. Yet even as we accept this reality, we reject the conclusion of Pichois and Rousseau (African literature was also curiously omitted from Étiemble's list quoted below), who write: "Les littératures africaines et polynésiennes occuperont d'autres chercheurs." This same French logic and prudence is expressed in their proverb, "Qui trop embrasse, mal étreint." Excepting this exclusion of Africa, one may agree with their general premise about world literature: "l'histoire universelle de la littérature n'est pas l'histoire de la littérature universelle." Aficionados of African or Polynesian literatures can of course feature them in theses written for their degrees in World Literature.

African literature has been given more and more academic attention recently. It is no doubt a portent that the language problem will be minimal, for two courses initiated at the University of Washington in the seventies, Modern African Literature and Afro-Occidental Literary Relations, are typical in stressing respectively English-speaking authors and francophone poets and novelists. ICLA congresses at Utrecht and Bordeaux have included panels on African literature. One issue of the *Revue de Littérature Comparée* (1974) gives further assurance by its theme that the language problem is no impediment: "Littératures francophones et anglophones de l'Afrique noire."

African Universities have begun to pay attention to comparatism. The University of Ife in Nigeria offers Studies in Comparative European Literature, African Literature in Relationship to French and German Literature, and to French and Brazilian Literature. The University of Cairo has combined its Department of English and Comparative Literatures. Ain Shams University offers a degree in Comparative Islamic Literature.

There is one dissenter to this complacent view about the language issue. Charles Larson writes in *YCGL* (1969):

> Mixing African writing in English and French (that is, from the two main colonial areas) in one course, then, would conform to our basic definition of Comparative Literature, but such a solution would be too simple and hardly fair to those Africans who are writing in the vernacular languages . . . the several hundred languages and dialects spoken on the continent.

This objection may be more ethical than reasonable, or even valid, for one can hardly expect a comparatist to know these minor languages that not even the Africans themselves read. Furthermore, in the long run, a masterpiece in a minor African tongue, like one in a minor Indian tongue, will eventually be translated into a more available language. To satisfy Larson, we should be required to translate fully from these "several hundred languages and dialects," something that is not undertaken in Russia, China, or India.

The Asian Language Problem

No such linguistic capitulation as Africa's is visible in Asia and Indonesia. English, although an official "third" or "international" language in India, is now spoken by only some five percent of the population, although there is strong sentiment in the Indian PEN Club for Indo-Anglian narrative and poetry, voiced typically by Bhabani Bhattacharya as follows: "The Indian writer must be free to use any language he likes, unharassed by criticism, either tacitly implied or plainly stated, and by any kind of compulsion, direct or indirect, which may come out of the strengthening mood of linguistic chauvinism." Yet nationalism is strong throughout Asia. The Indonesians have rejected Dutch for Bahasa Indonesia. Many Philippine writers reject Spanish and English for Pilipino.

China retains its linguistic xenophobia. The greatest problem for World Literature courses in this area is that there are almost no Asian specialists able to participate who know Asiatic languages other than their own—or even other Asian literatures, which is still more serious for literary internationalism. Fortunately the linguistic imperialism of English and French still clings in Asia, though less than in Africa, of course, and this enables Asians to have indirect access to their continental literatures. Thus, at a recent triennial meeting of the Asian Writers' Conference, the Korean Ko Yo Sup complained that Koreans wishing to translate Asian works must get hold of the English, French, or German versions of such works before turning them into Korean. Sc complicated are Asian languages even to close neighbors that Ryoto Sato of Tokyo claimed that it takes him an entire year to translate one Chinese novel into Japanese.

Thus Americans and Asians face the identical problem in mastering Asian literatures. This problem of linguistic intercommunication within Asia, where more natives know English or French than the *Sprachräume* of their neighbors, has reduced Indian comparative literature courses to feature English-Indian literary relations and led the University of Tokyo to emphasize English-Japanese relations. (Similarly, a dean of Cairo University recently boasted that his teachers were secular pioneers in comparative literature through their Hispano-Arabic researches.)

As suggested above, the inability of Asians to read Asian languages other than their own parallels an ignorance of their neighbors' literatures. Thus the aforementioned joint NYU-Indian program of East-West Literature, although finalized on paper and assured a subsidy from the Fulbright Commission, lurched to a sudden halt. It was only during the FILLM congress in Australia years later that DasGupta explained what had gone wrong: he could find no Indian colleagues who could or would read in the original (or conceivably even in translation) the various Asian epics and drama that were to constitute the Asian component of the projected courses. It is possible that projected World Literature courses in America may be partially staffed by the young comparatists of Asian birth now being trained in our own graduate schools. Their course work makes them familiar with the great texts of the Western Heritage, while their theses often encompass Indian, Chinese, Korean, or Japanese authors.

The Institute of World Literature

Let us turn now to another dream shared by many: the Institute of World Literature. It has been widely accepted that a dissemination of such institutes would support the spread of the discipline of Universal Literature. Étiemble writes, "The Institute I dream of would naturally include Hellenists, Latinists, Egyptologists, Slavicists, Hindi and Bengali specialists, sinologists, Semiticists, Germanic, Romance, Turko-Mongol, Dravidian and Japanese scholars." Such an institute would have to be in Paris, says Étiemble (who ironically claims to be an internationalist surrounded by chauvinists). "In Paris only can one learn all those languages which I believe indispensable." London and New York, not to speak of Hong Kong, are apparently out of the running.

It was this same dream, strengthened by some political motivation, that created Moscow's Gorki Institute of World Literature. It was Gorki's dream that such a clearinghouse could bring the peoples of the world together through literature. It is a research center, a library, and an advisory resource to the state publishers on their extensive programs. Many of the books recommended for translation and printing derive from Asia, Africa, and the uncommitted nations whose favor the government is currying. The Institute favors the "scientific" approach to literature, which Gorki chose to call social realism. In a *New York Times* report that I wrote after visiting the Institute I concluded that whereas the bibliographies and translations and researches cannot fail to be useful, the Institute's subjugation to political pressures cannot fail to hamper its prestige. It has not even begun to be effective in shaping curricula in World Literature.

Holland has also shown an interest in an institute of world literature, as have some of us in New York. We have had some meetings at New York University about such a project, encouraged by the many surrounding resource bodies: the Asian Literature Committee (chaired so effectively by Bonnie Crown), the Afro-American Research Institute, the American Library Association, PEN Club International, UNESCO, and others. However, it turned out that to carry on such an institute's five areas of activity (translation, publication, bibliography, symposia, and study groups) would require an annual subsidy of $250,000. Such a project was impossible, or seemed so at the time. An institute of World Literature in America, England, or France would be useful, yet its absence need not hold back the tide of literary cosmopolitanism. There are other, more attainable projects to be carried out.

Politics and World Literature

Here let us pause over an inevitable problem that will become intensified by the creation of World Literature curricula. Syllabi of all comparative literature courses, whether Western Heritage or East-West or World, must of course acquaint the student with a bibliography of background readings, commentary, and interpretation of the assigned texts. Time was when such a bibliography should be sure to include criticism by individuals of other nationality than the author evaluated. François Jost reminds us of the venerable attitude that "because foreign criticism is not immediately 'involved,' 'committed' or 'engaged,' it can sometimes reach more valid verdicts than indigenous criticism." It was traditional, he adds, to hold that the Abbé Desfontaines wrote better criticism on Fielding than anyone in London and that Swinburne was a superior analyst of Hugo. Indeed it was thought that criticism of an author by a conational tended toward shortsighted or one-sided judgments, overgenerous or overhostile.

The politicization of literature after Marx to a point unheard of since feudal-clerical scholasticism makes a luxury of discussions such as the one above. Such politicization may have embarrassed even its chief apostle Gorki, who in September, 1923, invited Stefan Zweig to write an article for *Beseda*, a journal which, he assured, "has nothing to do with politics." Controlled criticism, often fickle, spares insiders no more than outsiders. One day the *Hungarian Quarterly* equates József Lengyel with "some of modern literature's greatest writers," whereas the next he is a villain whose *Confrontation* must be suppressed. Literary criticism of outsiders is best illustrated by the two massive cultures of Russia and China, both of which would be inevitably well represented in East-West or World Literature curricula. Let me illustrate how this replacement of criticism by polemics becomes a very real problem for the future development of World Literature.

The monthly journal *Chinese Literature*, published in Peking, is the most valid document from which to learn the trends of Chinese letters and criticism. It contains original writing in the form of poetry, narrative, drama, film scripts, and opera libretti, such as the famous *Red Lantern*, recalling the war of resistance against Japan. Perhaps its most vigorous element is its literary criticism. Indeed the section reviewing books has borne the significant rubric "Literary Criticism and Repudiation," a franker admission of its role than one finds in Moscow's *Literaturnaya Gazeta*. To illustrate its international tenets of criticism, we shall sample expressions of disapproval of three books well known to the West: Mikhail Sholokhov's *And Quiet Flows the Don*, Ilya Ehrenburg's *People and Life*, and Konstantin Simonov's *Days and Nights*, the epochal novel centered on the Battle of Stalingrad.

Russia's third Nobel laureate is branded by critic Shih Hung-yu as a counterrevolutionary and lackey of revisionism who has been betraying the October Revolution since his 1926 *Tales of the Don*. After a lengthy indictment, the review concludes: "Today we expose Sholokhov to the bright light of Mao Tse-tung's thought, and tomorrow Sholokhov will not be able to escape a trial before the revolutionary peoples of the Soviet Union. It is certain that the Soviet people will sweep him into the dust-bin of history, alongside Brezhnev, Kosygin, and company." Critic Chung Yen-ping turns his attention to Ehrenburg's memoirs written under the brief thaw of Khrushchev, memoirs arraigning that Stalinism which the Maoists still view as a beneficial dictatorship of the proletariat. Chung's repudiation reads: "This big poisonous weed is a long, revolting series of anecdotes dealing with certain historical events and figures from the time of the February Revolution to the eve of the Great Patriotic War. Ehrenburg's intention was to borrow the tongues of the dead to attack the road of the October Revolution, to resuscitate ghosts to take part in the fight for a capitalist restoration." To clinch his point, Chung recalls that the revered pioneer writer Lu Hsün (called by Mao in 1940 "an unprecedented hero on the cultural front") dismissed Ehrenburg thirty years ago as a right-wing bourgeois author.

Finally, critic Hsieh Sheng-wen demythicizes the Siege of Stalingrad as chronicled by Simonov. "Analyzed and examined critically with the sharp weapon of Mao Tse-tung's thought, *Days and Nights* proves to be a black specimen of revisionist war literature, and Simonov a cowardly traitor who traded upon the glory and dignity of the soldiers of the Red Army." In sum, by an insistence on the people's sufferings, Simonov is accused of interpreting Stalingrad as "an unprecedented catastrophe which brought the people nothing but death and destruction" instead of viewing it, in Chairman Mao's words, as "the turning-point in the history of all mankind."

This type of criticism obviously must be prevented from plaguing and impeding the development of World Literature. Such polemicization of criticism, albeit more subtly presented, has found its way into comparative literature congresses in both Eastern and Western Europe. A great effort is needed to conciliate views to the point of producing intellectually honest manuals, literary histories, and bibliographies for the implementation of future courses in World Literature. The bibliographies on symbolism, Renaissance literature, and other topics now being undertaken by the International Comparative Literature Association will, it is hoped, demonstrate that zones of varying political persuasion can produce useful tools for the study of World Literature. If not, then the syllabus and bibliography for a course in contemporary poetry (see p. 46) will be different in Western Europe and America from those in Russia or in China.

Moving Ahead toward World Literature

The ACLA Report II on Professional Standards does not see a need for any immediate concern for World Literature:

> But for the study of those literatures further-flung from Europe and the Americas, perhaps all that can be reasonably said today is that methodological prudence must be tempered with flexibility. We are still lacking the concepts and tools which will permit us truly to study literature at the global level. These concepts and tools will gradually materialize. While waiting and searching for them, we must beware of ever again confusing "world literature" with the literature of our inherited culture, however rich; conversely, while working toward global perspectives, we will still need the virtues of precision and integrity our inherited culture

has taught us. It goes without saying that we cannot begin to absorb the wealth of exotic literatures before firmly possessing our own.

Returning to what we were characterizing as "more attainable projects to be carried out," the first and most lengthy step is to undertake a census of the texts available for a pilot graduate program in World Literature, as well as existing translations of these texts. Bilingual texts will be especially desirable. The M.A. in World Literature could in prospect require a knowledge of seventy-five or more texts on the part of a candidate, including twenty to thirty in his own native literature. The Ph.D. would require considerably more but would demand also a far greater number of background and theoretical works, which ideally should exist also in translations. The books selected for these literary courses are those which, as Fritz Strich has qualified them, have already won international recognition and display enduring values. In addition, they will be clearcut examples of the themes, forms, and movements that will structure the World Literature courses.

For this essential first step there are many bibliographical tools. UNESCO has been most useful in two ways, not only by the remarkable registry of translations all over the world in its *Index Translationum* but by its remarkable *Connaissance de l'Orient* series. Other bibliographical tools include *Books in Print*, England's *Bookseller*, and the European national bibliographies subsidized by governments. New retrieval-of-information techniques in our libraries will be most helpful. Microfilm and microfiche bibliographies will facilitate our enormous task. The Franklin Book Programs, a nonprofit organization with fifteen offices on three continents, has made a useful contribution. The PEN Clubs in many corners of the world publish literary bulletins, some of which I receive and which contain important bibliographical news. University presses and those of learned societies will have to be canvassed. *World Literature Today* will continue its dissemination of information useful to World Literature courses. All the bibliographical sources of the West will require investigation in our search for translations of Asian and African works into a Western language, preferably into one of the three foreign languages that we shall continue to require of our doctoral candidates. We are at this moment at NYU entering a request for a two-year subsidy to undertake such a census.

Naturally, the same preparations have to be undertaken for World Literature courses as have been made for comparative literature courses: curricular requirements established; course syllabi written; lectures, readings, and reports determined. The technical aspects of World Literature we are all familiar with. It might be useful if in addition we request the ICLA or FILLM —or possibly even the staff of *World Literature Today*, who have demonstrated that they can achieve what is impossible for others —to compile of a roster-by-region of comparatists whose knowledge of literature bridges East and West or two totally dissimilar areas.

We are in need as well of two or three major histories of World Literature compiled with an eye to the needs and practices of comparative literature. Jan Brandt Corstius has already issued a call for these in *YCGL* (1963), rejecting as inadequate the superannuated type of history that is merely a gathering of histories of national literatures.

Once the syllabi are constructed and the bibliographies compiled, we confront one last time the linguistic vehicle of our courses. We have committed ourselves to the principle that the texts of World Literature, like those of the Western Heritage, should be taught by instructors who read them in the original. Let us see how this principle operates in a hypothetical course on the world's great national epic poems, perhaps the most challenging and productive genre of all. Ideally, in a course including six Western and four Asian epics (leaving Africa and other areas in abeyance for our demonstration) a polyglot Western and a polyglot Asian scholar should suffice for the teaching. However, we have already observed that Asian professors usually choose as their second or third foreign language one from the West. Thus the course planner faces one of three solutions.

First, he may resort to group teaching by instructors of differing nationalities and specializations not too alien to epic, a practice occasionally tried in comparative literature departments. This is sometimes possible in a large metropolitan university or community. Yet there are inevitable difficulties of scheduling, teaching load, and lack of remuneration. Furthermore, a guest lecturer cannot always grasp the direction a course is taking and make the most pertinent contribution. Second, the instructor may lean on foreign-language-speaking graduate students as resource personnel, entrusting to them the reading aloud of a text, adjudicating the assigned translation (when necessary), and making further clarifications. Finally, the instructor may build his course with a maximum of Western epics (nine? ten?) he can read and teach himself and take a chance on finding a willing *suppléant* to teach the others. In case of failure, he must hope to have assigned the best possible translations and rest his case at that point. Certainly, if he feels that *Gilgamesh* must be included as one of the world's greatest national epics (and one that probably influenced the *Odyssey*), he may be forgiven for not reading Babylonian, Hittite, or Hurrian. It must be conceded that in comparative literature (and especially World) there will be frequent cases when an instructor will have to discuss a book he cannot read in the original, whether an assigned text or a background commentary. As the first Report on Professional Standards of the American Comparative Literature Association put it, "It would be highly puristic to exclude some reading from more remote languages in translation."

Paradoxically, this point is often raised by carping nonlinguists as yet another objection to comparative studies. It is a logical and facile argument, like the insistence that no graduate student in fine arts should work from slide projections but only from studying the original paintings or sculpture, or that historians, philosophers, anthropologists, and theologians should not use sources they cannot read in the original. We all stand behind the principle of linguistic versatility, but it is of course a question of degree. For someone to teach a course, graduate or undergraduate, on Dante without knowing Italian and Latin is unethical and reprehensible. Yet we should not suggest that the planner of the course on world epic described above abandon it. Many English or joint departments that administer the undergraduate literature-in-translation courses impose the *quot opera, tot linguae* principle on graduate literature departments while their instructors abandon it totally at the undergraduate level. When we have developed several World Literature graduate programs in several major universities, we shall have a good idea of what constitutes an ethical compromise on this issue.

Misuse of the Term "World Literature"

Rather than conclude with a bad conscience, I return for a moment to those ninety-one percent of college courses entitled "World Literature" listed by the SCCLA. If one is truly devoted to literature, one can only have mixed feelings about them. One may object that they tend to follow without method the random Homer-to-Arthur-Miller zigzag path through Western literature. One may object that they are often taught by instructors who do not read easily two or three European languages—and occasionally even one—that they usually require not one single command of a foreign language on the part of the student, that they are tokenist in their approach. After all, in the *YCGL* back in 1952 Henry W. Wells already complained, "Where in our American academic system a department or course in World Literature has been established, this has been in most cases undergraduate work with use of translations only. Such an understanding remains merely inaccurate." Still, any literature is good literature in these days of simplified college curricula and widespread abolition of the foreign language requirement. Furthermore, the schools' misuse of the term "World Literature" is not entirely of their own doing.

Our textbook compilers and editors have indeed decided that "World Literature" is a "sexy" rubric, to quote one publisher. Time was when a Western Heritage anthology would be called by Ginn *The Heritage of European Literature*, by Lippincott *Readings in Western Civilization*, or by Ronald Press *Literature of Western Civilization*. When the dike broke, Dryden (*Masterworks of World Literature*), Norton (*World Masterpieces*), Odyssey (*Types of World Literature*), and others opportunistically claimed a global viewpoint that was totally lacking. More ethically entitled were Scott, Foresman's *The World in Literature*, American Book's *World Literature*, Holt, Rinehart and Winston's *Heritage of World Literature*, and Macmillan's *Anthology of World Literature*, which led the American undergraduate to a few well-edited samplings of texts from the Orient and the Near East. There seems to be no reason why publishers cannot separate such clearly identifiable areas of literature as

Western, East-West, and World and describe their anthologies accordingly.

Not all undergraduate courses in World Literature are a travesty on the term. At SUNY-New Paltz John Alfonso Karkala has succeeded despite financial pressures in maintaining four World or East-West courses: Non-Western Books in Freshman English; the Asian Novel; Myth, Symbol, and Fable; and Western and Eastern Epic. East-West graduate courses are offered on Poetic Imagination and Mystical Experience and Literary Criticism. Courses at the graduate level are not entirely lacking. A major course at Indiana is C-595-596: Seminar in World Literature described as study of genres, epic and fiction, drama and poetry, and analysis of selected literary works.

We are sometimes soothed by assurances that such piecemeal phenomena as Pound's interest in Japanese haiku, Yeats's interest in Tagore, Joyce's knowledge of the Koran testify that we are on the way to World Literature. To paraphrase Joseph Bédier's shattering question, one may ask, "Mais où sont les programmes d'études?" Once we organize our courses and syllabi and get on with the task, getting the bugs out of them, as the scientists say, we shall achieve Ivar Ivask's goal of World Literature today. Goethe's challenging words of January, 1827, echo within us: "The epoch of world literature is at hand, and everyone must hasten its approach." We are getting closer. As the Russian proverb reminds us, "Patience is the mother of genius."

World Literature courses as we have conceived them in this chapter are intended for gifted and motivated graduate students. A candidate in this outermost extension of comparative literature is bound to be a true elitist (see p. 52).

If we do not have as yet institutes of World Literature, we have in America important departments and institutes of large segments of non-Western literature and culture that could contribute to courses in World, and especially East-West, Literature. The Program in Asian Studies at the University of Iowa grants an M.A. in East Asian Languages and Literatures. It includes a hundred courses in Chinese, Indian, Japanese, and Southeast Asian literature. Iowa's library has 32,000 volumes of Chinese literature alone. Indiana offers course work in Japanese-Western, Arabic-Western, and Chinese-Western literary relations as well as two

courses on African literature. Harvard offers courses relating
European literature and the Orient, as well as the strong curriculum of the Yen-Ching Institute. Ohio State has a strong and
varied program in East Asian literature. Columbia's rich Department of East-Asian Languages and Cultures is one of the world's
best; it supports an active publication program of translations of
Asian literature. The University of Pennsylvania has long supported Near Eastern literature and culture, and its museum in
this area is famous. Chicago not only boasts of an equally famous
Oriental Institute, offering the M.A. and Ph.D. in Near Eastern
Language and Civilizations, but also supports a Department of
Far Eastern Language and Civilization. There are many centers
of Hebrew Studies such as the Jewish Theological Seminary in
New York, Spertus College, Dropsie University, and the Hebrew
departments of California-Berkeley and New York University.
This representative roster, covering only Asian areas, indicates
the educational resources available for the planning of future
courses in East-West and World Literature.

We have in this chapter discussed the setting up of a curriculum in World Literature at either the Ph.D. or M.A. level. Once
curricula at these two levels have been established, their syllabi
(with bibliographies, lesson plans, sample examinations, etc.)
could be circulated to graduate departments countrywide. We
should not forget that colleges or universities without the personnel or library resources to undertake an entire curriculum for the
Ph.D. or even the M.A. could nevertheless enrich their offerings
and broaden their students' horizons by inserting an occasional
World Literature course into their regular offerings, just as graduate students in English, French, German, or other frequently
take a course or two in comparative literature to broaden their
knowledge and experience in a different approach and dimension
of literature.

We have in this chapter heralded an exciting epoch of World
Literature. In practical terms, the enrichment of certain comparative literature courses by extending their content to embrace
Asian and African texts need not imply that all courses within the
department need or even could assume a global dimension. If a
course on Western epic poetry (see p. 143) can be extended to an
East-West dimension (see p. 45) or a course on contemporary
sociopolitical poetry to a World dimension (see p. 46), such a

course as romanticism or neoclassicism, within their Western Heritage precincts, could hardly qualify. Comparative courses on myths and themes will probably be the easiest to expand to a World dimension, as Stith Thompson's lifework has demonstrated, with interrelations in second position. Forms and genres (tales, comedies, long narratives, lyric forms) will allow for selective expansion into global courses, whereas movements and periods will be the least convertible. Those more convertible courses, moreover, once become World Literature, will not thrust Asian or African letters into a majority role. In any case it will not be difficult to plan a 30-point M.A. in World Literature or a 60-point Ph.D. of which all courses or a portion of the courses would be actually global in content.

Thus a large department in the future could offer its comparative literature degree in any one of three dimensions: World, East-West, or Western Heritage. One cannot at this point even hazard a guess at what future dimensions (such as Asian-African) there may be. Most students in this century will opt for the Western Heritage, but they may sample World courses more and more for further enrichment. It must not be forgotten that World Literature is not a rival major to comparative literature, as some misconceive it, but merely the widest extension of comparative literature, strictly a dimension. Thus, converting a course on the novel or epic to a broader geographical selection of readings requires no administrative or curriculum committee action changing its category or code number.

FIG. 1: *Syllabus of Course in East-West Literature: Epic Poetry*
(Compare this syllabus with that of Western Heritage course on epic poetry on p. 143.)

CLASS ASSIGNMENT	CLASS REPORT
1. Nature of Epic; Theories of Epic	
2. *Gilgamesh* (2000 B.C.)	
3. Homer, *Iliad* (ca. 850 B.C.)	Rameses II as epic hero (12th century B.C.)
4. Homer, *Odyssey* (ca. 850 B.C.)	Apollonius, *Argonautica* (3rd century B.C.)
5. Vergil, *Aeneid* (29–19 B.C.)	*Beowulf* (ca. A.D. 725)

CLASS ASSIGNMENT	CLASS REPORT
6. *Mahabharata* (ca. A.D. 350)	*Shah Nameh* (10th century A.D.)
7. *Ramayana* (ca. 4th century A.D.)	*Dede Korkut* (11th century A.D.)
8. *Chanson de Roland* (11th century)	*Poema de mio Cid* (ca. A.D. 1140)
9. *Slóvo o Púlku Ígorevĕ (Campaign of Igor)* (early 13th century)	*Nibelungenlied* (ca. A.D. 1200)
10. Luis de Camoëns, *Os Lusíadas* (1572)	*Volsung Saga* (13th century)
11. Tasso, *Gerusalemme Liberata* (1575)	Lope de Vega, *Jerusalén Conquistada* (1609)
12. Voltaire, *La Henriade* (1728)	Milton, *Paradise Lost* (1667)

13. Course conclusions; national vs. religious epic; Western vs. Eastern epics

Students will read foreign language epics in languages for which they are certified.

FIG. 2. Syllabus of Course in World Literature: Twentieth-Century Sociopolitical Poetry

Note: All poems unavailable on reserve shelves will be made available in class.

1. Introduction on world poetic forms. Importance of thematic courses in this area. "Poetry is of its nature more personal than 'straight' propaganda" (C. D. Lewis). Social and political themes to be examined through poetry. English and French as international languages.

2. WAR AND PEACE: Yeats, "An Irish Airman Foresees His Death" (Ireland); Louis Aragon, "Ballad for One Who Sang at the Stake" (France); Paul Éluard, "La Victoire de Guernica" (France); W. H. Auden, "September 1, 1939" (England); James Dickey, "The Forebombing" (U.S.A.); Wilfred Owen, "Dulce et Decorum Est" (England); Denise Levertov, "What Were They Like?" (U.S.A.); Leopold Senghor, "Aux Travailleurs Sénégalais" (Sénégal); Amado Hernández, "The Soldier and the Huk" (Philippines); Suresh Koli, "After the War" (India); Salmi Manja, "For Mankind" (Malaysia); Kim Kyu-dong, "Army Cemetery" (Korea); Usman Awang, "Peace" (Malaysia); Ai Ch'ing, "Protect Peace" (China); Ku Sang, "Enemy's Graves" (Korea); W. S. Rendra, "Ballad of the Men of the

Limestone Soil" (Indonesia); To Huu, "Little Luom" (Vietnam); Che Lan Vien, "On the Way Home" (Vietnam); Mao Tse-tung, "The Long March" (China); David Wagoner, "To My Friend Whose Parachute Did Not Open" (U.S.A.); Max Jacob, "La Guerre" (France); Hans Bender, "Der Junge Soldat" (Germany).

3. POLITICAL PROTEST: Robert Lowell, "The March" (I and II) (U.S.A.); André Vosnesensky, "Self-Portrait" (Russia); John Ciardi, "At a Concert of Music, Remembering the Dead in Korea" (U.S.A.); John Robert Colombia, "The Central Intelligence Agency" (Singapore); Amado Hernández, "The Structures of Class" (Philippines); Gieve Patel, "My Ambiguous Fate" (India); Aimé Césaire, "Pour saluer le Tiers Monde" (Martinique); Fen Chih, "Northern Wanderings" (China); Tran Dan, "Victory Is Certain" (Vietnam); S. N. Masuri, "Voices and Speech" (Malaysia); Edouard Maunick, "Fusillez-moi" (Mauritius); Tchicaya U'Tam'si, "Le Contempleur" (Congo, Brazzaville); Kim Su-yong, "Words of a Certain Poet" (Korea); Toto Sudarto Bachtiar, "On the Subject of Freedom" (Indonesia); Günter Grass, "Gleisdreieck" (Germany); Boris Pasternak, "Koniets" (Russia).

(These first two lessons [classes 2 and 3] are illustrative of the variety of poets and their geographical dispersion in a world literature course. For lack of space only the topics of the remaining classes are listed hereafter. Note that a dozen poems by European poets will be added to lessons 2 and 3 for a more just proportion.)

4. ONE WORLD
5. PATRIOTISM, THE HOMELAND, NATIONALISM
6. SENSE OF SOLIDARITY: COUNTRY, REGION, FAMILY
7. COMMUNISM VS. NATIONALISM; CAPITAL VS. LABOR
8. RACES AND PEOPLES: XENOPHILIA AND XENOPHOBIA
9. CUSTOMS AND FOLKWAYS
10. RELIGION, PHILOSOPHY, SUPERSTITIONS, BELIEFS
11. LIFE OF STUDENTS, TRADESMEN, AND THE POOR
12. A BETTER FUTURE FOR ALL
13. Final class discussion. Dominance and value of English and French as the world media of poetry. Geographical, political, and linguistic alignments. Objectivity or subjectivity of the poetry; propaganda vs. true sentiment. Effectiveness of sociopolitical poetry; freedom and security of the poet. Values of the course.

III

Department and Faculty

Bald heads, forgetful of their sins,
Old, learned, respectable bald heads
Edit and annotate the lines
That young men, tossing on their beds,
Rhymed out in love's despair. . . .
WILLIAM BUTLER YEATS, "The Scholars"

The Graduate and Undergraduate Department or Program

The comparative literature department is designed to meet the
needs of those who wish to study literature as an intercultural
and in some cases interdisciplinary medium, whether concentrators in the department or as occasional registrants from one of
the departments of national literature. The department may on
rare occasions function as a program, an "interdepartmental program" (UCLA), or even, within an English department, an
"interdepartmental Committee on Comparative Literature" (Columbia). The department offers to those with appropriate
qualifications, including reading ability in foreign languages, an
opportunity to study literature extranationally through movements, periods, genres, themes, and the fifth catalyst of literary
history: theory and criticism. The department recognizes the
second objective of comparative literature, the sustained comparison with music, psychology, fine arts, etc. (see Ch. ix), but
only when two or more national literatures are involved. The
thesis on "Bossuet on Politics" (see p. 22) may be interdisciplinary, but it is hardly comparative. Some departments, indeed,
require that the two national literatures must not be composed in
the same language (Portuguese/Brazilian, Spanish/Hispano-

48

American, British/American), a point to which we shall return below (see Ch. v).

The dual objective of the department is to impart not only broad knowledge to the students, but a comparative viewpoint, so that they, if future teachers, may be adequately trained to accept courses in comparative literature, world literature, great books, the humanities, or even—as is sometimes the case—to teach in a broader context a national literature of their concentration. No department congratulates itself on "making" comparatists full-blown like Pallas by graduation time, but it can prepare students by teaching and example to develop into comparatists during their careers. The extreme conviction voiced by Michelangelo that "one attains lofty things only near the end" is implicit in the fact that teachers in the comparative literature department, certainly at the graduate level, are usually or should be full or associate professors who have published in this interrelated field.

The graduate department enables students to have a point of departure in a literature of concentration. Sometimes this concentration is represented by the M.A. in such a national literature; sometimes it may be a required accumulation of courses in that literature. Possession of the M.A. in a national literature not only is evidence of an excellent groundwork in literary history but may be vocationally expedient for future employment. There are, however, other meaningful course structures, as we shall see in Chapter iv, that do not involve the M.A. or even its equivalent of academic points in one literature.

The student is placed in contact with a maximum number of personal approaches and positions through the frequent participation of other professors than the nuclear few who constitute the departmental staff. In some universities, comparative literature departments even bring back their own Ph.D. alumni not only to form an ideological continuum, but to inspire the doctoral candidates by example. The candidate not only acquires the broad vocabulary and conception of literary history in its several national settings, but observes the impact of given cultures on cross-cultural movements, themes, and genres. Since the courses are intentionally sweeping in their coverage (see p. xvi), the frequent emergence of masterpieces on reading assignments becomes inevitable.

Unity in Program of Study

Comparative literature operates with a minimum of courses, leaving further integration and correlation of literature to the students as they take the regular literature courses of one co-operating department (sometimes more). Unity is achieved by the recurring patterns of many chronologically vertical courses (epic, tragedy, satire, lyric poetry), which trace a subject matter from its Greco-Roman origins to its present Western Heritage extension. Similarly, in a chronologically horizontal course (symbolism, baroque) there will be materials familiar to the students through their literature of concentration. Comparative courses that would not unify the specific interests of a maximum of students enrolled in them (e.g., Nineteenth-Century Drama in Germany, Denmark, and Sweden) are not offered.

A further unity is lent to the formal preparation of comparative literature candidates by a required semester seminar in this field, relating the discipline with problems of criticism, philology, stylistics, linguistics, library resources, research tools, evidence, and other pertinent matters. (See below, p. 96.) Unity of admission standards is in some schools preserved by each cooperating department's retaining the right of vetoing borderline applicants from concentrating (taking 28 to 32 points) within that department.

Unity of purpose would seem to be more attainable in a department than in a program, and therefore more difficult to achieve at the undergraduate level, where the curriculum is so commonly identified as a program.

Nevertheless, among the interesting discoveries of the Nichols Committee Report on the undergraduate major and minor is that programs have apparently turned out to be more feasible than departments. The passage that explains this state of the discipline must be quoted in full:

Although the original mandate of this committee specified that we concern ourselves with the content of undergraduate programs, rather than modalities, the question of staffing and the program organization has a bearing on the curriculum. Indeed, it may, in some instances, be a decisive factor as to whether there will even be a curriculum at all in these days of shrinking budgets. We have tried to suggest (section 3) that a viable Comparative Literature program can reinforce language departments. To do so effectively, the Comparative Literature program should be as flexible as possible in its institutional organization. This would seem to argue for the program model, rather than the more traditional department. By program, however, we mean a semi-autonomous organizational entity with its own budget and one or two "core" staff members—usually trained comparatists—associated full-time, or a majority of their time, with the program. They may hold joint appointments with another department (often an FL department). Complementing these core staff members are a variety of other part-time personnel drawn from contributing departments, most frequently FL and English. Such people may have a regular course or courses, or teach one every two years; they generally do not teach more than 2/5 of their time in Comparative Literature. It is here that the flexibility of the FTE (Full Time Equivalency) can be beneficial to Comparative Literature and to contributing departments. Because the FTE is not tied to specific individuals, it is often possible to pool portions of FTE's to make joint appointments between a department and Comparative Literature in cases where neither would have been able to make an appointment alone. In such cases the person hired may well be a recent Comparative Literature Ph.D., another reason for stressing basic FL competence in graduate schools to assure that our graduate students are competitive with FL graduate students in a tight job market.

The Nichols Report concludes that the kind of program described in the paragraph above is the most widely followed organizational model for comparative literature in use today in North America. The Report notes that the University of Kentucky undertook a revision of its program in 1975 to conform with the model described above. The Committee finds it noteworthy that the impetus for the revision came from the university administration, which saw in this model a possiblity for greater flexibility in hiring and development of personnel within the humanities, and consequently a financial advantage.

The Comparative Literature Student and the Question of Elitism

The chairmen of the first two ACLA Committees on Professional Standards were from Harvard and Yale. Colleagues in other parts of the country were quick to look for a note of New England "manifest destiny" or "mission" couched in their reports, both of which were rich in ideas and provided a real service to the profession. However, the honest inquiry the two reports voiced concerning the readiness of many faculties for this demanding new discipline was quickly viewed as elitist. The Levin Report voiced great caution.

> A preliminary question arises as to whether it is necessarily desirable or practical that Comparative Literature be represented in every institution; whether it does not make special demands, in the way of linguistic preparation and intellectual perspective, which ought to reserve it for the more qualified students; and whether it does not presuppose an existing strength in language departments and libraries to which not very many colleges, and indeed not every university, can be fairly expected to measure up. At this point we venture to suggest that, where it is not yet represented in a curriculum, it should not be introduced without a good deal of institutional heart-searching and a careful scrutiny of the facilities and requirements elsewhere.

Or again,

> It should be frankly recognized that a Ph.D. in Comparative Literature may take longer to acquire than one in most of the separate areas of language and literature; and if a candidate has any hesitations between the straight degree and ours, he may well be encouraged to take the more traditional choice. If we profess to cover more ground than our sister departments, we should honestly acknowledge that we must work harder, nor should we incur their suspicion by offering short-cuts.

Critics were quick to read condescension toward the majority of American universities in the first paragraph quoted above and condescension toward the less demanding degree requirements of individual-literature departments in the second. After all, if small colleges like Mills or Reed or Oberlin boasted of outstanding colleagues in other fields, why could they not boast of them in ours?

The second ACLA Report backtracked somewhat. "The elitism, the pursuit of the highest standards within a few, small departments—this idea which seemed so desirable and so feasible ten years ago has been challenged for better or for worse by rapid historical change." Yet some critics vigorously attacked the second report as elitist, perhaps the most vocal being a dissident member of the second Committee on Professional Standards itself, Dean Herbert Weisinger. The first report had supported the view that only universities that could and would grant full tuition scholarships to all comparative literature students should be allowed to offer our discipline. In the 1976 Report the plea for scholarship help for students is more moderate, even while making a condition of admission that every student receive some scholarship help.

> A major responsibility of a graduate program in comparative literature is to admit only that number of capable students it can truly educate, as they deserve, as the discipline requires, and as available fellowship funds permit. Wholesale admission of students by institutions with little or no scholarship help is, we believe, reprehensible. Few universities in the seventies can offer blanket support, as some did in the sixties, but some assistance toward the most needy and most gifted abbreviates the long test of stamina which graduate study can become. It is wiser to admit a realistic number of students among whom available help can be meaningfully distributed, than a number so large that a sense of community is lost and study becomes associated with penury.

Of this passage and others Dean Weisinger objected in an open letter:

> I know of no department which would not prefer fewer but better students, fully supported; more faculty; increased support costs; reduced teaching loads . . . and the like, but if their argument were carried through to its ultimate conclusion, there would be neither students enough nor money enough to satisfy their desires. . . . To perpetuate, and indeed to foster, the spirit of elitism which breathes through the document is to cut off the

future of comparative literature just at the moment it is ready to take its place among the major disciplines. . . . If the committee believes that the graduate study of comparative literature should in fact be restricted to the few institutions in which its [the committee's] standards can be said to apply, it should say so directly.

When I first read this discussion, I thought of the extraordinary ways other than teaching by which a few of our better students have been obliged to earn their living: dancing, acting, editing, translating. One student was working as a stagehand in off-Broadway productions. Even if this student completed his degree brilliantly—a reasonable prediction—by the arcane thinking of the ACLA Report he had no business being among our graduate candidates. Others among our past candidates would have been equally ineligible, including four whose theses have appeared as books, since our established departmental policy has been to distribute the number of scholarship stipends as widely as possible on the theory that all candidates admitted and retained were of such a comparable quality that we had to distribute equally the modest tuition allotment. Most must therefore find supplementary funds for tuition. "Intellectual perspective," fortunately, is not limited to such a happy few that they would have carried off the lion's share.

The spirit of the 1976 paragraph quoted is quite clear. A literal reading notes that four degrees of financial help are mentioned: full (blanket), some, little, or none. Full or some justifies one's being admitted. Where little or none is available, it becomes unfair to admit a student—no matter how willing the candidate may be to take the risks. Students take such risks in other literature departments, but those in comparative literature were not to do so—another invidious comparison setting comparative literature apart from its congeneric departments. A fifth quantity of financial aid is also mentioned, this being denoted by the indefinite adjective "available." This is the amount that we at NYU have spread widely and equally among the many qualified students who request scholarship assistance. Our students are willing to accept this egalitarian approach to the disbursement of "available" tuition funds, knowing at least that the system eliminates favoritism. Occasionally of course the department loses a potential applicant of merit who receives a larger financial offer from another institution, but our departmental standards and student spirit remain high.

The paragraph of Report II quoted above raises a crucial problem of departmental policy somewhat alien to the matter at issue. This is the Report's allegation that if a department restricts its admissions to those applicants receiving "full" or "some" (but not "little" or "no") tuition money, then a "sense of community" is retained. This ideal or desideratum of the *beati pauciores* is suggested in both reports without being justified. This sense of community, so important to a department, results more easily, from our own departmental experience, when a large and diversified student body is present and available for the various types of departmental activity we engage in: quarterly colloquia, annual regional conference, receptions, student parties, a student newsletter, and so on. Since our students take many classes in the national literature departments, it becomes all the more important to have such gatherings where they may meet and exchange ideas. Indeed, in a large comparative literature department, the various communalities have an opportunity to mingle: the Orientals, the Indians, the Scandinavians, the Israelis, and so on. Other standards being equal, a full-bodied department brings a greater sense of solidarity than one limited to the Plautian concept of the happy few. Later on we shall view this desideratum of a broad, international student group in another context.

Rather than entering more deeply into the matter of students' financial problems, which is the deep concern of every chairman and adviser—and discussion of which occupies a major part of consultation hours—let us merely grant that during periods of diminished federal and state assistance, most universities have fewer resources (scholarships, loans, funds for thesis writing, grants from special societies, alumni groups, etc.), and chairmen and advisers who spend an infinite amount of time on their students' behalf can hardly accept being libeled as "reprehensible" for admitting willing and deserving students with only "little" help. Dean Herbert Weisinger, in his comments on the elitism of Report II, entered the following vigorous dissent:

The report also seems to find an immediate correlation between the number of students in a department and the quality of those students. This may often be true at the undergraduate level, but if a graduate department has fixed standards of admission and a firm philosophical stance, I do not see the correlation as necessarily true. It is a question of governance. On this matter, the idea that departments should accept only the number of students whom it can financially subsidize is out of touch with reality. Some of our most prominent students are the poorest, but the decision whether they will pursue their degree with little help is theirs, not ours.

The elitist view, however, will continue to attract adherents, who are wise enough, however, to dissociate elitism from concepts of numerus clausus, financial subsidy, library census, and the rest. Fred Nichols of CUNY is one of these:

> I guess I do think that Comparative Literature is an elite discipline. You do have to know more and use more languages, keep track of more things going on, to get a job in the field. It should be a little harder to get a comparative degree than one in a single literature, language exams should be tougher, and so on. Yet it's been my experience, at all three institutions where I've been involved with it, that the discipline attracts more mature and more sophisticated students. We should take advantage of that.

Admission Qualifications and Standards

The 1976 Report of the Committee on Professional Standards of ACLA is a well-written, basically conservative document, and its section on admissions does not vary from its general excellence. The prescriptions for admission read as follows:

> Overpopulation in our graduate schools will be reduced if we weigh scrupulously the credentials of each applicant for admission. A critical criterion of each applicant's application is his acquaintance with foreign languages. Normally, he or she should bring to graduate study considerable knowledge of at least two languages. After one or two years this number should rise to three. Of these, one should be an ancient language. Thus, by the time the student begins his dissertation he should be capable of dealing with texts in at least four literatures, including English.
> In addition to these linguistic requirements, which should be

stringently maintained, some philological training is highly desirable. Most graduate programs, moreover, continue to require a single major language and literature [concentration], and in view of the present job market this requirement seems to rest on solid logic. Since it tends to direct students toward positions in single language departments and thus toward the teaching of elementary language courses, it further increases the need for strong linguistic training.

This is of course good and prudent counsel. However, there are two underlying premises that are not necessarily valid. The first is a blind acceptance of the belief that large departmental enrollments ("overpopulation") are necessarily bad, worse for comparative literature than for other departments of literature. *Over* as a prefix is a pejorative not really applicable here. We are back to the restrictive elitism of the first Committee Report (see p. 52). In any case, the current decline of enrollments in the humanities makes a concern over excessive student population irrelevant. As for the tenacious loyalty to the requirement of Greek, Latin, "or an equally ancient language," this debatable policy has been treated below in Chapter v. It is often honored in the breach, even in comparative literature departments with the highest standards, and for understandable motives. The other points in the paragraphs above are well made, as is the appeal for traditionalism, which follows:

> To be admitted into an adequate program, a candidate ought to be able to offer two other requirements in addition to linguistic proficiency. He or she must have had extensive undergraduate instruction in at least one literature, and preferably in two. Such instruction should include training in the analysis of texts, as well as in the forms, meters, traditions, genres—the idiom and particularity of the literature or literatures he has chosen to learn. This requirement already implies a second: a lively awareness of the past itself. Despite some tendencies to permit students a nearly exclusive engagement with the present century, Comparative Literature as a discipline rests unalterably on the knowledge of history. The student who wants to specialize in twentieth-century literature needs to know just as much about the past as his fellow students if he is truly to understand his chosen period. Arguably, he needs to know more since the cultural inheritance of our century is in the nature of things richer than any earlier period.

In sum, it is sufficient to repeat that in a period of decreasing enrollments in large and well-staffed graduate schools it is anomalous for a standards committee to propose that enrollments in comparative literature be made more restrictive than in the national literature departments. Or to propose that only students who can receive all or some scholarship funds may be considered for admission. This creates a most difficult rapport with the graduate school deans and budget officers, which will scarcely benefit the comparative literature departmental budget.

When a new department of comparative literature joins the company of well-established and respected departments of literature, it can and should gear its admission requirements to the high standards already entrenched—especially since graduate applicants with only the B.A. in some schools like Cornell are admitted directly to Ph.D. candidacy. If the local standards require high achievement on the Graduate Record Examination, a B plus or better in one's college major (or over 3.2 to 3.4 minimum score on a 4-point maximum), and reassuring letters of recommendation, these should suffice for a decision to be taken, without invoking a rule that comparative literature be "tougher" than its cooperating departments. On the other hand, comparative literature chairmen should encourage candidates when possible to drop by for an interview, to check on the candidates' languages, travel, and peripheral studies and interests, if not also to double-check their financial needs. At some universities a visiting applicant is urged to visit a couple of comparative literature classes to see what they and the students are like. Frequently applicants welcome this opportunity. Yet the values of the personal interview are not unique to comparative literature. Such interviews are encouraged by the departments of science especially.

Student Progress Evaluation

The ACLA Report II rightly reminds us that

> . . . at some point during his graduate career, the student's performance needs to be evaluated, not only for its mere adequacy but also for its real promise. It is unfair to the student, to the

department, and to a profession afflicted with unemployment, to retain in the academy the weak and the mediocre. We urge the directors and staff of graduate programs to give this question of retention serious periodic scrutiny.

The Report reminds us that in this area the judgment of colleagues in neighboring departments is especially useful.

The initial precautions must of course be taken during the admissions phase, as we have seen. Yet once in a while students, especially those absorbed in personal or financial problems, do not bear out their promise. Some large literature departments, especially English, have special qualifying examinations for the Ph.D. required of M.A. holders who wish to proceed to the doctorate. Most comparative literature departments, being smaller in student population, do not impose such an examination when a student completes his M.A. work, since the student's transcript now tells a chairman or graduate adviser what he needs most to know: quality of class work, quality of written papers, initiative and assiduity, progress in foreign languages, and a grade level. Some departments supplement the transcripts by requiring end-of-semester comments on students. Even so, in busy and understaffed comparative literature departments the chairmen and advisers must double-check periodically to see if the transcript bears out their generally satisfactory impression of the student, verify whether any conditions imposed on admission have been met, make sure that incompletes are being duly repaired, and so on. Registration period, when students are present, would seem an appropriate time to check on their records, if appointments are staggered to avoid crowding. Some universities impose a statute of limitations on the acceptance of late grades (usually delayed by term papers), and even though it is the students' responsibility to be aware of this, their chairman or adviser would do them a service to remind them of the danger.

The Staff and the Budget

The full-time professors within the department at the early stage of its development need not be a large number provided the department has backup manpower resources inside and outside the university. The familiar pattern of staffing is to have two or three professors completely assigned to the department or program with a number of colleagues from neighboring departments offering part-time or occasional teaching and sometimes carrying a dual title (e.g., English and Comparative Literature). In a recent Harvard bulletin, for example, of the twenty-nine professors sharing the teaching, three held full-time appointments in comparative literature. Thus an adequate staff is available to supervise examinations and theses. There must be, as at Harvard, a nucleus of two or three professors dedicated to maintaining without compromise an integrity of principles and methods, *sans peur et sans politique*. This nuclear group must give continuing evidence of its dedication, as, for example, when examiners are lacking during the marginal weeks of the school year and during vacations and sabbaticals of crucial personnel. The most frequent reason why an otherwise supportive colleague will beg off serving on a thesis jury is that "the topic is beyond my field of competence," a refusal that must be accepted even when you know that he is closer to that field than any other incumbent in his department.

These exhibitions of professorial reticence, even when dictated by the laudable quality of modesty, are of course discouraging. When a Victorian specialist invited to interrogate on Trollope declines on the ground that he or she has not read Trollope for several years, we have an example of overspecialization creating a problem for the comparative literature department. The implication is left that the comparatists are less demanding and need to be reminded of the fact. It is an even more acute problem when the search for thesis readers is initiated. For here the candidate may have included some less familiar figure like Aubrey Beardsley or Pierre Loti in his or her cast of characters. It is a paradox that comparatists, sometimes suspected by their rivals of seeking to know less and less about more and more, in such circumstances expect their colleagues in the national literatures to know something about everyone in their own literature. I once heard a comparatist at a Great Books examination chide an English professor who claimed to be too rusty on *The Scarlet Letter* to interrogate on it by suggesting, "O.K. You interrogate on *Bovary* and I'll take *The Scarlet Letter*." The point is that the Great Books examination calls for information in extenso as well as in depth on the candidate's part, enlarging upon generic, thematic, and periodic issues raised by the texts.

The problems of staffing are of course inextricably tied in with the budget, a subject awaiting our attention.

The Annual Budget Hassle with Dean Midas

The recent boom of the narrative told in the second person, so successfully exploited by Michel Butor, is based on the theory that the reader empathizes more easily, and indeed becomes personally involved, when directly addressed. Our department has already contributed two Ph.D. theses to this boom. Since any chairman past, present, or future has had or will inevitably have a conversation such as the one reproduced in this section, I shall cast it in the second person. The subject of the exchange is the lack of personnel to handle the many duties required by a typical graduate department (or program) of comparative literature. I know of no department that has such adequate personnel that it must not make constant and insistent demands on the other departments of literature.

If yours is a typical—or medium-sized—department, we may set the background for your battle of the budget. Your department offers six individual graduate comparative literature courses each semester, not counting the guided individual research course whose instructors are listed vaguely as "staff." Your department has each semester a student complement of forty candidates for the Ph.D. and thirty for the M.A. Of these candidates ten will receive the Ph.D. during the course of the academic year and ten will receive the M.A. As usual, the nuclear teaching staff in your department this year consists of yourself and the graduate adviser, both of you teaching two courses each semester. This year, as during others, you have invited two guest professors from the national literature departments to teach one comparative literature course each for the first semester and two to teach the same number the second semester. The teachers in your department this year thus add up to two full-time and four part-time. You have thus a teaching staff of six to call upon for departmental duties—or more pessimistically, four each semester. Your dean obviously assumes that you are well staffed for a new department, much smaller than the English department, which operates, at the graduate and college levels, with a staff of twenty-some full-time personnel. We pick up your conversation with Dean Midas as you are explaining your need for a budget increase.

"I hope you notice that we had an increase in registrations this year, especially since we're discussing budget needs."

"Yes," says Midas. "The French, German, and English departments had an increase also. Admittedly, not so much as yours."

"Of course they did. Look at these statistics. We sent comparative literature students to take courses in the five national literature departments to the amount of 180 graduate points. They should show an increase."

"But they sent you students, as well."

"Not many. They're feeling the pinch. They sent us a total of 24 registration points during the same period."

"All right, but if you're teaching only twelve courses a school year, why do you need more money?"

You sigh. You explained all this last year at this time.

"Teaching is not the problem. It's the extra chores. This June we shall grant ten Ph.D.'s. This will require fifty people to sit on ten thesis defenses. We shall grant ten M.A.'s, for which we shall need twenty thesis readers. We shall have ten students taking their final oral exams preceding the thesis, which will require another fifty examiners. Not forgetting the volunteers to staff the guided research courses and the long-term theses in progress— about twenty more at least. Since you have your calculator here on your desk, you can confirm that we shall need 140 units of noninstructional manpower next year just as badly as we do this year."

Dean Midas' face has not assumed the expression of caritas you were hoping for. He says, "One hundred and forty divided by six is twenty-three point three hours. There are six of you teaching comparative literature this year."

"No, there are only four teachers each semester, and two of these part-time. Furthermore the examinations and defenses run from two to three hours or more. Even this doesn't explain the problem adequately. You are thinking in terms of the other literature departments where Ph.D.'s in French or English can be somewhat familiar with the content of their own departmental examinations and theses. Our theses and examinations wander all over two or three continents at least. Sometimes we cannot find an adequate complement of jurors or readers here and have to bring in specialists from outside."

"This surprises me. You must have a great potential source of specialists in the full-time professors in Romance languages, German, Slavic, classics, and Near Eastern studies."

"True," you explain, "in those five departments there are forty professors certified to teach at the graduate level, within limits. But they're not on call. Even their own chairmen don't feel they can tap them at will for tasks in their own department, let alone ours. With their narrower interests, they often turn us down with the remark that such an examination or thesis is outside their field. And they are usually right, of course. Out of these forty professors in neighboring departments we have perhaps a dozen with wide interests and willing dispositions we can count on—a few sometimes teach for us—for our household duties. But even these few we can't use more than two or three times a year, because they are busier than ever in their own reduced-staff departments. If we multiply twelve by three, we can thus count on 36 units of interdepartmental manpower per year. Even if we require our intradepartmental annual teaching staff of six to contribute 8 units apiece each year, eight chores of reading theses, reading examinations, serving on juries, we come up with only 48 units. We cannot ask more of the four intradepartmental teachers, for we use one quarter of their teaching time and they have many duties in their own departments. This situation is even worse when we invite a distinguished professor from elsewhere to teach an occasional course for us, for we cannot use such visitors as additional manpower."

"Why couldn't you use them? At least while they're on your staff."

"When you authorize us to pay distinguished visitors the unit cost of an instructor, they're being exploited even if they merely teach and race back home. As I was about to say, if one's department needs manpower, beyond teaching needs, for theses and exams alone, 140 units of manpower, and with the best will in the world one has only 48 plus 36, that is 84 units, where am I to find and pay for the missing 56?"

Dean Midas maintaining an honest perplexity, you continue:

"Could you at least put on our budget an allotment of $25 for each one unit of service? Better yet, an honorarium, which is another way of saying a miserably inadequate payment."

Dean Midas shakes his head.

"There's no precedent for it."

"How about giving us two more assistant professors in comparative literature? That would help solve it. After all, we're making a profit for the university."

"Not enough," answers Dean Midas, who this year raised your estimated departmental charge for library purchases from $8,000 to $35,000 so that your budget could not possibly show a profit.

You start to grasp for straws.

"How about letting each cooperating department reduce one professor's teaching assignment by one course and assign him or her to help on these comparative literature chores that have to be done?"

Dean Midas does not bother to answer this one. You suggested it last year and he refused you then.

Finally Dean Midas brightens up and you sense that he may have found the answer—or an answer. He resets his cigarette on the ashtray. He strokes his jowl for a moment. His thick gold ring has never shone so brightly.

"Look," he asks, "why don't you keep a record of all these services and then be sure to invite all these chaps to your spring departmental cocktail party?"

We lower the curtain on your painful interview. You are back where you started. The more students you attract, the more difficulties there will be in finding volunteers to help them through theses and examinations, not to mention the other legitimate needs of students. So long as comparative literature has as many full-time and part-time students as—or even more than—the other established literature departments and yet must be staffed by fewer professors, deans will be willing to thrust the difficult problem of manpower back onto the department head. The issue must be raised again and again until the administration finds a solution. Not all chairmen find themselves reasoning in vain with a Dean Midas, known as the "bottom-line dean." Yet any potential chairman, if urged to take over direction of a comparative literature department, must endeavor to have the matter settled before assuming his difficult new charge and losing his bargaining power. Otherwise, he will face continual frustration. The solution I should propose is an honorarium of $25 for each unit of manpower contributed from outside the department. If you multiply the missing 56 manpower units by $25, it is clear that the entire problem can be solved for the cost of a single instructor at current rates.

The Formation of the Comparatist: Why Not Take Assistant Professor Nesposobny?

Since we are discussing the typical comparative literature department's urgent manpower needs, we must refer to an unsatisfactory solution recently proposed in those institutions faced with reducing enrollments in the language and literature departments. This solution is surely just as undesirable a tactic as the merging of comparative literature and the foreign language departments into a giant bouillabaisse, a thoughtless solution entertained recently by many adminstrators and one to which we shall return in Chapter xiv. The solution now discussed is a fragmentary example of the bouillabaisse solution. Let us return to Dean Midas and yourself and pick up your dialogue where the above-mentioned indecisive colloquy came to a halt.

Dean Midas has just remembered that the slump in Slavic studies has left that department overstaffed. Indeed, there are six professors with too little to do in that reduced department. All of them have tenure. He suddenly brightens up and says to you:

"Of course. Just the man to help you. We could transfer him to your department and he could be very useful. Dr. Nesposobny!"

Your heart sinks. This elderly assistant professor has a reputation of being a timeserver. He published in Minsk his thesis on Ukrainian dialects, his only work in print. He has mastered three languages: Russian, Ukrainian, and Polish. His English is really understandable only if you know Russian. He has held his present rank for thirty years.

"Nesposobny? But what does he know about comparative literature? He's a linguistics scholar."

"He could help you on Russian exams and theses. You could make him retool. You could have him cheap. In fact, you're in luck. He'll be retiring in two years. Anyway, we couldn't get you anyone from outside. We're overcommitted financially to the language and literature departments."

There are various irrelevant and dubious motivations behind the staffing of comparative literature from within the university. One sees cases where departmental feuds and divisions break out, and comparative literature attracts some as a possible refuge. One sees individuals who know only French and English literature and feel that their natural home is the comparative literature department; they either try to transfer or keep proposing binary courses on Diderot and Swift or Byron and Foscolo. One must contrast these narrow specialists with versatile polyglots in English or German or other departments who can retool and slowly develop useful courses of truly international breadth. These are the scholars the comparative literature departments need to incorporate for full-time or part-time service. Indeed, it is precisely when lowered enrollment leaves the national literature departments overstaffed that comparative literature should accept only competent literary scholar-linguists able to retool themselves into comparatists, even if only on a part-time schedule.

Comparative literature, in a period when it is a fashionable major or graduate curriculum, will attract a few professors to retool who do not have what Paul Van Tieghem called the *équipement* for it. F. M. Guyard (see Bibliography) enumerates these qualifications as (1) a knowledge and sense of history, (2) an acquaintance with several literatures, (3) a reading ability of several languages, and (4) a knowledge of such research tools as national bibliographical manuals, comparative literature bibliographies, a chronological repertory (such as Van Tieghem established in 1937) of modern literatures, outlines of comparative literature like that of Friederich (1954), and the bibliographies kept up to date by literary journals themselves. Others in the field would have no quarrel with this list of requirements, although Pichois and Rousseau at one point summarize the comparatist as a tripartite being: polyglot, philologist, and globetrotter. We perforce underemphasize foreign travel as a requirement; graduate students who cannot travel or study abroad before obtaining their degree can console themselves that travel will become more possible—with travel grants, it is hoped—once they have their final degree.

The rapid growth of comparative literature without appropriate budgetary increase can have only two optimum solutions. Slowly, as tuition income increases, more of this income must be allotted to maintain the necessary teachers and faculty manpower for theses and examinations. Moreover, the situation of having to depend on French, Spanish, German, or other colleagues to retool and become latter-day comparatists should very soon become unnecessary with several generations of Ph.D.'s in comparative literature by now tested and proved as scholars and teachers, available for and worthy of senior professorships in our profession. Those of us veterans who have had to convert to comparatism from Romanistik and other studies were adequate for the task during the first decades of the postwar revival of comparative literature. *La nouvelle relève* is waiting and eager for the change of guard. They can only watch with dismay as they see the positions for which they were trained being usurped by the retooled professors of national literature, no matter how talented the latter may be.

This author would be less than grateful if he neglected to mention with gratitude a group of volunteers who have sometimes saved the day when no other personnel could be enlisted as thesis readers and examination jurors. These are the dozen or more distinguished emeriti professors in the several national literature departments who have been eager to "keep their hand in" and have performed brilliantly. Their conscientious preparation and enthusiastic participation have proved not only helpful but often inspiring. Other chairmen, and especially those in universities with early retirement policies, who are desperately trying to solve the manpower problem described above, might well keep in mind retired Professor Chips.

The Training of Teachers

Graduate degrees in comparative literature must be as vocation-oriented as the degree in any other of the humanities or social sciences. This does not mean that those few special cases (intellectuals, true dilettantes, early retirees) who are studying for the mere excitement of it are not welcome or that they cannot make unique contributions to classroom discussions. The vocationally motivated are the vast majority, even if the goal is not classroom teaching, but rather library work, publishing, journalism, or other. Most of our graduates, it must be recognized, would "gladly teach" rather than anything else. Teaching is an art that cannot be taught of itself. We can help by example. We can help by sharing experience. We can help by communicating knowledge, demonstrating techniques, evaluating materials, and serving as models—the gamut of broad didactic functions that Confucius called simply "the teacher's rubbing off of himself on his students." One cannot be too self-congratulatory. We sometimes educate our students by bad as well as good examples.

The influence we exert on our graduate students out in the field is only partially apparent to us. Sometimes a student will write that he has adopted a book of ours as a reading text in a course. Sometimes a student will write that he is using a course syllabus of ours and basing a new course on it. We are aware that they are advancing in the profession as we are requested to update our letters of recommendation and mail them to successive deans. When the alumni send back news notes of books, articles, reviews, jobs, etc., for the annual departmental newsletter, we all feel that we are doing—or have done—a creditable and rewarding job.

The true introspection comes, however, when the job situation tightens and students begin to question their training. Professor Leland Chambers has recently published in the *ACLA Newsletter* some comments on their vocational preparation made by recent Ph.D.'s in comparative literature from a number of graduate schools. The replies to his questionnaires leave one concerned, even though it may be logically assumed that the unemployed Ph.D.'s would be the most vocal and critical. Chambers comments on the many replies:

> Quite often they wrote what they did because of some breakdown of rapport between them as individuals and the institutions which had either trained them or employed them or refused to hire them, and their comments often sprang from an active sense of betrayal and rejection, whether legitimate or imagined. In some cases they give the impression of a basic inadequacy before the current conditions of the profession, while in others one is convinced of a gross institutional insensitivity to the needs of our graduates.

Several of the replies stress the irrelevancy of their graduate training to the teaching posts available:

> I have to teach large sections of Freshmen and Sophomores whose background in literature and communications skills is very poor. I was trained, in contrast, to teach highly educated and highly intelligent Ph.D. candidates.

> I received no training on how to teach undergraduates.

> My advice is to trim graduate programs and encourage the development of broad, critical intellectuals rather than narrow specialists.

> Much of graduate education seems madly irrelevant to most undergraduate teaching. It is narrow and lacking in that philosophic perspective that might relate specialized knowledge to human pursuits generally.

If the two last Ph.D.'s quoted had indeed been trained to narrow specialism, they surely had a just grievance against the departments that trained them. Indeed, it would seem that some departments have not yet assumed the great breadth which lends the excitement to comparative literature. One suspects courses narrow in their subject matter, their geographical breadth, their approaches. One is also likely to be critical of departments or programs that offer perhaps too few courses to boot.

To some extent lowered standards of college and high school training are making young minds less adaptable to what some have called the elitist discipline of comparative literature, even in its most restricted dimensions. This deterministic decline, the depreciation of foreign languages, the rise of remedial reading at even the college level, and the financial crisis of the colleges have indeed changed the vocational situation in the past decade. Ten years ago, we could take satisfaction that all our Ph.D.'s were gainfully employed. At the present writing, it appears that four of our seventy Ph.D.'s out in the profession are momentarily unemployed and a few are busy in alternate careers—a defensible statistic when compared with a nine percent national unemployment figure, but hardly one to make us complacent. (See also the suggestions in the job market section of Chapter xv.)

Under the present circumstances the new Ph.D. will probably

spend a longer apprenticeship teaching sophomore and junior literature and humanities courses before facing advanced or graduate classes. Yet this is surely appropriate. Under these circumstances that curious phenomenon of modern education, the A.B.D. (all but dissertation) degree may fall—unregretted, many will say—by the wayside. The employment situation for Ph.D.'s is now so tight that a C or two on a transcript, one or two reservations in a letter of recommendation, one or two incompletes on a record sheet may cost a graduate a teaching position.

This manual is being written during a period of recession, one of three since the Great Depression of the thirties. Since the education cycle, like the business cycle, fluctuates about normalcy—a fact of which one must occasionally reassure candidates—most of the counsels herein will assume normalcy, but will be valid, it is hoped, for any situation. One cannot train comparatists one way when the wave is at crest and another when it is in the trough.

The Graduate Seminar in Comparative Literature

The classroom training of a comparatist should start with the Seminar in Comparative Literature, a basic baptism-by-fire that entrants must undergo their first semester. A traditional subject matter is presented in Frederick Garber's course at SUNY-Binghamton: C.L. 301. Methodology, which covers the following areas:

1. The nature and scope of comparative literature as seen by the various schools. The Sorbonne and positivism. Wellek and the integrity of literature. Other commentators. Implications for theory and criticism, especially practical criticism, in the various approaches.
2. Traditional concerns and areas of comparative literature. Influence studies. Thematology. Problems of literary periodization; historicism vs. uniqueness. Étiemble and internationalism, etc.
3. Illustrations of method: Wellek, Frye, Spitzer, Auerbach, etc.
4. Translation: theory and problems, especially in relation to comparative literature. Student class presentations of translation, with discussion.

5. Literature and interdisciplinary studies, with emphasis on study of literature and the other arts. Examples, problems, basic issues.
6. Term paper submitted.

This seminar is a variant of the course known in other national literature departments—where one exists—as the methods-and-bibliography course. It is variously called Problems in Comparative Literature (North Carolina) or Introduction to Graduate Studies in Comparative Literature (Indiana). At New York University the course extends to discussion of practical professional problems and matters in order to meet some of the complaints that Professor Chambers uncovered in his polls on recent Ph.D.'s. The full title of the course indicates its pragmatic orientation: Methods, Bibliography, Resources, Comparative Techniques, and Professional Concerns. The list of topics discussed indicates the course's "busy" nature:

1. Comparative literature and its geographical dimensions. East-West problems. Role of the classics, history, organization, goals, and unity of comparative literature as an academic discipline.
2. The literary scholar-adventurer. Publish or perish. The excitement of scholarship. Literary and philological adventures and detectivism.
3. Libraries, bibliographies, the retrieval of knowledge. Researching, organizing research, styling. Learned societies and their journals. Microfilms, Microcards.
4. Literary schools, movements, generations, periods.
5. Comparative literature by genres: the epic.
6. Comparative literature by forms: ode, elegy, ballad, sonnet.
7. Themes and myths; plots and topics; archetypes.
8. The many interrelations of literature. Politics, censorship, the Index. *Littérature engagée*. Other interrelations.
9. Literature and language. Linguistics. Semantics, stylistics, taste. Auxiliary languages and their literary implications. Basic English. Pidgin. The loom of language. International Phonetics Alphabet.
10. Translation. Electronic translation. Can translation be taught?

Les Belles infidèles. The PEN Club Bill of Rights for Translators.

11. Textual accuracy. Evidence. Establishing a text. Determining chronology. Influence and seepage. Literary impact. Editing a text. Textual explication.
12. The scholar and the publisher: various relationships. Textbooks, scholarly books, trade books. Criticism in action: book reviewing.
13. The teaching of comparative literature. Special problems. Techniques. Content of syllabi. Textbooks, anthologies, dictionaries, etc.

The pragmatic nature of this syllabus is obvious and might worry a traditionalist expecting a larger infusion of literary theoretics. In NYU's department, as elsewhere, however, this matter is covered in the year-long survey of the theory and practice of criticism, summarized in Chapter x below. Even the term paper is a pragmatic one, consisting of the composing of a syllabus (with exercises, examinations, term paper topics, and bibliographies) described in detail in Chapter xii below. A veteran of this course will not be at a loss for a most explicit and comprehensive reply when asked to define comparative literature. Students from the national literature departments often wander into this course, either because many such departments have abolished their traditional methods course or because the visitors are attracted by the practical, vocational nature of many of the lectures, equally valuable for any and all debutants in literary studies.

In view of the disappearance of the methods-and-bibliography course in the smaller national literature departments, comparative literature can indeed service other graduate students than its own. As Professor Levin's report stated back in 1965, "proseminars in theory of literature and in textual methods or technical problems . . . often seem to attract, and profit from the presence of, the more adventurous students in other graduate fields. Comparative literature performs a service for the other literary departments, and repays its incidental obligations to them, by widening the critical orientation of their students." If a few elements of the methods course, such as bibliography, will differ from those of the national literature seminar, by far most of the staple items will provide meaning and utility to all graduate students of any literature: library resources, retrieval of knowledge, establishing chronologies, utilization of evidence, principles of influence and source study (see pp. 153–57), organizing research, and so on. A typical discussion on evidence would feature Morize and Schoenbaum. Schoenbaum's Eight Principles of Scholarly Inquiry, for example, established originally for verification of Shakespearean texts,[1] are valid for authors of other nationalities and even other genres. They were no doubt used by Thornton Wilder as he studied the authenticity and chronology of the plays of Lope de Vega. Thus, the classes devoted to research tools and methods would have value as well for "adventurous students in other graduate fields."

[1] 1. External evidence cannot be ignored, no matter how inconvenient such evidence may be for the theories of the investigator.
2. If stylistic criteria are to have any meaning, the play must be written in a dominant style.
3. The investigator must always work with the most reliable texts, preferably directly with the early prints or manuscripts.
4. Textual analysis logically precedes stylistic analysis.
5. Plays of which all the early or manuscript texts are continuously defective offer no fit quarries for evidence and are not fit subjects for canonical investigation.
6. For any author proposed, a reasonable amount of unchallenged dramatic writing, apart from collaborations, must be extant.
7. Intuitions, convictions, and subjective judgments generally, carry no weight as evidence.
8. Whenever possible, stylistic evidence should be supplemented by bibliographical evidence.

IV

Curriculum and Courses

Ecce tibi est exortus Isocrates, magister historicorum omnium, cuius e ludo tamquam ex equo Troiano meri principes exierunt.
MARCUS TULLIUS CICERO, *De Oratore*

Setting Up a Graduate Curriculum

There are several principles to be kept in mind in establishing a definitive curriculum of courses in comparative literature. The major principle is to provide a complement of graduate courses with a balanced assortment of themes, genres, movements, and interrelations. Another is to establish a satisfactory rotation of courses corresponding to the urgency of the subject matter and the availability of the authority who is to teach the course. It is self-evident that some themes or some movements may be more productive than others, of course, but the important thing is that there be a florilegium of themes, forms, and movements so that the student may sample one or two demonstrations of each approach every academic year. It is also true that some courses must enjoy a higher priority than others. Thus, the very basic Seminar in Comparative Literature not only must be given annually, but must be scheduled for the fall semester in order that a student may obtain a proper orientation during his first period of study. It is also true that the crucial history of literary theory and criticism should be given at least every other year, in its role that we characterize in Chapter x as catalyst.

Courses may be established on a one-, two-, or three-year rotation. We have learned from experience that only basic courses should be set on a two-year cycle, for over two thirds of our candidates cannot study full time and require two years or more to complete the M.A. requirements and three or more to complete the Ph.D. course work and examinations. The reader will find below a list of a desirable triennium of graduate courses. More of these courses are set on a triennial rotation than on a biennial one, for the number of courses budgeted for comparative literature is always a small core—since students take a third or more of their courses in the cooperating literature departments—and the selection is much reduced if all the courses are set on a two-year cycle. Although students may regret once in a while that they could not catch a certain course on a two- or three-year cycle, their disappointment is as nothing compared to that of the students who see their meager choice narrowed even more at registration by encountering a course or courses they have already taken.

Course Rotation and Variety

An effort must be made to offer the student each semester as varied a selection as possible among approaches (genre, theme, period, interrelation), especially those students who are limited to enrolling for only two courses per semester.

The triennial program below is based on the principles just posited. It is based on the courses currently being offered in the comparative literature graduate program at New York University, subject obviously to sabbatical leaves, availability of colleagues, and visiting professors. It is based also on a fixed number of six 4-point courses each semester. The courses on an annual or biennial rotation are taught by the nuclear members of the comparative literature staff. As at Chapel Hill, the basic courses in comparative literature are announced as rotated biennially. The other courses on a triennial cycle are taught by the nuclear staff, professors from cooperating departments or neighboring institutions, or sometimes from our own departmental alumni. In view of this widespread source of staffing, we are fortunate to be able to follow the course curriculum depicted below. Naturally, the availability of comparative literature specialists from neighboring institutions enriches our offerings. To be realistic, we can affirm that the thirty courses listed here are the courses we give and have given, even though an individual staffing problem may vary the pattern on occasion. It is to be hoped that for departments just initiating a graduate program or those hesitant to call on an evaluating committee for advice (see Ch. xiii) the enclosed mosaic of courses may be helpful or suggestive.

Each course is identified by its category and frequency. The letters T, G, M, I, and C denote themes, genres, movements, interrelations, and criticism. The numbers 1, 2, and 3 signify annual, biennial, and triennial. Thus the "Faust Legend in Literature" becomes T-3, a thematic course offered on a triennial cycle, and so on. Each class is of two hours' duration, meeting once a week, and earns 4 points of graduate credit.

Triennial Program of Graduate Courses[1]

First Year of Rotation: Fall Semester

1. Seminar in Comparative Literature (S-1)
2. Metamorphosis of the Modern Novel (G-2)
3. History of Literary Theory and Criticism, 1st semester (C-2)
4. Faust in Literature (T-3)
5. Literature and Music (I-3)
6. The Nature of Tragedy (G-3)

First Year: Spring Semester

1. Arthurian Literature in Europe (T-3)
2. European Romanticism (M-2)
3. History of Literary Theory and Criticism, 2nd semester (C-2)
4. Epic Poetry (G-3)
5. Literature and Law (I-2)
6. The Picaresque Novel (G-3)

Second Year of Rotation: Fall Semester

1. Seminar in Comparative Literature (S-1)
2. The Symbolist Movement (M-2)
3. Contemporary European Poetry (G-3)
4. Interrelations of European Literature and Art, 1st semester (I-2)

[1] Individual research courses are not included.

5. Avant-Garde Theater (G-3)
6. Traditionalism and Change in Twentieth-Century Fiction (T-3)

Second Year: Spring Semester

1. The Surrealist Movement (M-2)
2. Interrelations of European Literature and Art, 2nd semester (I-2)
3. Themes and Forms of Renaissance Literature (T-2)
4. Realism in the European Novel (M-3)
5. The Rise of Comedy (G-3)
6. Oedipus in Literature (T-3)

Third Year of Rotation: Fall Semester

1. Seminar in Comparative Literature (S-1)
2. Metamorphosis of the Modern Novel (G-2)
3. The Don Juan Theme in Drama (T-3)
4. Literature and Cinema (I-3)
5. History of Literary Theory and Criticism, 1st semester (C-2)
6. Baroque and Classicism in Literature (M-3)

Third Year: Spring Semester

1. Literature of the Enlightenment (M-3)
2. Literature and Law (I-2)
3. Themes and Forms of Mediaeval Literature (T-3)
4. History of Literary Theory and Criticism, 2nd semester (C-2)
5. European Romanticism (M-2)
6. Literature and Psychology (I-3)

In addition to the courses listed above, there are of course two or three summer courses that receive supportive enrollment. A reasonable policy is to choose such topics as will retain interest during hot summers. One staple course has been The Development of the *Novella* from Boccaccio and Chaucer to Cervantes, which, even as it demonstrates how the social criticism in these tales paved the way for the Renaissance and Reformation and illustrates the careful structuring of a genre (see p. 144), guarantees entertaining "dog days" reading. Another is Don Juan in Literature. The summer, at least in urban areas, reduces the number of resident instructors. However, the demands of students for advice and information and letters of reference last straight through the summer, and one of the small nuclear staff has to stay around to "mind the store."

Guided Research Courses

Another course that is not listed on the triennial schedule is the graduate research course. Graduate students, as was said of Thucydides, have interests which go off in all directions. They often beleaguer an understaffed department with requests for permission to register for guided research in areas of all sorts. These courses often are listed at two levels, the 2000 level denoting a course taken before completion of course work and the 3000 level indicating work on the doctoral thesis. The 3000-level course was invented in order for students writing a dissertation to receive federal or state subsidy usually restricted to "course work."

Some graduate departments do not offer the research course at any level. This policy is the easiest way to discourage candidates from registering for it either to explore an extraneous topic or to use it merely to make up for lacunae in their reading, a special temptation in such a vast field as comparative literature. Departments with very small offerings unfortunately buy off their consciences by a permissiveness about students taking research courses. These are actually less demanding than the classroom course, with its disciplines of class attendance, class reports, recitation, term paper, or examination.

Enrollment in the guided research course must be permitted with caution, as suggested above, for further reasons. When a student becomes enthusiastic over a research paper that has nothing to do with his eventual thesis, it is sometimes alleged as research for an article he plans to publish. A suspicious adviser may of course wonder whether it is a *remaniement* of some paper done elsewhere before, and whether only this could explain the student's zeal to do an exegetical paper explaining, let us say, some new aspects of Rilke's *Duino Elegies*. I choose this topic with a wince, for early in my career one of my best students convinced me in an unwary moment that he had something new and comparative to say about this specific work and was authorized to undertake the research paper more or less on his own. The paper turned out to be adequate, but the textual references were keyed to an English translation and I further noticed that only two British and two French critics were cited throughout. As you may have quickly surmised, this excellent paper was "researched" by a student whose three foreign languages were French, Spanish, and Modern Hebrew. When I became aware of this, I explained to the student that whereas we talk much about the need of foreign languages to read the novel or play in the original language—in this instance, German—there is the additional need to know whether the German critics have not already published the results the candidate believed to have uncovered. The story has a happy ending. The student, abashed, declined credit for the paper on Rilke and eventually worked up a more appropriate topic. A safer precaution, which should be generally adopted, is to have students write out an abstract of their proposed topic for a research paper, just as they must do for a thesis, including mention of the foreign languages they control.

The 2000-level research course, as it exists in most graduate schools, can be and should be controlled. The department should not permit it to be taken before the candidate has received the M.A. It should be limited to the last phase of course work, when the candidate has presumably passed the three foreign language examinations and has given evidence of being able to profit by research with a minimum of guidance, and when the investigation is devoted to the determination of a valid Ph.D. thesis topic. Thus, it would usually be taken during the student's last semester of course work and limited to 6 or 8 points.

It is useful for the research courses at both the 2000 and 3000 levels to be listed as offering from 2 to 8 credits. Thus, when students are finishing their course work with only a few credits to complete the point quota, they may register for 2 to 8 points, not only for research purposes, but also to avoid paying for extra points in excess of the required 70 or 72 points.

Touching All Geographical Bases and Approaches

It is obvious that the rotational course curriculum we have supplied here is limited to the Western Heritage—the dimension most widely accepted in universities at this date. We touch upon global course curricula elsewhere (see p. 40). However, an examination of the content of the rotated courses above shows that each course concerns itself with five or six or more areas within that Western tradition. Thus, the "generic" course The Rise of Comedy will start with Aristophanes and cross the European terrain slowly until it ends with Wilde and Ionesco. The thematic course on Oedipus will traverse European drama, poetry, and narrative all the way from Sophocles to the Atlantic countries and back to Alberto Moravia. The movement course of neoclassicism will circulate like a will-o'-the-wisp from Aristotle to the eighteenth-century classic playwrights of Russia. They will perforce, as we saw in Chapter i, feature major works of literature.

It is obvious from these and other examples on the rotational schedule that classical Greek and Roman literatures permeate much of the curriculum. Instead of neglecting the Greco-Roman classics, the rich heritage of Greek comedy, tragedy, satire, lyric poetry, and epic is preserved in the comparative literature curriculum when carefully and conscientiously planned. The graduate student who wishes further contact with Greco-Roman literature can of course elect courses in the classics department. Indeed, we have seen several classico-comparative theses in our department: the influence of Horatian satire on Byron, Scaliger's *Poemata* and neo-Latin poetry, a brilliant thesis entitled "The Complex Oedipus," and others.

During their first year of incumbency, students learn in the required comparative literature seminar the values of the four approaches to literature and are instructed to keep a balance among them in selecting courses within and without the comparative literature department. The same principle applies whether a student is embarked on the master's or the doctoral program.

Finally, another valid factor in the student's choice of course must be acknowledged. This is the attraction or inspiration generated by an outstanding and learned teacher. Some professors will conspicuously exemplify or illustrate one of the various approaches to literature. Choosing instructors will depend not only, as we are reminded in ACLA Report II, "on the interests and competences" of available instructors, but as well on their "various critical and scholarly approaches."

One final but important comment must be made here. The Report's reference to "the interests and competences of those instructors who are available" seems to imply that the course offerings should be determined to a great extent by the available subjects and specializations vested in the incumbent faculty instead of by carefully planned coverage of the Western Heritage, through the recognized approaches, worked up deliberately in advance. Except for rare coincidences, "hand-tailored" should be preferred to "ready-made" courses. A curriculum of courses should be planned to make sure all the approaches are included and that the widest meaningful geographical latitude should be represented by the individual courses. The students' interests take precedence over the instructor's. The brilliant monographic courses should be taken in the national language departments. As a colleague puts it, "To teach comparative literature courses required considerable retooling."

In devising such a biennial or triennial pattern of courses, the principle of touching all bases has multiple applications. First of all, the courses selected must be geographically broad, involving four to six or more literatures, as the syllabi at the end of Chapters vi, vii, and viii demonstrate. As stated elsewhere, the student class reports can contribute importantly to the geographical breadth of a course. Without the experience of these broad courses, the candidate might well settle for a narrower and safer thesis topic later on, perhaps even a binary subject that even the comparatists in France now discourage. A second application of the principle refers to the five bases of approach: genre, period, theme, interrelation, and theory-and-practice. If one considers that comparative literature theses will necessarily fit into one of these five approaches, it is obvious that students should have the opportunity to take three or more courses during graduate work —or one or two during their undergraduate program—in the approach of their future thesis. A graduate student who has taken from the triennial curriculum above the Faust, Oedipus, and Don Juan courses is well prepared to undertake a thematic course on Orestes or Mary Stuart with a minimum of outside help. In some departments, which legislate that their three oral and written examinations must be based on the five approaches above, it is obvious that the more the students have "touched bases" with these approaches in the classroom, the more fortified they will be to cope with these examinations. Preparation for writing theses and examinations is usually effected better in the classroom than in guided individual research courses taken under some overburdened adviser.

Students themselves can be concerned over the principle of touching all geographical bases in the courses offered. From one instructor's Western Heritage course, which, most exceptionally, did not assign the reading of a single German text, a recent German-born registrant came to my office to resign forthwith from the department. Attempts to explain and placate fell on deaf ears.

A cosmopolitan body of students will sometimes wish to include in theses, as is understandable, a major author from a less taught literature. Touching a remote base through a thesis can sometimes prove to be an exciting innovation, even though it may require finding guest readers from outside the university or even community. Thus, recent theses at NYU have concerned Japanese surrealists, Asian dramatists, Afro-Cuban poets, Sanskrit texts, Indian disciples of Tagore—usually tying them into the Western Heritage. Unfortunately university budgets do not normally provide for such outside assistance as was required for these theses. In fact, administrations often set up obstacles by insisting that outside readers submit to them their vita for approval by a curriculum committee even though they may appear in all the who's whos in their field. Rather than humiliate the outside specialist, one should photostat the vita from a register in the library.

The principle of requiring a course on a given theme or genre to include examples from four to six national literatures (with usually one or two conspicuous examples from each) will seem less stringent when one realizes that the assigned readings represent a genre or form even more than they represent a country. Thus, Professor Barricelli's course on comedy at Riverside carries the catalog description: "The works range from the Greek to the Middle Ages to Modern Literature, but the approach will be modal and generic rather than historical." To make the point even more clear the course is entitled The Comic Mode. His course on romanticism is announced with two such demurrers. It is entitled "Studies in Romanticism" rather than "History of." Even though it inevitably includes several European literatures, the touching of all bases is acknowledged modestly: "Selected texts drawn primarily from the literatures of Germany, England, and France, but with excursions into other European literatures." That literary anthologies should honor this principle of extension is illustrated by Howard Hugo's carefully edited anthology of chosen texts on romanticism, often adopted as a text in the course in question. Hugo omits important texts from Russia, Italy, and Spain that could have rounded out the picture in a most useful way.

Double-Listing and Cross-Listing of Courses

ACLA Reports I and II on Professional Standards make passing references to double-listing of courses as a good thing, apparently considering it an evidence of interdepartmental cooperation and harmony. It is a common practice. For example, at the University of Iowa seventeen of the twenty-two comparative literature courses are double-listed with English or Spanish. At Illinois twenty-one of twenty-six are at the undergraduate level. Columbia lists many courses doubly as comparative literature and English.

Double-listing is not that simple a matter. If the Departments of Comparative Literature and Psychology, for example, decided to offer in common the familiar course uniting their two disciplines, sharing staff and budget, each listing the same title and course description, and each registering its own students to the double-listed course, this is indeed an ethical and valuable example of cooperation. The same collaborative effort between comparative literature and the other departmental disciplines mentioned below in Chapter ix could only be applauded, especially if the two elements of the interdiscipline receive equal emphasis. It goes without saying that in such cases each departmental listing will carry its own catalog code or serial identification, ensuring that candidates in each department can apply the credit to their appropriate major degree. The NYU course Literature and Law (see p. 200) is double-listed, for example, in the Law and the Arts and Science Schools.

When the double-listing involves comparative and a national literature instead, however, it could be evidence of a soft or inaccurate definition of the scope and identity of a comparative literature course. At Pennsylvania State, for example, Anglo-American Folk Song is listed understandably as English 593, only to reappear with the international billing of Comparative Literature 593. Careless double-listing can thus deny the integrity of a course. It is too often a compromise to divide student enrollment or to please a budget officer by getting two courses taught on a single teaching budget. An actual case, and a troubled one, comes to mind. A professor of national literature agreed to give a comparative literature course on, let us say, contemporary tragedy. The course was accepted and announced in the bulletin with the comparative literature code and number. Playwrights from five literatures, it was agreed, would be read. Just before registration week, unbeknown to the comparative literature department, the professor circulated within his own department a syllabus of the identical course under his own departmental code and number. His desire to win registrations at another department's expense was, alas, understandable, even though his own department offered twice as many courses as comparative literature. What was most unacceptable was the notion that a single course content could be at the same time both national and comparative. The case was referred by the dean to the curriculum committee, which ruled that such a course could not be double-listed. (Ironically, no students from the professor's home department registered for the course when he offered it.)

The lesson of this episode is twofold. Maneuvers to increase enrollments in one's own department under budgetary pressures are ingenious and varied; the integrity of double-listing should not be endangered. The second lesson is that if professors of literature become careless about distinguishing between national and plural-literature courses, a curriculum committee made up of professors from liberal arts and social and physical sciences, by their unanimous decision, have to correct their logic. The solution to such double-listing of a course that must be intrinsically either comparative or national in scope, but obviously not both at the same time, is to assign it ethically to the right department and then permit the two-way, interdepartmental student traffic to move back and forth more freely. With such reciprocity each interested department will sooner or later get its share of registrations.

It is true that rivalry for student enrollment in the forties and fifties slowed the establishment of comparative literature departments. There was no doubt as well an uneasiness about comparative literature's ambitions and awareness of its legitimate precincts. However, when it became clear that the new departments were often attracting more students from outside than within the university and that these new students were going to take a third or more of their courses in the national literature departments, the latter departments not only accepted the new arrival, but offered it many manpower units of assistance.

One of the early hopes of both the comparative and national literature departments was for a stream of two-way student traffic between them. This hope was reflected in ACLA Reports I and II, strong in their loyalty to the national literature departments. Although at least one university in America unwisely allowed graduate comparatists to take all their courses in their home department, most agreed that the M.A. candidates should take two or three courses for their M.A. in national literature departments. For the Ph.D. a larger ratio was reserved, although for credits in national literature or literatures a student could substitute other humanities courses. Thus a student wishing to work up a specialization in myth, let us say, could take myth courses in classics, religion, psychology, anthropology, fine arts, or other. Even so, the two-way traffic principle was generally preserved.

Cross-listings, as opposed to double-listing, of courses between comparative literature and its neighboring departments is an admirable and sure guarantee of interdepartmental cooperation, widely practiced. Since graduate candidates in comparative literature have an option of taking courses in other literatures—are indeed obliged to do so—the comparative literature pages in the bulletin frequently list a few courses from other departments that would be especially valuable for them. As Fred Nichols rationalizes the matter, "The advantage of being a student in comparative literature is that you can take good courses in the national literature departments and avoid the bad. It is a good idea to nudge students in the right directions, selectively cross-listing good courses in other departments." Similarly, the English, French, or other department reciprocates by listing comparative literature courses of general value. Since most national literature departments, for example, have abandoned the traditional course on research methods and bibliography owing to financial retrenchment, this is a comparative literature course that has a universal value for registrants from other departments and is often taken by them. It is cross-listed, however, rather than double-listed.

The principle of two-way enrollment, so desirable for all concerned, declines in periods of decreased enrollments. During the stringent years of the seventies even though national literature courses were overstaffed and comparative literature was still understaffed, it was inevitable that fewer national literature students would come to register in comparative literature courses. A brief statistic from that period is available from NYU records. The unit of comparison is the 4-point single-semester course. Comparative literature students' points in national literature courses were:

1974–75	72
1975–76	76
1976–77	72

National literature students' points in comparative literature courses were:

1974–75	48
1975–76	40
1976–77	36

Such statistics demonstrate how budgetary considerations in times of crisis defeat the splendid ideal of heavy two-way traffic, or more specifically the ideal of having national literature students profit occasionally from the experience of taking the intercultural, international, or interdisciplinary courses available to them. In such times of crisis, free trade gives way to protectionist policy.

The Master's Degree Requirements

As if symptomatic of the numerical growth of candidates taking the Ph.D. during the last twenty years, the M.A. degree is generally viewed as less demanding and less important than it used to be. Some states and institutions have eliminated the thesis requirement, as we note elsewhere. As the employment market has not kept pace with the larger number of students issuing from graduate schools, the M.A. is no longer a guarantor of a job in any area. A few graduate students are enrolling for the M.A. in education after obtaining it in a literature department.

The classical values of the traditional M.A. in literature have been expressed recently by Professor James Mirollo of Columbia in a report to the Regents Board in New York State. It complements and supports the ACLA Committee on Professional Standards reports on the value of the Magister Artium in Comparative Literature.

> Our experience has been that the M.A. is necessary and useful to our students, in obtaining part-time or full-time positions as instructors and lecturers, for which the degree is a requirement; in transferring to other graduate schools, for whatever personal and professional reasons, where the M.A. is required as a preliminary to beginning doctoral study; for certification credit and consequent salary increments when the student is teaching in the school systems; and last, but not at all least in these times, as a token of a milestone having been reached, a unit of advanced study having been accomplished, for the student who decides to discontinue graduate study, whether temporarily or permanently, before going on to the Ph.D. I might add that these remarks would be confirmed by the experience of all twenty-eight departments of the arts and sciences at Columbia, as was recently confirmed when the Graduate School decided to maintain, strengthen, and carefully define M.A. programs.
>
> As to the specific degree in Comparative Literature, in addition to the values stressed above, there is the special attraction of a degree which suggests a broader training of the kind towards which we are rapidly moving, partly in response to our own sense of the needs of the future and partly because the demands of the academic market now center on interdisciplinary and cross-cultural preparation for teaching world literature, literary genres, history of culture, etc., rather than the traditional narrow fields of national literatures.

The ACLA Report II finds the M.A. in Comparative Literature valuable both as a qualifying or trial-run experience anticipating the Ph.D.—weeding out those unprepared to venture further— and as a rewarding fulfillment in itself. It would normally be a four-semester curriculum of three courses per semester, thus requiring 36 rather than 30 credits. The Report cautions:

The M.A. in our field would *not* be a teaching degree but would lead to careers in research, library work (usually in conjunction with a degree in library science), translation, etc. A combination of both these functions may indeed make such a degree useful in many institutions. It could attract a larger number of graduate students than the Ph.D. program would allow. It would permit departments and programs in Comparative Literature to offer career options outside the teaching profession in a declining job market.

Assuming that a candidate has some background in literature and commands at least one language, he would, according to the Report, take three courses in literature A, two courses in literature B, four courses in comparative literature, including methodology, and three electives. After concluding this course work, the candidate would take a comprehensive examination and write a master's essay. Whereas there will be inevitable and allowable variances in the course structure of the M.A., it seems that this proposal reduces unnecessarily the student's contact with comparative literature courses to only four out of a total of twelve. The NYU master's degree, made up of eight 4-point courses, requires that five be taken in comparative literature and only three in other literatures (or literature), thus giving students a majority experience in comparative literature though sharing them with other departments of literature. The methods course (see p. 96) is required and indeed must be taken at the very outset. The vast majority of M.A. programs require demonstration of the reading knowledge of two foreign languages before the M.A. paper is undertaken.

The Undergraduate Major and Minor

Let us survey the situation of the undergraduate literature major before the definitive revival of comparative literature in the forties. The pattern was definitely a one-literature major, usually a very demanding one requiring not only a reading knowledge of French, Spanish, German, Russian, or other single language, but a fluency as well. Many of these majors included an honors program, which demanded a research paper in addition to the other requirements. Some schools, like Harvard, experimented with a prestigious major in history and literature, using a tutorial method and allowing for the study of literature in breadth.

Present in the undergraduate program were national literature surveys lasting two semesters, the teaching and reading remaining in English. These surveys were common in classics and Russian departments. After the abandonment of the undergraduate foreign language requirement in many colleges, such surveys were initiated by the other national literature departments. Indeed, in the early seventies some colleges that did not have an undergraduate comparative literature major offered a general literature or literature in translation minor made up of several of these single-literature surveys. Taught by individual specialists, they constituted a very useful background for graduate work in comparative literature—perhaps more valuable than a minor in a single literature. In fact, ACLA Report II on Professional Standards, fearful that the undergraduate major or minor may provide too much slippage into translation, warns, "Not all directors of doctoral programs are convinced that the undergraduate major is the best preparation for graduate study in Comparative Literature, however admirable it may be for general and liberal education." Furthermore, such courses constituting a minor helped to save some departments like Italian, classics, Portuguese, or Russian after the foreign language requirement was dropped.

The English departments do not figure, of course, in the discussion above, since they had long engaged in the survey courses of Western Literature in translation discussed in Chapter ii. These sophomore or junior courses in Western Heritage, Great Books, Literary Heritage, or even the misnomer World Literature were undeniably the antecedents of the undergraduate courses in comparative literature.

The first Report of the Committee on Professional Standards set down what it considered "certain minimal standards" to be met by the new undergraduate major curriculum. These included the benign presence of strong classical and modern language departments. It stipulated that the program be guided by a staff member with the doctorate in comparative literature or "equivalent" training. The library holdings should be strong. The undergraduate program should meet the needs of students preparing for either graduate work in the discipline or other graduate literary study. The program should include courses on the major periods, movements, and genres. Independent study of special topics was recommended. Yet the compilers of the second report eleven years later were obliged to conclude after a study of many college catalogs that "at more than one institution, the titles of comparative literature course offerings do not exclude the dilettantish, the modish, even the frivolous."

The requirements for the undergraduate major usually include courses at the junior-senior level in at least two literatures, with study in depth of at least one. If one of these literatures is English, the student must still acquire a reading knowledge of two foreign languages. Advanced courses in comparative literature demanding reading of original texts, taught by a trained comparatist, should be taken. A final requirement is "some acquaintance with the major writings of Western Literature from classical antiquity to the present."

The ACLA reports also approved as legitimate service courses those available to nonmajors, provided they are taught by a recognized comparatist-linguist. When the Western Heritage courses require no reading in foreign languages, majors and minors in comparative literature should steer clear of them. Courses dealing with a single national literature should not be designated as comparative literature. (This restriction more than contradicts two former presidents of ACLA, who have claimed that a course on a single author, if taught by an exceptionally cosmopolitan colleague, could qualify as comparative.) Finally, "majors in Comparative Literature should be separated for instructional purposes from students who read exclusively in translation. When such separation is not possible, measures should be taken to insure reading in original texts by majors in comparative literature." It is proposed finally that the presence together in the classroom of majors and monoglots might well affect the standard of instruction. The Report concludes by stating that the undergraduate major provides a solid foundation for graduate study, that it inculcates depth and breadth. Its final sentence is unexpected, for it is binding equally on undergraduate and graduate levels: "It cannot be sufficiently emphasized, however, that study in comparative literature must proceed hand in hand with intensive work in the individual national literatures, at undergraduate as well as graduate levels."

Although there were inevitably dissenters to some of its ideas, including its alleged elitism, ACLA Report I was immensely important for two reasons. It was the first broad statement, albeit brief, of principles for the governance of comparative literature as an academic discipline. Its second importance was its timing, for it was written at the very beginning of the boom of comparative literature in American education, when some guidance and coherent principles were sorely needed.

ACLA Report II reaffirms the premises of the Levin Report concerning undergraduate curriculum, and echoes its deep concern about language competency:

> At the undergraduate level the most disturbing recent trend is the association of comparative literature with literature in translation. Many courses taught today under the rubric of comparative literature are not in fact properly labeled. The college lecturer who is truly a Comparatist should at the very least have read the text he is teaching in the original, and should *use* this experience to advantage in the classroom. He should also draw on the insights of those members of the class who are able to dispense with translations. Indeed, by his frequent references to the original he should make the remaining students aware of the incompleteness of their own reading experience.

In other words, the instructor must make students aware of the fact that, in the words of Cervantes, even the best translation is like the reverse side of a Flemish tapestry. It is even easier to prove that two such reverse sides will in themselves be quite dissimilar. To show students the inexactitude of even the best translations, one needs only to point out the various competitive Englishings of Verlaine's "Art poétique" or—even more striking— of Mallarmé's "Après-midi d'un faune."

The Undergraduate Curriculum; the Nichols Report

In 1974 the Committee on Undergraduate Programs in Comparative Literature submitted an excellent, informative "profile" on the subject to the ACLA. Since the chairman was Stephen G. Nichols of Dartmouth—one of the pioneering colleges in our discipline—the document is often called the Nichols Report and is usually so identified in this volume. The names of the other valuable members of this important committee are recorded in our Foreword (see p. xxi). Their inquiry into our discipline "looked at what our colleagues have said it ought to be [an obvious reference to the Levin Report] and to examine in fact what it seems in practice."

The group found that roughly fifty percent of the typical American colleges responding to their questionnaire offered an undergraduate program in comparative literature. Confirming what Haskell Block was to call "the most dramatic development" in our discipline, some individual colleges like Dartmouth (900 comparative literature students at the time) were already teaching hundreds of students in their undergraduate comparative literature programs. The number of majors was found to be very small, "often a mere six in a departmental enrollment of 300 to 500. These figures indicate that the number of students willing to subject themselves to the rigors of our discipline are in a distinct minority as compared to those students who eagerly turn to our offering as a change from other humanities courses." This disparity of majors and nonmajors, the Committee found, led to a "difficulty in enforcing linguistic standards. Not without justice colleagues in other disciplines point to such courses as essentially literature-in-translation." The wide gap between majors and mere registrants would also in 1976 surprise members of ACLA Report II, which had found ratios ranging from $\frac{1}{10}$ to $\frac{1}{90}$. The Greene Report commented later:

> This state of affairs is probably a given fact for the near future, and it allows of many interpretations. It may testify first of all to the rigor of the comparative literature major. But it may possibly also testify to a compromise with that rigor in the education of the less committed student. Reflecting on programs like that which reports 6 majors and 500 enrollments, we are tempted to discern there two faces of contemporary comparative literature— the one demanding and severe, the other accommodating, searching for its own place in the sun at its own institution.

Then the ACLA II Report concludes with the honesty and frankness that marked the Nichols Report:

Apparently many comparatists throughout the country have tacitly accepted a trade-off in which large-scale popularization with minimal requirements is accepted in exchange for the right to provide rigorous training for a small number of students. Much of the recent expansion of comparative literature, especially at the undergraduate level, seems to be based on an uneasy compromise between qualitative and quantitative norms, with the balance shifting more and more toward the quantitative rationale of large enrollments and relatively low instructional costs. In at least some colleges and universities comparative literature seems to be purveyed in the style of a smorgasbord at bargain rates.

The five basic components of the curriculum leading to the undergraduate degree in comparative literature are listed by the Nichols Committee as "the foreign language requirement; the introductory course; a course in theory, criticism or methodology; a specified number of courses taken in comparative literature; the thesis, or honors thesis."

The course structures and topics were found to allow for a great variety.

Some programs prefer a conceptual and contextual approach in which genre, theme, period, tradition, aesthetic theory constitute the organizing principles of the program, while others choose the more traditional genre and period approach. The difference between the two paradigms is primarily one of emphasis. In the former case, theory and criticism tend to be dominant (e.g., courses like "Topics in Literary Periods," "Topics in the Themes of Literature," "Music and Literary Communication: A Study of Goals"), with historical coverage definitely subordinate, while in the latter case, the reverse is true. Naturally, many programs combine the two, which seems prudent. Happily, a majority of the programs surveyed confirm, by their requirements and their course offerings, the definitions of Comparative Literature.

The structure of the undergraduate curriculum will perforce be less standardized than that devised for the graduate degrees. There will be less unanimity concerning the distribution requirements, although the Nichols Committee uncovered a curious principle of "rules of three." This meant that students could be asked to take (1) courses in literatures read in the original language, (2) courses in literary theory, and (3) a seminar on methodology. The rule of three as adopted at Indiana, Berkeley, and Princeton will require undergraduates to take core courses as follows: (1) a period course in comparative literature, (2) a genre course in comparative literature, and (3) four upper-class literature courses read in the original language.

In other schools, such as Beloit, Stanford, Irvine, San Diego, and Dartmouth, a "conceptual" rather than period-genre approach is preferred. This alternative, allowing for several freer structures, encourages one area of specialization, buttressed by literary criticism courses, tutorial, research methods, foreign study, and especially the interrelating of literature with another discipline: science, philosophy, music, etc. The Committee allows that this latter option may encourage specialization prematurely, but feels that the period-genre approach "requires students to accede to an organizing principle for their concentration which presupposes a commitment to the discipline that extends beyond the undergraduate level. . . . Obviously some compromise between the two extremes is desirable." One must lay the foundation for a thorough grounding in literary history, while nevertheless allowing students to undertake individualized research projects in specialized areas that interest them.

> One note of warning. If historical coverage can be achieved only by means of broad survey courses taught mainly in translation, then it can hardly be worth the sacrifice of rigorous language-study emphasis. If, on the other hand, coverage can be achieved— as it is in some existing programs—by specifying advanced work in literature departments, the two goals of historical coverage and language competence may be squared very well.

The Committee finds that Northwestern's "rule of three" blends historical and linguistic goals quite naturally, even integrating the conceptual approach as well. This tripartite approach is constituted of (1) literature in a foreign language, (2) a period core with choice of five periods (with generic emphasis on narrative or poetry or drama), and (3) courses in literary theory and criticism.

The Committee discovered that whatever course options were open to undergraduates, many schools required either the introductory course, the methods course, or the course in literary criticism. The criticism course varies from college to college, emphasizing variously history of criticism, literary theory, or contemporary criticism. The Committee also found much variance and "lack of focus" concerning the required methods course, wandering from the history of comparative literature, theories of comparative literature, and types of scholarship to critical and historical method. It is obvious that whereas a number of college-level anthologies and histories of literary theory are in current use, special textbooks or anthologies directed specifically to the problems of the discipline (as the Committee puts it) and edited specifically for comparative literature students would be a precious tool, and would bring uniformity into these universally offered undergraduate courses and seminars.

Since many colleges operate a standard service course such as the Western Heritage or Humanities Survey, open to undergraduates of many disparate majors, the perplexing question still remains: Should undergraduate comparative literature majors and minors take this course? The Nichols Committee takes a definitive stand:

> Practical politics may dictate the implementation of service courses—such as the "humanities survey"—within a given program. There is no objection to such a contingency, especially at the introductory level, provided that some way be found to apprise students of the general nature of the comparative approach. This can be accomplished by means of the organization and presentation of service courses and by the inclusion, in the reading list, of one of the current introductions to Comparative Literature presently on the market.

Among the Summary Recommendations of the ACLA Committee on the Undergraduate Curriculum are three concerning the course composition of the comparative literature major in the college:

1. Comparative literature programs should encourage majors to work in contributing departments, particularly foreign languages.
2. Requirements for the major should be realistic, given the con-

straints of the ordinary two-year major. While a balance must be struck between background preparation and comparative literature training, it is better, at the undergraduate level, to err on the side of background preparation.

3. Accordingly, as much as sixty percent of a major's preparation may be done in foreign language and English (at the advanced level).

The Undergraduate Methods Course

The Nichols Report on undergraduate standards and practices found that a foundation course was widely required, and that it showed up in three guises: as introductory, methods, and criticism. Yet the Nichols Committee, as stated earlier, found a much wider lack of consensus, purpose, and focus in the methods or introductory courses. The Report enumerates the variety of course titles and subject matter in current use: Methods of Research, Studies in Comparative Literature (a topic course including methods and theory), Comparative Method in Literary Studies (bibliography, approaches, methods), Studies in Comparative Literature (directed research and writing, group discussion, lectures on periods, movements, and themes), Comparative Studies (interdisciplinary study), Comparative Approaches to Literature (examinations of parallel texts from drama, poetry, narrative), Introduction to the Study of Comparative Literature (majors only; reception, influence, themes, genres, periods, and translation).

The Report concludes pessimistically of this diversity of structures:

It does not seem perverse to wish that the uniformity of agreement on the necessity for some kind of methods course could be translated into a more general agreement on the basic nature of such a course. Without imposing any one view of the discipline, it should be possible to evolve a methodological course paradigm which could be generally adopted. Failure to do so might suggest to our colleagues in other disciplines that we really do not know what we are about.

To achieve the optimum methods course, and reassure our colleagues, as is suggested in Chapter xi, appropriate textbooks must be compiled specifically for comparative literature.

It might console the Committee to realize that the traditional methods and bibliography courses in our graduate literature departments, with their training in philological method, seem slowly to be disappearing. Indeed, again referring to the graduate-level situation, the comparative literature methods courses described in Chapter iii occasionally attract students from other literature departments that offer no such courses of their own.

The Nichols Committee, understandably calling for a uniform methods course, finds that its syllabus, reading list, and course description would help to indoctrinate a colleague not trained as a comparatist drawn from another department.

Stephen Nichols has reflected for some time on an ideal undergraduate introductory course by which to both attract and indoctrinate newcomers to comparative literature in the most effective way. After finding undergraduates getting a false start in some colleges with such introductory courses as Rilke and Bob Dylan, he turned to the planning of the ideal introductory course. Shifting his concern from a course to a purpose, he hit upon a two-stage sequence of courses (macrocourse and microcourse) predicated upon a progressive integration of the student with the discipline. The macrocourse, required of all majors, demonstrates *how* comparative literature does, leaving the *why* and *what* to later courses. His solution was introduced at Dartmouth. The macrocourse is described in the college bulletin as follows:

> The course will consider ways in which literature can provide pleasure, knowledge about the world, knowledge of self and others, experience of history. As a focal point the course will examine the theme of Hell in works by Homer, Aeschylus, Sophocles, Euripides, Petronius, Dante, Rimbaud, Gorky, Sartre, Camus, Faulkner, and Jerzy Kozinski. Slide lectures will explore the interaction between written and visual art forms.

The microcourse, or seminar, is on the other hand a narrowly focused, limited-enrollment seminar devoted to pursuing in depth a particular problem or topic in a specific period. The relationship of the two courses becomes clearer if one thinks of the seminar as giving a closeup view, within that specific period, of the same concerns treated in the macrocourse. The emphasis in both courses seeks to clarify the variety of forms of literature, the difference between pleasure reading and study, the variety of literary themes, literature's interdisciplinary relationships, and so on, adding up to a "strategy whereby we might effectively resolve the crisis of confidence and the crisis of conscience foisted upon us by changing times and trends. It would surely be a healthy sign in the movement to strengthen the standards of our undergraduate program as well as those of literacy in the humanities generally."

This summary cannot of course do justice to the full rationale and details of this promising plan, but the thoughtful two-level experiment has much more in its favor than the usual introduction to comparative literature by the zigzag contents from Homer to Joyce or Miller that characterize most undergraduate anthologies, of which a few more words must be said before concluding the present chapter.

Schools that have recently established a major or minor in comparative literature at the undergraduate level almost inevitably took over the venerable Western Heritage survey frequented by sophomores and juniors, along with one of the many trade book anthologies entitled variously Western Literature, Western Heritage Literature, Western Classics, Great Books, Our Literary Heritage, or even mistitled World Literature. As the Nichols Report suggests, the new program or department inherits both the course and the textbook. It suggests philosophically that comparative literature can live with the course and the anthology.

> Although trained comparatists might deplore the incorporation of such courses into the Comparative Literature curriculum the leverage is greater on the side of those who favor them. For one thing, it can be argued persuasively that the inclusion in the program of the Western Classics survey will assure a high enrollment for at least one course or sequence, thus offsetting the necessarily lower enrollment of some of the more rigorous, advanced courses. Second, deans often look with disfavor on departments refusing to teach their share of the "service" courses. Inevitably the introductory course in Comparative Literature

suggests itself, at least to outsiders, as a logical place to situate the "great books course." . . . It seems an inevitable fact of life in American and Canadian universities that an introductory course based on a synthetic overview of Western Classics will figure in many undergraduate Comparative Literature programs.

My own solution to this dilemma is a simple one: to accept the situation pragmatically but to organize an undergraduate anthology to implement it. There is no reason why this Western Classics course and anthology must cling to the above-mentioned anthological zigzag pattern "from Homer to Joyce," when it can instead present many of the same materials in an authentically comparatist disposition of texts by themes, forms, and genres. Such an anthology, as this writer has designed it, is described below (see p. 226).

V

Foreign Languages and Linguistics

What shall it profit our students to gain Swahili and have no Latin?

HARRY LEVIN

The Foreign Language Requirement

America, with its heterogeneous society, was ideally endowed with the major foreign languages of Europe. By the mid-forties, however, when comparative literature was undergoing its major resurgence, second- or third-generational students were losing—in some cases deliberately—the language heritage of their parents. Ancient and modern languages that in the early nineteenth century represented one third or more of the college curriculum were under attack from many quarters, especially the social sciences. Social scientists saw no reason for their students to read Hegel, Freud, Jung, and Engels in German. A minority of scientists were arguing that mathematics was the language of science (the computer languages of Fortran, etc., were yet inexistent) and that it obviated the distracting study of foreign languages. Ironically, World War II not only helped to prolong the foreign language requirements but spurred the government to subsidize the study of them. Having invested millions of dollars in the language courses of the Army Specialized Training and the Civil Affairs Training Programs (ASTP, CATP), which were eminently successful (although anthropologists and linguists played as great a role in shaping their methodology as language teachers did), the government maintained its commitment in the postwar period. Its impact on the new discipline of comparative literature is noted in ACLA Professional Standards Report I.

> The recent proliferation of Comparative Literature in colleges and universities throughout the country could hardly have materialized without the support of the National Defense Education Act (NDEA): but it marks the coming-of-age of a movement which has been spurred for some time by the revival of interest in language teaching, the introduction of programs and courses in great books, and the international cross-currents and exchanges of postwar years.

An even earlier force in the uniting of literature and languages was the Modern Language Association, which, with its emphasis on "philological method," had concentrated more on literary study than its title would indicate. In the period during and after the war (see rear Appendix), it was the then conservative Modern Language Association of America that obtained great sums from the government and the Rockefeller Foundation for the support of a wide range of languages. Yet the military enterprises of the fifties and sixties (Korea, Vietnam) were not of a nature to stem the return to linguistic isolationism that invaded the colleges in the seventies, when language requirements were reduced and even abolished. The commitment of comparative literature to foreign language study was thus an unusual reaffirmation. Some schools went so far as to state in their bulletin copy that comparative literature was designed specifically for "students who have greater than average linguistic competence and preparation" (Illinois) or "students with the drive and ability to master foreign languages" (Stanford). The ACLA Report had demanded of young comparatists inter alia linguistic competence to a high degree. "In practice [linguistic aptitude and critical aptitude] often tend to be weighted somewhat more on one side or the other. We should seek for balance in this respect, just as we balance the counterclaims of coverage and depth." The Report also noted that some languages—notably French and German—must be studied as auxiliary languages even if the student is not to specialize in their literatures. The Report recommended not only Greek and Latin (see below), but also Sanskrit "substituted in the increasing number of programs where a span is attempted between Occidental and Oriental literature." Finally, the Report stressed the need of polyglots as teachers: "Is it too much to expect that the teacher of literature, while not professing to be an expert in everything he teaches, should have some access to all the original languages involved?"

Although they might disagree on other issues, the comparative literature departments of America have largely agreed on the language requirement at all levels, making it clear that the requirement was minimal and that more enterprising candidates would exceed it: one foreign language for the B.A. major, two for the M.A., and three for the Ph.D. Fred Nichols has voiced the unanimous opinion, writing, "In a society becoming more relentlessly monoglottal than ever, comparative literature is where we ought to hold the line." Yet a comparison shopper who wants a cut-rate Ph.D. with only two languages should shop around among the various graduate school bulletins available in the college library. The student will find such schools as Pennsylvania State University satisfied by two foreign languages and English, UCLA by two foreign languages with a third "recommended," and Columbia University by two foreign languages (1976 bulletin). In fact, the ACLA Committee on Graduate Programs reported (1974) that of typical language combinations that may satisfy the Ph.D. requirement, ten combinations out of thirty-one listed permitted certification in only two foreign languages! There is usually unanimity that the requirement should be fulfilled at the latest before a dissertation is undertaken at any level. Since airline stewardesses on SAS and other international airlines must learn three foreign languages, it seems a modest requirement to impose on a Ph.D. in our discipline.

Which Languages?

The three foreign languages that the first generation of American comparatists commanded (often they knew more) were Latin, French, and German. The wide command of German had resulted from the veneration of things German by Emerson and Longfellow. Much of the early researches undertaken (as we have seen) involved English and one of these three tongues, a fact borne out by early theses. Because of the abundance of great authors in these three idioms, it was obvious that they would long remain the most prominent of the Western Heritage group.

Leaving aside the question of the classical language requirement (see below), the student of today is usually given considerable latitude in choosing his required languages for examination. A few schools, like Wisconsin, may forbid that all three languages be from the same linguistic family, although the values of this could be debated, since Romanistik is no longer an area of research in the disunited neo-Latin language departments, and could profitably be encouraged within the context of comparative literature.

The splendid isolation of English, American, French, and German literatures alongside the classics of antiquity is no longer unchallenged. If Spanish literature has suffered from controls and censorship (Spain had only six years of parliamentary government during two millennia), the tables have turned in Spanish America, and Spanish is no longer studied as a "commercial" language. José Donoso, in his recent study *Historia personal del Boom*, makes it clear that Hispanoamerican writers are no longer influenced by American and French authors, but indeed are now being imitated all over the Western World. His thesis is modestly applicable also to Brazilian literature. Even though Russian literature began its *essor* only in the eighteenth century and has remained under censorship most of the time, its literature and language have vindicated its claims to primacy. The point need not be overstated. Because of the maturation of many Western literatures and because of a dissatisfaction with two-literature courses and theses, students must have contact with several literatures and as many languages as they have time to master.

In discussing the knowledge of foreign languages, Pichois and Rousseau recall that Proust, having only a rudimentary knowledge of English, was able to translate Ruskin and that Edmond Jaloux, using translations, discoursed intelligently on the German romanticists. They affirm that Frenchmen and Englishmen have a hard time learning foreign languages and that Russians, Swiss, and Germans find it easier. Others in the field are more implacable, and one may recall a recent proposal that Ph.D.'s be awarded upon the recipient's promise to keep learning further languages.

We might pause over the question, what is a foreign language?

I have been in Trois Rivières, Canada, with Parisian friends who shared my almost total incomprehension of the language we heard spoken. Yet for purposes of comparative literature, dialects and patois, even if existent in printed form, can hardly constitute a separate literary language. As we have pointed out in Chapter ii, some countries like Indonesia or India have over a hundred variants of their inherited language. Some graduate schools actually list the few foreign languages that they will approve as satisfying the language requirement. Such a list should be vastly extended for the comparative literature department.

One request that constantly comes up with our students from Europe and the Near East is for approval of ancient and modern Hebrew as two distinct languages and, similarly, of ancient and modern Greek. Since we view as distinct Latin and Italian, Anglo-Saxon and English, Gothic and modern German, consistency is in order. However, the student seeking shortcuts to language certification should probably not be in comparative literature. Another question often asked is whether the three foreign languages must coincide with the languages required for the Ph.D. thesis. Since the point is made in the ACLA Report that the foreign language requirement exists to master not only the foreign texts read but also the critical background studies, students might be able to justify their selection of languages as needed for background reading, but they ought not write theses involving a foreign language they cannot read. With this principle firmly established and protected, one can be sympathetic to students who learn finally the neglected foreign language of their grandparents and rationalize on its value to their future (postthesis) researches.

The Classical or "Equally Ancient" Language Requirement

"Tout le monde n'est pas forcé de savoir le grec," asserted Victor Hugo, a romanticism refuting directly the humanist creed of the great Erasmus: "Sine Graecis literis caeca est omnis eruditio."

Hugo's is a remark that has always troubled me. The classical literature of Greece and Rome is probably the richest for the comparatist, and indeed one certified by our dimensional phrase Western Heritage. My own senior generation studied Greek and Latin—indeed it followed close upon an earlier generation that strongly recommended as well the study of Sanskrit. And their masters before them studied ancient Hebrew and Chaldean—two languages taught during the early nineteenth century at New York University. Yet as early as 1883 the hegemony of classical languages was undermined by the very change of opinion that led to the establishment of the Modern Language Association (see Appendix).

At the Harvard faculty meeting that voted to drop the classical language requirement for undergraduates, the present writer cast his vote with the minority. Classes in Greek and Latin brought thrills and even excitement, like those of a Winckelmann or a Keats rediscovering the psychagogic impact of Greek canons of art and culture.[1] Captured by their lyricism, many of us could recite odes (of Anacreon especially). When we took our courses on Renaissance poetry, with its endless plagiarisms by Ronsard of Pindar and Anacreon, we could measure the seminal role that Greek literature played in the comparative endeavor. Many genres and forms of Hellenic invention persist to the present day. In view of this undeniable role, could the language requirement of Greek or Latin, implicit in the ACLA Committee Reports on Professional Standards, ever become a controversial or divisive issue within our profession? Could we really find fault with Harry Levin's question in his presidential address quoted as the incipit of this chapter?

The classical language requirement did nevertheless become an issue for a short time. For a certain period the Washington office of the NDEA withheld scholarship funds from comparative literature departments that did not include the knowledge of one classical language among its Ph.D. requirements. Since NYU had not imposed such a blanket requirement, I visited the NDEA offices to verify the facts. I was informed that the government did not associate itself with the requirement, rather remaining neutral and accepting policies by which its advisers executed their mandate.

Further inquiry among colleagues around the nation showed that many were introducing the ancient language requirement not

[1] To confirm my own objectivity in this question, I have studied in the classroom Greek, classical Latin, Vulgate Latin, French, Italian, Spanish, Portuguese, Provençal, German, and Russian and have taught five of these languages. I have audited an Arabic course at the University of Bordeaux and Professor Chiu's Elementary Chinese course at NYU.

out of conviction, but for the benefit of their students who might thus become eligible for government grants. Two chairmen stated that they were introducing the requirement, but with discretionary exceptions, or in a minimal or diluted form. Fortunately the government changed its policy and removed what could have become a truly divisive issue.

In any case the division made us all do some hard thinking about the requirement and for whom it should be applicable. A policy committee at NYU that included two distinguished classicists and two Renaissance specialists decided that the requirement should not be a blanket one, but one applied to specific groups of candidates. The articles of this loyal-opposition committee report can be simplified as follows:

1. The great tradition of Greek or Roman literature is not necessarily transmitted by the study of four semesters of their language. A student taking four semesters of Latin may not pass far beyond Caesar's bridge—or in Greek, beyond the seashore of Xenophon. The implication that four semesters of an ancient language afford an understanding of the literature in that language has troubled some universities to the point of offering as alternative to study of an ancient language a year's survey of that ancient literature in English translation.

2. Comparative literature course topics and theses are usually either chronologically horizontal (contemporaneous) or vertical (of long duration). European surrealism, its *Blütezeit* running from roughly 1916 to the late 1920s, is a horizontal movement. For someone working on a thesis on this movement, a knowledge of three modern foreign languages is imperative, indeed minimal. Courses on European epic or tragedy are obviously vertical in time, starting with Homer or Aeschylus. Someone doing a thesis in this completely vertical field, or such other topics as the Oedipus theme—any theme, in sum, rooted in Greece and Rome —would be expected to know Latin or Greek.

3. In certain horizontal fields involving antiquity, Middle Ages, Renaissance, or neoclassicism, a knowledge of at least Latin is of course fundamental. A student would be required to demonstrate a reading knowledge of Latin, which remained a lingua franca from Dante to Erasmus and a literary language to Boileau. Even Renaissance Greek, if the coinage is justifiable, remained a free-trade language among the elite, and a Renaissance scholar must

acquire it sooner or later. This reasoning is more than supported by the UCLA program, which recommends a classical language for students "with periods of specialization prior to the nineteenth century."

4. An insistence on Greek or Latin for all candidates as one of the three required foreign languages would mean that someone working in three modern foreign literatures might be required before his degree to learn Latin or Greek as a fourth requirement. One of our earlier theses on the Spanish Civil War in the novel necessitated a facility with English, French, Spanish, German, at least. Surely a fourth foreign language is an eventual desideratum for a comparatist, as is a fifth and a sixth—but a burden for a Ph.D. candidate working under temporal and financial pressures.

5. A poll taken by the registrants in our department at that time revealed the agreeable statistic that three out of five of our comparative literature candidates had come to us with two or more years of Latin on their record. Yet even a few of these stated that an ancient language requirement would have deterred them from entering the department, since they wished to spend time perfecting three modern foreign languages more closely applicable to their thesis fields. Their feelings about a more "open" language requirement seemed to coincide with a telegram from President Jacques Voisine of ICLA read during the Indiana meeting of the ACLA. It called for more global coverage in our researches. At that period our students were beginning to find a need for the more unusual languages to complete their theses, such as Polish, Modern Greek, Modern Hebrew, and so on. New generations take new directions.

6. The ancient language requirement favored at that time by the officers of ACLA and the advisers to NDEA foundered on the allowed substitution of "an equally ancient language." Such a language is Hittite. If Hittite can be substituted in the case of a thesis involving inscriptions in ancient Syria, or Babylonian in the case of a thesis on *Gilgamesh* (see Ch. ii), then why not allow substitution of Russian for ancient Greek if a candidate is doing a thesis on the demanding topic of the realistic novel in Europe? The value of a last-resort "equally ancient language" meets all sorts of objections involving logic and cultural history that need not occupy us here.

7. Most comparative literature departments work closely and

profitably with departments of national literature that do not require Latin or Greek. Of the cooperating departments—English, Romance, German, Slavic, classics, Arabic, and Hebrew—only two require a knowledge of Latin and in one of these cases (Romance) Vulgar Latin (almost devoid of a literature to justify it) will satisfy the requirement.

It is obvious that the ancient and "equally ancient" language requirement was predicated on courses and theses neatly contained within the dimension of a classical heritage. The requirement, logical as it seemed at the time, failed to fit the expanding-universe drive of comparative literature itself. Dean Herbert Weisinger, whose familiarity with classical languages was apparent in his writings, realized that the boundaries of our discipline would inevitably have to be expanded. He wrote, "Indeed, many comparatists, having managed to emancipate themselves from the thrall of nationalism, promptly enslave themselves in the larger, but still confining, concept of the Western literary tradition. They insist that without mastery of Greek, Latin, German, French, and English, the study of comparative literature cannot be pursued." It is perhaps ironic that a recent Harvard graduate bulletin does not list an ancient language requirement, although four or five of the comparative literature courses listed would make such a requirement understandable. Despite all attempts to legislate the nature of the language requirement, candidates' needs will depend on the subject and compass of their theses, and the corpus of criticism on those subjects. Common sense, shared by students and advisers, can dictate the choice. Thus, paving the way toward theses in East-West or World Literature, Wisconsin had legislated by 1968 that the classical language could be replaced by Sanskrit, Tamil, Chinese, Arabic, Persian, or other Asian language.

Once in a while students will elect as their three foreign languages French, Spanish, and Italian. They may even be apologetic about it, since these are an easier challenge than one Romance, one Germanic, and one Slavic language, for example. Some schools, as stated above, even legislate against a student's satisfying the requirement with three languages from the same linguistic group. One need not agree with this, for the great early comparatists like Vossler, Meyer-Lübke, and others were Romanists of the highest order and set a level of scholarship for all

Europe. Their native language was German, of course, and they mastered as well Latin and Greek. As we have already remarked, they were the first scholars in Germany to use the comparative method. Their disciples in America, including Nitze, Wilkins, Ford, demonstrated that the Romance area (including Portugal, of course) was a logical and fruitful area of comparatism to cultivate.

Professor Nichols of CUNY, a Neo-Latinist who did his thesis on Scaliger's *Poemata* and has edited a volume of late Latin poetry, is a most eloquent partisan of the Latin or Greek requirement. This section will close with his rebuttal:

A Comparative Literature person, whatever his specialization, is always expected to be more of a generalist than his colleague who is a Shakespearean, a Dante man, and so on. There is a particular way in which he should know Western literature, and Latin is the central—and in a way, the defining—language of Western culture. Whereas I should not go so far as to say that every comparatist must know Latin well, I think a department that requires it is placing its students in an advantageous position in terms of their intellectual and professional lives. While Classical Greek is not quite so central, substituting it for Latin can be justified by the tremendous intrinsic importance of the texts written in it. And a Comparative Literature person with Greek has a tremendous professional advantage because really few people nowadays except Classicists learn the language otherwise.

Testing Procedures and Standards

A graduate student usually satisfies a single-language requirement by completing with a B or better a second-year college course in the language, by passing a special examination offered by the appropriate language department, by passing a graduate course requiring reading in a foreign language, by appropriate schooling in a foreign country, or by passing the Graduate School Foreign Language Test of Princeton's ETS (Educational Testing Service). (Moreover, at schools like SUNY-Binghamton the English department awards credit of one foreign language to a student who passes with an honor grade a course in comparative literature.) The ETS tests are administered and governed by the

Graduate Record Examinations Board, an independent board affiliated with the Association of Graduate Schools and the Council of U.S. Graduate Schools. They will validate candidates, if they pass, in French, German, Spanish, or Russian. The examinations are given four times yearly, in October, February, April, and June. They guarantee a unanimity of standards across the entire country. They last 100 minutes each and are administered locally. They consist of two parts: Part I includes sixty multiple-choice questions in the selected foreign language that measure basic knowledge of vocabulary and structure essential to a reading comprehension. Part II measures the ability to read material containing information within one's field of study (humanities, natural or social sciences). It is generally agreed that two years of study of a language completed with a final honor grade would prepare one adequately for this test, although often someone with less preparation and a keen mind can outguess the multiple-choice tests. The test fees, which are minimal, are paid to one's own graduate school and not to ETS. Departments may obtain copies of the GSFLT information booklet by sending a request to the Educational Testing Service, Box 591, Princeton, New Jersey 08540. In many schools the ETS examination is not necessary if the candidate qualifies by resorting to one of the four alternatives listed above. For languages other than French, German, Spanish, or Russian one of the alternatives above must replace the ETS.

Although the minimal scores may fluctuate each year depending on the difficulty of the individual tests, the average passing scores based on a minimum-maximum range of 200 to 800 hover around the following tabulation:

French	540
German	520
Spanish	510
Russian	480

Sometimes students feel more secure if they can at least see a copy of the type of test ahead of them. For this reason there follow at the end of this section sample questions of two types offered by ETS for French, Spanish, and German.

There is no such national organization as GSFLT for assessing the language skills of undergraduates, since college students usually satisfy their language requirement by passing the fourth semester of a foreign language. Otherwise the local language departments provide a variety of examinations to certify both undergraduates and graduate students to be tested in languages not processed by GSFLT.

A few schools, like CUNY, dispense with this useful service provided by the GSFLT. Fred Nichols explains why:

> It doesn't take long to pick out two passages, one narrative and one critical, and grade them. A student doesn't pass unless he really does have a working knowledge of the language. Our kind of examination has the advantage of approximating the real uses to which a student is going to put his knowledge of a language, which a multiple-choice exam, however ingenious, doesn't really do.[2]

Most departments, however, favor the ETS examinations for their convenience and objectivity. They present another advantage. Students preparing for language examinations inevitably worry about their level and nature, coming to their graduate advisers to question whether they are sufficiently prepared—a question difficult to answer. It is therefore helpful—and sometimes reassuring—for them if the department office keeps on hand copies of the easily obtainable current GSFLT sample examinations, such as these on pages 111–19, for candidates to inspect.

FIG. 3. *Sample Pages of Foreign Language Proficiency Tests*

SAMPLE QUESTIONS

Sample questions for each of three Graduate School Foreign Language Tests follow. While these questions are representative of the general content and level of difficulty of the tests, they should not be regarded as clues to the specific vocabulary, points of grammar, or texts likely to occur in a particular examination.

The directions preceding each group of sample questions are those used in actual tests.

---

[2] Students who oppose the ETS examinations allege three somewhat subjective criticisms: that students can pass these examinations without a real understanding of a literary text; that a fee of (currently) $15 is levied at each examination; and that in rare cases a student carrying a friend's identity card can take the examination for that friend.

FRENCH

Section I

Directions: Each of the sentences in this part has a blank space indicating that a word or phrase has been omitted. From the four choices select the ONE which, when inserted in the sentence, fits structurally and logically with the sentence as a whole.

1. Pendant les famines du Moyen Age, beaucoup de gens devaient . . . nourriture.

   (A) passer sans   (B) passer   (C) se passer de   (D) dépasser la

2. On retrouve ainsi des conditions de photographie comparables à celles . . . connaissent les cosmonautes.

   (A) que   (B) dont   (C) qui   (D) quoi

3. Personne n'a jamais pu interpréter ce rôle . . . que Caruso.

   (A) tant   (B) comme   (C) bien   (D) mieux

4. Les experts ont écrit un rapport sur la situation de la compagnie . . . les années 1920 à 1929.

   (A) entre   (B) par   (C) puisque   (D) pendant

5. Comme il n'a pas compris la question, il a demandé une mise . . .

   (A) au jour   (B) au point   (C) en scène   (D) en pages

Directions: In each of the sentences in this part, a word or expression has been underlined. From the four choices select the ONE that is the best translation of the underlined portion of the sentence.

6. Cette œuvre est très représentative d'un aspect permanent, <u>même</u> classique, de la littérature.

   (A) very   (B) even   (C) though   (D) also

7. Le mécanicien s'est <u>rendu compte</u> de la cause de la difficulté.

   (A) discounted   (B) anticipated
   (C) accounted for   (D) realized

8. Pendant l'hiver le jeune peintre <u>ne chauffait plus que</u> la pièce où il travaillait.

   (A) no longer heated more than   (B) no longer heated even
   (C) no longer heated only   (D) no longer heated at all

9. <u>Il est bien peu probable</u> que le public le prenne au sérieux.

   (A) It is indeed likely   (B) There is probably very little
   (C) It is highly unlikely   (D) There are probably very few

10. Cette image de la France est partielle, sans nuances. Elle <u>se borne</u> aux caractères typiques et pittoresques.

(A) is related   (B) reverts   (C) is limited   (D) appeals

Section II

Directions: Read the following passages carefully for comprehension. Each passage is followed by a number of incomplete statements or questions in English. *On the basis of the content of the passage,* select the completion or answer that is best.

HUMANITIES

Vers un nouvel humanisme

On sait ce que fut l'humanisme du XVe et du XVIe siècle; c'est à un nouvel humanisme que conduisent les études de littérature comparée, humanisme plus large et plus fécond que le premier, mieux capable de rapprocher les nations. En effet, au fur et à
(5) mesure que la notion de nationalité a fait plus de progrès, le danger des autarcies[1] intellectuelles s'est révélé plus grand; les différences entre les peuples ont passé des moeurs à l'esprit. Contre cet isolement si essentiellement dangereux pour l'unification pacifique du monde, nos méthodes réagissent[2] heureusement. Elles mettent
(10) en relief les ressemblances entre les peuples, ces tendances générales de l'esprit humain sans lesquelles aucune influence ne saurait se produire. Mais elles soulignent aussi les différences entre les divers génies nationaux. "Que ces petites différences," comme le dit Voltaire "ne soient pas des signaux de haine et de
(15) persécution!" Il ne suffit pas de s'accommoder de ces contrastes irréductibles, il faut se les représenter, avec Montesquieu, comme des ressorts[3] nécessaires à la vie harmonieuse de l'humanité. La littérature comparée impose ainsi à ceux qui la pratiquent une attitude de sympathie et de compréhension à l'égard de nos
(20) "frères humains," un libéralisme intellectuel, sans lesquels aucune oeuvre commune entre les peuples ne peut être tentée.

---

[1]autarcie: self-sufficiency, independence

[2]réagir: to react

[3]ressort: incentive, spur

1. The first sentence states that in comparison to the old humanism, the new humanism has a greater capacity to
   (A) study national literatures in breadth as well as in depth
   (B) help to draw nations closer together
   (C) approach the study of each nation through its literature
   (D) understand feelings of nationalism

2. In the second sentence, the author states that growth of nationalism has
   (A) been proportionate to the differences in customs
   (B) exaggerated the notion of national self-sufficiency
   (C) contributed ultimately to international understanding
   (D) turned cultural differences into ideological differences

3. In lines 12–13, the author maintains that comparative literature
   (A) stresses differences in national character
   (B) plays down individual geniuses in a nation
   (C) is subject to divergent national problems
   (D) is not affected by genuine national differences

4. The author says that Montesquieu believed that differences among peoples
   (A) are inevitable but acceptable to some
   (B) may eventually disappear if one has an open mind
   (C) can be lived with if they cannot be eliminated
   (D) should be considered advantageous

5. In line 12, *elles* refers to
   (A) general tendencies   (B) similarities
    (C) methods   (D) differences

GERMAN

Section I

Directions: Each of the sentences in this part has a blank space indicating that a word or phrase has been omitted. From the four choices select the ONE which, when inserted in the sentence, fits structurally and logically with the sentence as a whole.

1. Fragen Sie Dr. Merker. Er . . . auf diesem Gebiet lange gearbeitet.
   (A) wird   (B) hätte   (C) hat   (D) würde

2. Ein sehr guter Artikel erklärte die Methoden . . . Erfinder.
   (A) dieser   (B) eine   (C) unser   (D) deren

3. C. ist drei Jahre . . . als die anderen Patienten der Versuchsgruppe.
   (A) alt   (B) jüngst   (C) jünger   (D) ältester

4. Viele Leute finden moderne Kunst und Musik schlecht, . . . sie sie nicht verstehen.
   (A) als   (B) während   (C) seit   (D) weil

5. Der Universitätsverlag hat Dr. Bergers neues Buch . . .
    (A) geschrieben   (B) herausgegeben
    (C) kritisiert   (D) komponiert

Directions: In each of the sentences in this part, a word or expression has been underlined. From the four choices select the ONE that is the best translation of the underlined portion of the sentence.

6. Herr Baumann hat sich die Hühe gemacht, meine Arbeit durch-zusehen.
   (A) had trouble in   (B) could afford to
   (C) went to the trouble of   (D) caused difficulty by

7. Mehrere Umstände haben dazu beigetragen, die politische Lage zu verschlimmern.
   (A) have been added   (B) have been rumored
   (C) have brought about   (D) have contributed

8. Professor Grothe spricht am Donnerstag über seine Ausgrabungen in Kreta.
   (A) is speaking every Thursday
   (B) is going to speak this Thursday
   (C) will speak today, Thursday
   (D) spoke last Thursday

9. Diese Hypothese is falsch, so einleuchtend sie auch scheint.
   (A) therefore also   (B) also when
   (C) and even   (D) no matter how

10. Er sagte sehr wenig über das Resultat seiner Expedition. Er wird wohl damit unzufrieden sein.
    (A) I assume he is dissatisfied with it.
    (B) He is going to be dissatisfied with it.
    (C) He ought to be dissatisfied with it.
    (D) He has a right to be dissatisfied with it.

Section II

Directions: Read the following passages carefully for comprehension. Each passage is followed by a number of incomplete statements or questions in English. *On the basis of the content of the passage* select the completion or answer that is best.

HUMANITIES

Trauersitten im griechischen Altertum

Die Opfergaben begannen wohl meistens gleich bei der Be-stattung.[1] Hierbei Spendegüsse[2] aus Wein, Öl und Honig darzu-bringen, mag allgemein üblich gewesen sein. Blutige Opfer, wie sie bei Homer am Scheiterhaufen[3] des Patroklos, auch des
(5) Achill, dargebracht werden, können in älterer Zeit nicht unge-wöhnlich gewesen sein. Solon verbot ausdrücklich, ein Rind

am Grabe zu opfern, in Keos wird ebenso ausdrücklich durch das Gesetz gestattet, bei der Bestattung "ein Voropfer darzubringen, nach Vätersitte." Von der Bestattungsfeier zurück-
(10) gekehrt, begehen die Familienangehörigen,[4] nachdem sie sich einer religiösen Reinigung unterzogen haben, bekränzt[5] (während sie vorher der Bekränzung sich enthalten hatten), das Leichenmahl. Auch dies war ein Teil des Seelenkultes. Die Seele des Verstorbenen galt als anwesend, ja als der Gastge-
(15) ber; Scheu[6] vor dem unsichtbar Teilnehmenden war es, welche die Sitte eingab, nur lobpreisend seiner bei dem Mahle zu gedenken. Das Leichenmahl war eine Mahlzeit für die überlebenden Angehörigen, im Hause des Toten ausgerichtet. Dem Toten allein wurde an seinem Grabe eine Mahlzeit aufgetragen
(20) am dritten und neunten Tage nach der Bestattung. Am neunten scheint nach alter Sitte die Trauerzeit ein Ende gefunden zu haben. Wo diese länger ausgedehnt wurde, erstreckte sich auch die Reihe der ersten Totenspenden auf eine weitere Zeit. Sparta hatte eine Trauerzeit von elf Tagen; in Athen schloß
(25) sich bisweilen dem Opfer am dritten und neunten ein wohl auch mehrmals wiederholtes Opfermahl am dreißigsten Tage an.

[1]Bestattung: funeral

[2]Spendeguß: libation

[3]Scheiterhaufen: funeral pyre

[4]Angehörige: relatives

[5]bekränzen: to garland

[6]Scheu: awe

1. The sacrifice called a *Voropfer* (line 8) seems to have been a
   (A) sacrifice preceding the funeral
   (B) libation of wine, oil, and honey
   (C) bovine or other animal
   (D) human sacrifice

2. The first thing the members of the family did upon returning from the funeral was to
   (A) put garlands on their heads (B) purify themselves
   (C) pour a libation to the soul   (D) hold the funeral banquet

3. During the funeral banquet, the soul of the deceased was considered to be
   (A) present as host
   (B) on its way to the nether world
   (C) hovering near the grave or funeral pyre
   (D) the guest of honor

4. According to custom, the period of mourning was usually
   (A) three days (B) nine days   (C) eleven days   (D) thirty days
5. Which of the following was a feature of the funeral banquet?
   (A) Family and friends of the deceased took part in it.
   (B) It was held three days after the funeral.
   (C) It was held at the graveside.
   (D) The participants praised the deceased.

SPANISH

Section I

Directions: Each of the sentences in this part has a blank space indicating that a word or phrase has been omitted. From the four choices select the ONE which, when inserted in the sentence, fits structurally and logically with the sentence as a whole.

1. El grupo del Instituto Gómez persistió en su encuesta . . . todos los obstáculos.
   (A) sin embargo   (B) a pesar de   (C) además de   (D) para
2. El equipo técnico llegó a Hatogrande antes de que . . . la expedición científica.
   (A) llegue   (B) llegaba   (C) llegó   (D) llegara
3. Los guardias civiles pasaron de nuevo . . . del palacio.
   (A) por delante   (B) entre   (C) opuesto   (D) juntos
4. Se despidió del coronel y siguió . . . despacio.
   (A) a andar   (B) andando   (C) de andar   (D) andar
5. Simón Bolívar y José de San Martín son los grandes libertadores de Sudamérica; éste es de la Argentina y . . . es de Venezuela.
   (A) aquél   (B) eso   (C) él   (D) aquello

Directions: In each of the sentences in this part, a word or expression has been underlined. From the four choices select the ONE that is the best translation of the underlined portion of the sentence.

6. No lo podemos esperar todo del trabajo de unos cuantos.
   (A) as many   (B) how many   (C) only one   (D) a few
7. Este estudio debe hacerse desde otro punto de vista.
   (A) must be carried out   (B) ought to make
   (C) must make   (D) must become
8. Ni siquiera es suficiente el mero diagnóstico sicológico, como no sea vinculándolo a las alteraciones de naturaleza social.
   (A) be that as it may   (B) however it may be
   (C) unless it is   (D) as it is not

9. Los abogados convinieron en solucionar el problema cuanto antes.
   (A) as before   (B) as soon as possible
    (C) whenever feasible   (D) much earlier

10. El segundo aspecto de la teoria está casi sin tocar.
    (A) is rarely tested
    (B) is of very little importance
    (C) has been almost completed
    (D) has hardly been dealt with

Section II

Directions: Read the following passages carefully for comprehension. Each passage is followed by a number of incomplete statements or questions in English. Select the completion or answer that is best *according to the passage.*

HUMANITIES

Literatura y lenguaje

El estudio de una lengua limitado a los textos de las épocas literarias es incapaz de ilustrar ciertos aspectos de la vida del lenguaje. La literatura nos presenta el idioma, si no fijado, como suele decirse, al menos muy cohibido por la tradición letrada, y el hecho lingüístico suele aparecer bajo una sola de sus facetas, la escogida por esa tradición. De ahí que el dialectólogo, deslumbrado por la abundante variedad de hechos que ofrecen los lenguajes vulgares modernos, más movedizos, más libres de las trabas eruditas, siente orgullo de "nuevo rico", y desprecia el patrimonio señorial del filólogo que se aplica sobre todo a los textos literarios.

1. With respect to certain aspects of language, the author states that they are
   (A) best illustrated by literary texts
   (B) limited to certain literary periods
   (C) not represented in literary texts
   (D) common to all literary periods

2. The author states that literary tradition tends to inhibit the development of
   (A) idiomatic expression
   (B) literary forms
   (C) language, although much less than commonly assumed
   (D) language, although it does not arrest it

3. The dialectologist finds himself in a position in which he

(A) tends to be confused by the wealth of material with which he
has to deal
(B) tends to scorn the philological method that confines itself to
literature
(C) would do well to collaborate more closely with the philologist
(D) has considerably more difficult material to deal with than the
philologist

Undergraduate Foreign Language Requirements

Before the mid-seventies an undergraduate aiming at any
liberal arts and sciences major was required to take foreign
language courses or at least demonstrate a reading knowledge of
one foreign language. After that time many colleges dropped the
foreign language requirement, an unfortunate policy with repercussions also on the graduate offerings in foreign literatures. The
Nichols Report (1974) found that all colleges with an undergraduate major in comparative literature required knowledge of
one foreign language, whereas a few required or strongly urged
acquisition of a second. It found colleges rationalizing the single
foreign language policy as follows: "It is preferable for undergraduate majors in comparative literature to acquire a thorough
grounding in a first foreign language rather than attempting to do
two concurrently, thereby risking over-extension" (p. 4). This is
supportive of the first ACLA Report on Professional Standards,
which urged a firm grounding in a single language and literature
as a departure for graduate work in comparative literature.

The Report notes the possibility that some undergraduate
majors may weaken the foreign language requirement as a
stratagem to attract increased numbers of majors. It notes that by
reducing its language requirement, Brown University increased
its majors from six to thirty.

It seems preferable, however, to look at the language requirement as a means of increasing fruitful relationships between
comparative literature programs and foreign language departments. One source of friction between comparative literature and
traditional national literature departments is the latter's fear that
a flourishing comparative literature program will deprive them of

students whom they badly need when budgets are so tight. A careful reading of the Princeton requirements [one foreign language plus completion of an upper-level foreign language course] shows an explicit strategy which works to the advantage of both comparative literature and foreign language departments. By requiring comparative literature majors to take a specified number of advanced literature courses in their foreign language departments, comparative literature programs actually contribute to an increased enrollment in precisely those advanced foreign language literature courses which have traditionally shown low enrollment. It is very much in the interest of existing and proposed comparative literature programs to work closely with foreign language departments, stressing the mutual benefits that may be realized.

With the collegewide abolition of the single foreign language requirement in the mid-seventies—an abolition that may unfortunately be with us for a long time—the competition for literature students, indeed for departmental survival in a few cases, became more Darwinian. One proof is that the practice of foreign language departments of offering teaching assistantships to comparative literature doctoral candidates in one major university declined from a total of eleven in the late sixties to none at the present writing. Assistant professors found themselves teaching elementary and intermediate foreign language courses. Rather than face the competition of an undergraduate comparative literature program, national literature departments, as we note elsewhere, instituted more Great Books courses, surveys of individual foreign literatures in translation, and humanities courses as understandable stratagems to keep adequate enrollments for survival. For this reason the Nichols Report sagaciously reminds us that the newly installed comparative literature programs were rather a spur to increased study in the foreign language departments:

The apparent loser in a situation where Comparative Literature majors' requirements are reduced from two to one foreign language, would seem to be English departments. Many students who would like to major in Comparative Literature, but are unwilling, initially, to make the investment in two foreign languages do turn to the English department as a logical major, while continuing to take courses in Comparative Literature. In a climate of reduced foreign language requirements, they may well turn to Comparative Literature for their major. There is probably a tendency to overestimate the number of such students, however, at least in the case of a Princeton-type requirement. As was pointed out above, one should not emphasize the reduction in language requirement, but rather the *increase* in language exposure. Students primarily interested in English with a secondary concern for another national literature will probably continue to major in English, taking an occasional course in the second literature. In other words, this approach to a single foreign language in Comparative Literature appeals more to the student who—without wishing to limit himself to one language/literature—is essentially language-oriented, than to the English major who has proficiency in a foreign language. This point cannot be overemphasized when talking with colleagues in other departments: one of the chief "scare" tactics used to deter the formation of new undergraduate programs, or to undermine existing ones, has been precisely the assertion that "it will take our students." In fact, in this case—as in the case of staffing, to be discussed later—not only need this not be true, but the reverse can apply: *undergraduate Comparative Literature can help increase foreign language enrollment.*

The valuable Nichols Report separates the undergraduate departments or programs that maintain a plural-language requirement. Among these are established comparative literature programs that still adhere to their original demand for two foreign languages and recent programs that require two foreign languages under special provisions. There are many variants of the latter. Most common is the honors program, which imposes special varying demands and levels of accomplishment in both language and literature study. In some schools, like SUNY-Binghamton, there is a two-track major (one allowing for an English minor), but each track requires two foreign languages. Stanford, Beloit, and Dartmouth are typical in demanding two foreign languages, although the latter has an alternate major permitting a degree with one foreign language. California-Berkeley is most demanding of majors in its honors program, requiring two foreign languages, plus classical Greek or Latin. This triple-language requirement looms in egregious contrast to the absence of languages in the majors in other humanities at the undergraduate level. Indeed, as we have observed, it is the conventional number of foreign languages required universally for the Ph.D. The Nichols Report, which not only reported the *état présent* of current undergraduate requirements, wisely accepted as part of its charge the interpretation of the statistics it garnered. Thus it concludes the investigation summarized above with a final observation on the relationship between language requirements and enrollments.

> Before closing the discussion of the language requirement, two observations must be made. While it is clear that strong arguments exist in favor of maintaining the multi-language requirement on the one hand, or, on the other, of maximizing exposure to a single foreign language, the choice between the two alternatives should *not* be made on the grounds that increased numbers of majors will automatically result from a reduction in the number of FLs required. Although the experience at Brown reported earlier would seem to contradict this observation, experience suggests that some other factors must have been at work in the increased numbers of majors experienced at Brown than the simple reduction of the language requirement. Many of the universities and colleges polled have had a single foreign language requirement for years and yet show the same low major to overall enrollment ratio as institutions requiring two foreign languages. It would thus not appear that the language requirement in and of itself is a determining factor in the number of majors a program attracts. At most the language requirement can be seen as only one of the factors contributing to the reputation of Comparative Literature as a "difficult" major.

Comparative Literature and Linguistics

As we conclude our discussion of foreign languages and comparative literature, it is appropriate to reflect briefly on the relevancy of the comparative science of language, linguistics, to the study of international literature. The infusion of linguistics into a course on literature can obviously be an enrichment if it is intelligently undertaken. If unintelligently done, it serves as an impediment to, and even an annoying intrusion upon, the student impatient to arrive at an intimate understanding of a proper interdiscipline for literature, which language should obviously be. Language areas or *Sprachräume* are the very units by which we separate the dimensions of our discipline. Period courses, such as mediaeval literature, often bring into focus the special factors and influences of language. Variants of the same language distinguish popular from "book" language, and writers like Kazantzakis become suspect for writing in demotic.

Comparative literature, like geopolitics, divides nations by speech isotherms. Linguistic atlases are called upon to settle boundary disputes. Languages are used as vessels of political hostility, with René Étiemble's and Charles De Gaulle's attacks on *le franglais* and Hitler's and Mussolini's attacks on anglicisms undermining their pure languages. Such struggles between languages account for dramatic literature, as in Daudet's "La Dernière Classe," in which Alsatian schools are forced to abandon French for Alsatian German. The suppression or limitation of the great Catalonian or Basque languages and literatures under Franco kept those regional writers in continual revolt. In some revolutionary countries, like Thailand and Russia, new leaders legislate changes in the very alphabets themselves of the native language—sometimes for the best. We have seen in Chapter ii how authors of emerging literatures launch linguistic and literary campaigns against the foreign occupants of their homelands. All these interlacings among politics, literature, and language make the study of comparative literature more fascinating.

Somewhere in their training, either in the methods or some autonomous course, students should be taught the relation with literature of phonology, phonetics, phonemics, semantics, semasiology, morphology, syntax, grammar—perhaps even euphonics. Such stylistic matters as the splitting of infinitives and ending sentences with "bobtail" syllables should be explained. (Examples: *He ought to unobtrusively leave* vs. *He ought to leave unobtrusively. The senators, after a lengthy discussion, vote* vs. *The senators vote after a lengthy discussion.*) Such principles of euphony operate similarly in all the world's languages. The mysterious mutations of meaning in etymology and semantics can make the analysis of a literary text a subtle exercise. Orthography will tell us many things about a literary work, including the dating of the piece. Calligraphy, which also helps us to establish and date texts, is in the Orient a total artistic achievement independent of the content of the writing.

Students of comparative literature especially should know about the International Phonetics Alphabet, created by linguistic scientists of three nationalities: Sweet, Vietor, and Passy. Late during the last century the phoneticians decided that every sound of human speech was classifiable and could be designated by a symbol just as invariable and international as the signs of weights and measures. The signs that characterize these many types of vowels and consonants have become the standard transcriptions of the sounds of the world's languages and dialects. Most dictionaries of Western languages include the phonetic transcription after spelling the word. Students working in comparative drama, epic, and oral folklore would do well to spend a weekend learning these symbols.

The field of linguistic statistics has been carried furthest by departments of foreign language. This field concerns itself with word and idiom counts, syntax counts, and lexicography. Its principal value has been for the preparation of high school and college grammars, textbooks, and readers, and thus it has less immediate interest for the comparatist.

A major branch of linguistics is of course stylistics, so important to literature study of all dimensions. Comparative stylistics would be a most demanding specialization, involving in plural literatures such basic concerns as prosody, metrics, versification, sentence structure, diction, word order, imagery, metaphor, epithets, coherence, emphasis, standards, and taste. This area of linguistics has been historically as involved with rhetoric as with literature.

This excursus into the relations of linguistics with literature is necessarily brief, but those interested will find further pertinent sidelights on the matter in two brilliant books no longer new but still available and welcome: *The Loom of Language* by Frederick Bodmer and the revised edition of Mario Pei's *The Story of Language*, both of which fall under the rubric of pleasure reading. W. Bernard Fleischmann reminds me of two further books that demonstrate that linguistic scholars have recently recognized literature as a subdiscipline in their field. Karl D. Uitti's *Linguistics and Literary Theory* devotes a chapter to the history of this relationship and to the difficulties of conciliating essentially ahistoric linguistic theories with the study of literatures moving in the streams of history and cultures. Donald Freeman's chapter on "literature" in Wardhaugh and Brown's *Survey of Applied Linguistics* demonstrates by contrast applications of insights gained through study of grammar and syntax to an understanding of style and poetic meter in specific literary texts. Freeman offers in addition an international bibliography on the interrelationship during the period 1945–75.

VI

Genres and Forms

ἃ μὲν γὰρ ἐποποιία ἔχει, ὑπάρχει τῇ τραγῳδίᾳ, ἃ δὲ αὐτῇ, οὐ πάντα
ἐν τῇ ἐποποιίᾳ.

ΑΡΙΣΤΟΤΕΛΟΥΣ ΠΕΡΙ ΠΟΙΗΤΙΚΗΣ

The Generic Approach: Aristotle

It is significant that Aristotle, to our knowledge the earliest
orderly theorizer on literature, saw fit to analyze "poetry" by
genres. The generic forms of literature that interested him are
distinguished mainly on the basis of form, but also, to a lesser
extent, of technique. In what remains to us of the *Poetics* Aristotle concentrated on epic and tragedy, which he considered the
most "important" genres. He intended to expand his probings to
comedy, and had he done so, his scientific mind would have had
to distinguish between the nature of comedy and that of satire,
another recognized genre, since the Old Comedy of Aristophanes
was viewed in later literary treatises as the ancestor not only of
comedy itself but of satire. The generic approach was of course
not the only one that Aristotle might have taken. Although by the
fourth century B.C. literature had as yet seen few developed
movements, he could have as easily hinged his discussion of
poetry on themes or on interrelations. Since, as it is important to
remember, Aristotle was writing an apologia for poetry (what
later critics called a defense), hoping thereby to justify the very
existence of imaginative writing, he might naturally have leaned
on the didactic values of the great national myths of his time:

Prometheus, Icarus, Antigone, and so forth. He could have stressed the close relationships of poetry with history, with politics, with philosophy, and with religion, for the chief attackers of poetry in his time were precisely the historians, politicians, philosophers, and high priests. He could also have stressed the connections of poetry with the law, noting that Solon the lawgiver composed his legislation in verse.

Yet, to justify poetry Aristotle elected to order his defense on genres—on the two genres most respectable in his time, tragedy and epic. He even engaged in evaluative byplay, debating which of these two genres was the greater—a question that has less relevance in our times, when the existence of imaginative literature needs no apology or rationalization.

Aristotle's example represented that antiquity, when literary theory remained preoccupied with the generic divisions. In ancient Greece and Rome, it surely occurred to Hesiod and Lucretius that, if they were not writing in a formally identifiable way, they were pioneering in a new genre. By the time of Horace, in the first century B.C., the theorists were writing not only of genres, the larger species of literature such as tragedy, epic, and comedy, but also of "forms," the subspecies such as elegy, pastoral elegy, epigram, and so on. Later criticism has evolved a number of generic hierarchies of literature in which structure and length—not content or tone—have been the determining factors in separating genres from forms. Even though a long pastoral play like *The Faithful Shepherd* (*Pastor Fido*) is an example of a genre, there also exist short pastoral elegies in the tradition of Theocritus, Bion, and Vergil (of which Milton's "Lycidas" is a fine example), which are "forms," even if similar to Guarino's pastoral play in tone and sentiment. Genre and content will make unpredictable matches. Thus we have picaresque, autobiographical, historical, and even surrealist novels.

Structure and length are paramount in defining the familiar term "novella," around which there is some current controversy. A recent book published in America endeavors to define the novelette or short novel by its functions as apologue, tragedy, medium of characterization, and satire. (For a contrary view on the short novel, see p. 138.) Even though the author approves the generalization that "a short novel is something in itself, neither a lengthily written short story nor the refurbished attempt at a novel," she insists that the short novel, novelette, or novelet borrow the established generic term "novella" for her purposes. Alas, the novella, a term not for hire, was already amply defined by Renaissance critics and perfected by mediaeval and Renaissance writers after a retrospective glance at many Oriental archetypes. It spread over Europe and maintained its structure and identity well into the seventeenth century. It contains its own common elements, listed on page 142—elements that are not relevant to such modern novelettes as those of Conrad, Mann, Kafka, Camus, and others. On this lively controversy over terminology—which separates *grosso modo* Americans from Europeans, revisionists from traditionalists, *novecentisti* from mediaevalists and Renaissance scholars—the debate will most likely continue, but only in America, since the *OED* has long since ruled in favor of the entrenched and historical meaning of the word.

Abundant evidence shows that on occasion the vogue of certain genres and forms heralds a new direction of literary history. The change is sometimes accompanied by the discrediting of other genres and forms branded as "old-fashioned." In Renaissance France Joachim du Bellay, the leading pamphleteer for the establishment of a great vernacular literature, based his campaign on the rejection of mediaeval poetic forms (ballad, song, virelay, etc.) and on the adoption of alternate forms, mostly with a classical antecedence (ode, sonnet, elegy, epistle, epigram). Du Bellay misjudged the worth of the mediaeval ballad, which within two centuries came back strongly if in a somewhat modified form. The rejection of the regular tragedy of neoclassicism was, as we well know, one of the principal objectives of the romantic movement. The romanticists rebelled against the neoclassical cult of form and structure and demanded freer forms. They speculated in various ways on the matter of generical divisions. Goethe set up his distinctions between three "nature forms" (epic, drama, lyric) and the lesser subspecies (*Dichtarten*) of odes, ballads, sonnets, and so forth. In his "Preface to *Cromwell*" Hugo divides man's history into epochs of ode (primitive times), epic (antiquity), and drama (modern times): "In a word, civilization begins by singing of its dreams, then narrates its doings, and lastly sets about describing what it thinks." The surrealists of the twentieth century also viewed conventional generic distinctions with disfavor.

Durability of Genre: The Epic

In his book *Comparative Literature*, M. Guyard brings up this fluctuating relationship between genres and historical periods. He meditates on the destiny of genres, which are born, grow up, and die, sometimes without apparent reason: "Why does one no longer compose verse tragedies in five acts? Why, at the beginning of the nineteenth century, were people writing historical novels in all the countries of Europe?" He finds that similar questions are raised by present-day literature, in which technique often operates against the maintenance of generic distinctions. For instance, the novel of today, as we shall point out more fully in Chapter ix, assumes such Protean, unprecedented forms as film scenario and tape-recorded transcriptions.

Thus, to watch two thousand years of Western literature follow its generic evolution is a complicated spectacle. Let us turn back to Aristotle's beloved epic. From prehistory to the time of the Roman Empire, epic poetry slowly evolved from its folkloric, oral phase to a learned, written phase. After the urbane nationalist Vergil composed his carefully metered epic on Aeneas, it seemed that epic would be henceforth literary epic, an erudite poem to be read, not sung. Yet, during the early Middle Ages oral epic had a revival, during which *Beowulf*, the *Chanson de Roland*, and the *Poema de mío Cid* were compiled by anonymous singers who knew nothing of Aristotle's theories. By the time that Voltaire penned his rich and readable *Essay on Epic Poetry* and composed his own epic, the pro-English *Henriade*, in memory of the popular Henri iv, the venerable genre was dying out, leaving open the question: Are there ages of epic poetry? This parallels the question that Voltaire himself raised: Are there nations with a propensity for epic? Frenchmen, he claimed, had no *tête épique*, no head for epic poetry. Similar questions have been raised concerning the other genres. Italian critics have long speculated on why Italy has no tradition of great tragedy. Paul Valéry claimed that it was because Italians had too much emotion in their daily lives. Others have attributed the lack of tragic theater in Italy to the Italian addiction to long, late, conversational, and wine-enriched suppers! It is also said that there is no such thing as contemporary tragedy; the phrase "death of tragedy," adopted by George Steiner as a book title, is commonly heard today.

In the case of epic, this genre was of course replaced by the historical novel just as poetic pastorals and romances were replaced by the sentimental and romantic novel. These changes, important as they are, were merely part of a much more comprehensive literary revolution that took place in the seventeenth and early eighteenth centuries: the disappearance of poetry as the natural vehicle for all extensive genres of literature.

Durability of Form: Lyric Poetry

The four major types of lyric poetry have undergone various changes of form and even content over the ages. The complex Greek ode as practiced by Pindar and Bacchylides derived from the tripartite choral songs of drama: strophe, antistrophe, and epode. Sapphic and Anacreontic odes were simpler and humbler. The homostrophic odes of Horace (each stanza being the same metrically and structurally) were also simpler and shorter. Renaissance poets adopted both patterns. Landor and Swinburne attempted to revive the three-part Pindaric odes, but Hugo, Wordsworth, Shelley, and Keats abandoned them.

The elegy in ancient Greece and Rome could be dedicated to war, peace, everyday matters, having nothing to do with death or melancholy. The name merely referred to a fixed form of verse set by Propertius, Tibullus, and Ovid, characterized by the alternance of dactylic hexameter and dactylic pentameter rather than by any special subject matter. The late, widespread idea that elegy dealt with death and mourning was enhanced by Gray's "Elegy Written in a Country Churchyard," with its description of the tomb-studded yard as "the place of fame and elegy."

A ballad can have its origins either in an individual composer or in a folk group. The many variant verses of early ballads lead us to conclude that they were the product of a people rather than a single poet. The search for folk stories and folk ballads in early romanticism led to the two texts that launched their vogue in England and Scotland, the collections by Bishop Percy and the evasive Macpherson. Chilling, emotional ballads were composed in Germany by Bürger ("Lenore") and Goethe ("Der Erlkönig"). Anyone who reads *The Ancient Mariner* of Coleridge knows how exciting the narrative suspense of a ballad may be. The crescendo of suspense is even more rapid and anguished in Lorca's two *romances*: the "Romance somnámbulo" and the lament for the bullfighter Sánchez Mejías, where the ballad refrain (envoi) "at five in the afternoon" constantly interrupts the narrative as though the inevitable clock over the bullring had stopped at the moment of the goring and death.

The sonnet is a curious ancient form that came out of Sicily in the late Middle Ages, compounded of an eight-line *strambotto* and a six-line stanza or sestet. It was Dante, followed by Petrarch, who raised the sonnet to the dominant form of love lyric for two and a half centuries, indeed a form practiced by major poets today.

The curious mediaeval amalgam of the sonnet (*abba/abba/cde/cde*) meant a special challenge for the poet. The structural division meant much to the complex, mediaeval mentality, if little to poets today. Dante felt compelled in his *Vita nuova* to keep explaining the logic and structure of his sonnets. This was of course typical of a scholastic mind trained in logic, grammar, and rhetoric. The curious structure of the sonnet was bound to satisfy the generation of mankind that first adopted rhyme. The surprising thing is that this structure with little variation has proved not only acceptable, but indispensable to poets up to and into the twentieth century.

Shakespeare not only defied the generic rules of Aristotle as a dramatist. As a poet he took issue with Dante and Petrarch and rejected the scheme of *abba/abba/cde/cde*, with its five rhymes, demanding seven possibilities of rhyme, as follows: *abab/cdcd/efef/gg*. His rebellion was accepted by the other Elizabethan poets, producing some of the greatest sonnets ever written. Even freer rhyme schemes have been devised by Ezra Pound, Robert Frost, Robert Lowell, Dylan Thomas, and Stephen Spender, who still have clung nevertheless to this ancient lyric form clothed in fourteen lines.

Categories for Investigation

In any case, now as in Aristotle's time, the generic approach characterizes much of literary criticism, including some of the best pages of Bowra, Empson, and Frye. Despite fluctuations in most of the conventional genres, they continue to serve as useful descriptive devices. A major Polish journal is devoted to genre study, and a recent American scholarly journal entitled *Genre* set up four categories of investigation for its contributors:

1. Theoretical discussions of the genre concept
2. Historical studies of particular genres and genre debates
3. Attempts to establish and define genres
4. Interpretation of works of literature from the genre point of view

These four approaches will prove useful to the comparatist in dealing with both genres and forms. As in the case of literary movements (Ch. vii), the reader can see how a unifying force operates on the genres and forms of literature, even as individual nations and writers are responsible for inevitable modifications. Also to be recognized through génre study are the echoes of one national literature within another, whether in the epic, with the Roman *Aeneid* mirroring the Greek *Odyssey*, or in the novel, with the American *Moby Dick* echoing *Don Quixote* in subtler ways.

The extent to which genre study is embedded in both intellectual and social history is emphasized in M. Guyard's concluding observations on the subject: "Literary forms respond to diverse needs of both authors and reading public. The functions they fulfill can develop in importance or can become useless. Far from remaining at the surface genre study penetrates finally, as deeply as other approaches, the history of ideas and sensibility."

Upon leaving the subject of genre study to proceed to the other major categories of movements and themes, it is fitting here to raise a possibility that could be entertained in either of the two following chapters. It is quite possible that courses may be restricted to a single category or approach (Literature in the Renaissance), to two categories (Lyric Poetry in the Renaissance), or to three categories (Themes and Forms of Renaissance

Literature), this latter title being precisely the first course this writer taught in our field. The temptation to tighten the title of Themes and Forms of the Literature of Humanism was strong, emphasizing thus the movement rather than the period. However, the very term Renaissance, as opposed to Sixteenth Century, Cinquecento, etc., implies a humanistic orientation in the choice of texts.

Textbooks for the Generic Approach: Anthologies

English-language textbooks for comparative literature courses on literary genres and forms are curiously in good supply, whether devoted to drama, poetry, or narrative. These few pages can merely summarize a few useful texts and discuss their content and editorial equipment, as Chapters vii and viii will do for other appropriate readers. As declared in Chapter xi below, a new series of several types of appropriate readers and anthologies is needed for both graduate and undergraduate courses in comparative literature. A few observations on their structures, viewpoints, and adequacy will conclude this section. So rapidly are the standard titles—hard-cover and paperback—disappearing from publishers' catalogs that the instructor will have to verify their availability in the current Bowker's *Books in Print*, to be found in every library and bookstore. These casualties include such basic paperbacks for both comparative and national litera-ture courses (one thinks of the much regretted *Elizabethan Lyrics* of Norman Ault) that the Modern Language Asssociation has invited members to submit a list of those that should be re-printed. We mention the following texts as interesting archetypes, whether or not they continue to be available, as we do elsewhere in this volume.

Several of the recent anthologies of Western literature, grand format, are structured on the generic approach. Two of them follow a similar technique to emphasize the variety of genres and forms they include. This comes in the form of a supplementary index to the types of literature included, which is found in each case at the end of the anthology. It strikes one that the concern for genres thus came as an afterthought. The final pages of Hib-bard's *Writers of the Western World* (Houghton Mifflin) remind us that its excerpts have illustrated the following genres and forms: address, autobiography, ballad, drama, dramatic monologue, epic, mock epic, essays, literary criticism, lyric poetry, odes, pastorals, philosophic verse, poetic narrative, prose narrative, romance, satire, and sermon.

Thompson and Gassner's *Our Heritage of Western Literature* (Holt, Rinehart and Winston) follows suit with an index of literary types, where the forms are not mentioned alphabetically but according to a vague connection with the periods that marked their apex: mythology, epic, mediaeval romance, tragic drama, comic drama, history and biography, diary, autobiography, philosophy and wisdom, fable, sermon, satire, prose tale, verse tale, and various forms of narrative and poetry. An "analytic contents page" in Beardsley et al., *Theme and Form: An Introduction to Literature* (Prentice-Hall), illustrates the editors' claim to have "included all the chief modes of literature, or genres." The modes listed include a few unexpected ones alongside the chief conventional ones. These are "expository analysis, questioning and reflection, and dramatic portraits." A glance at this list, or the lists of the two preceding anthologies, will demonstrate how the contemporary world has enlarged the number of eligible genres and forms to suit its purposes. Such emancipation of forms was demanded by the romanticists and apparently followed after romanticism, symbolism, and the literary revolts of our own century. With this multiplication and proliferation of genres and forms in the present century, definitions of many genres themselves have been expanded or diluted. Yet the prototypical approach to literature leaves the student with something to cling to as he confronts the Protean literature of the present day, with its antinovels, antitheater, and the antipoems of Nicanor Parra.

Drama, Tragedy, Comedy

Whether one is preparing a course on comedy, tragedy, or drama of an international dimension, the number of available textbooks—currently over twenty—still presents an *embarras de choix*. Since the collections usually include tragedies, comedies, and tragicomedies, the titles specify the contents as "dramas" or "plays." For plays not generically prescribed one has at one's disposal *Great Plays* (Holt), edited by Bloomfield and Elliott, pressing the extremes of the Western Heritage from Sophocles' *Antigone* to Edward Albee's *American Dream*. Caputi's six-volume boxed paperback anthology of *World Drama* (Heath) traces this same sweep from the *Oresteia* of Aeschylus through *A Month in the Country* of Turgenev, without any representation from the exciting theatrical experimentation of the twentieth century. *World Drama* (Dover), compiled by Barrett Clark, is a venerable two-volume collection that justifies its title by including the *Shakuntala* of ancient India, the anonymous *Chalk Circle* from mediaeval China, and three mediaeval Japanese classics. Another familiar two-volume anthology, *Treasury of the Theater* (Dryden) edited by John Gassner, is made up of a rich selection running from the *Agamemnon* of Aeschylus to *Death of a Salesman*. A collection stressing tragedy is Weiss's *Drama in the Western World* (Heath-Raytheon) running from Sophocles to Beckett. A mixed bag of light and dark plays is found in Bennett Cerf's *Sixteen Famous European Plays* (Random House) and Allison-Carr-Eastman's *Masterpieces of the Drama*. Most of these volumes are characterized by very little footnoting and critical apparatus. It would seem that professors of drama prefer to supply their own explanations and interpretations of these great plays. Only Sanders' *Discovery of Drama* (Scott, Foresman) emphasizes the generic distinctions among comedy, tragicomedy, poetic drama, and so on.

It would also appear that modern drama is just as important as the courses and texts that acquaint us with the earlier rise of the theater. For there is an ample choice of anthologies from Ibsen to the present. Block and Shedd's *Masters of Modern Drama* (Random House), richly illustrated with plates, does include clarifying footnotes. Other attractive collections of modern plays are Corrigan's *Modern Theater* (Macmillan) and Barry Ulanov's *Makers of the Modern Theater* (McGraw-Hill).

If anthologies of tragedies are rare, or are rarely so identified, such collections are currently available from Houghton Mifflin (Corrigan and Loney), Little, Brown (Barnet), Harcourt Brace (Levin), and Bantam (O'Brien). Anthologies of comedies have been prepared by Corrigan (Houghton Mifflin), by Felheim (Harcourt Brace), and by Barnet, Berman, and Burto in an unpretentious, inexpensive paperback *Eight Great Comedies* (Mentor). Both the Harcourt Brace and the Mentor collections include excellent essays on comedy, and they may be adopted in common since their plays and essays complement one another.

It is obvious then that four types of comparative theater courses are easily serviced by textbooks: the Western Heritage course from Sophocles to the present, the modern drama course from Ibsen to the present, the survey of comedy, and the survey of tragedy. Only the pioneer Barrett Clark collection includes Asian dramas, and these from the Middle Ages. It would seem that the one anthology we look forward to as comparatists is an East-West if not World collection of dramas selected to establish common aims, interests, and attitudes.

Fortunately there are a few drama collections on the great mythic heroes mentioned in Chapter viii. Oscar Mandel has edited a brace of the most important Don Juan plays (Nebraska), and if he has altered the texts occasionally to make them more "playable," he has atoned for this by appending some of the most significant essays on the theme of Don Juanism (see below, p. 173). The anthology of Oedipal dramas by Sophocles, Seneca, Voltaire, Gide, and Cocteau, edited by Sanderson and Zimmerman (Houghton Mifflin), as well as that publisher's theater anthologies on Medea, Phaedra, and Orestes—all of them including essays and study aids—seem what the doctor ordered for thematic courses in comparative literature (see below, p. 173). Such an anthology on the Faustus legend and prepared in German by Eike Middell (Reclam Verlag), as Doris Guilloton reminds me, rather than the volume by Bates, which reproduces only one Faustus completely, would seem to be a needed textbook here. An anthology of plays (or epics or other genres) in their original languages seems an ideal for the distant future.

Collections of Poetry

Poetry, the most ancient, lasting literary medium, plays a versatile role in the generic courses of comparative literature, as well as courses illustrating periods and movements, or even myths and themes. Poetry has the advantage that an instructor can measure out for his specific purposes the amount to be assigned in a graduate or undergraduate course. If one is fortunate, one may find bilingual editions to adopt in one's course (see Warnke's and Segel's texts below), just as professors of classics are able to do by means of the Loeb editions. There are numerous collections unified by genre, such as McEdward Leach's *Ballad Book, The Viking Book of Ballads,* and so on. Ballad collections, however, are usually restricted to a single language, so that a course would require several texts. The same is true for the sonnet. The value of the sonnet for comparative literature is stated by Bender and Squier in their anthology (Washington Square Press):

> The really remarkable thing about the sonnet is its endurance as a form. . . . It is after all virtually the only important verse form in poetry. . . . The endurance and utility of the sonnet as a form stems to a great extent from the fact that the sonnet is so flexible. The pattern can be violated in many ways and yet the sonnet remains a sonnet. . . . The sonnet provides the poet with a form and traditions which he can use nearly at will to say what he wants.

Poetry can become the exlusive genre in some period and movement courses, as illustrated by such comparative collections as Flores' *Mediaeval Lyrics* (Modern Library), Frank Warnke's bilingual *European Metaphysical Poetry* (Yale), or Harold Segel's *The Baroque Poem* (Dutton), which includes original texts even from Polish and Croatian. The periods may indeed be narrow ones, as one witnesses from collections entitled *Poems of the Nineties* (Verry), *Poems of the Twenties* (McCutcheon), *Poems of the 1939–45 War* (British Book Center), etc. Poems can be found for almost any thematic course in comparative literature. Indeed, Henderson and Lee point the way with *Poetry: A Thematic Approach* (Wadsworth). One of the most common areas of theme is political with *Poems of Protest Old and New* (Macmillan), whose editor Arnold Kenseth claims: "The strength of poetry as a vehicle of protest is that a well-wrought poem involves us, blood and bone, heart and mind, in the experience providing and provoking the protest . . . reenacting in the reader what has already happened to the poet." Other currently available collections are *Poems from Prison, Poems of War Resistance, Where Steel Winds Blow: Poets on War,* and others. That the genre of poetry overlaps with interrelated disciplines is illustrated by *Poetry and Mathematics* (Lippincott), *Poetry and Mysticism* (City Lights), and *The Poetics of Music* (Random House).

A course on poetry could well add to its required texts a handbook on this genre. There is a wide choice, including Babette Deutsch, *Poetry Handbook* (Funk and Wagnalls); Jean Hollyfield, *Poet's Handbook* (Young); Laurence Perrine, *Poetry: Theory and Practice* (Harcourt Brace); and the always useful *Poem Itself,* edited by Burnshaw (Schocken), with its comments on the translation of poetry.

Prose Narrative

Novels, either hard-cover or paperback, are usually assigned as reading in their simplest available and least expensive edition, and thus have little place in a discussion of textbooks for a genre course. There is, however, a recent and fortunate trend toward what the publisher Norton calls "critical editions," admirably suited to the needs of the student. A typical example is Norton's paperback edition of *Moby Dick,* which includes beyond the text of the novel maps of Melville's voyages, an explanation of whale-craft, reviews and letters of Melville, sources and analogues, contemporary reviews, academic critical pieces, an excerpt of a basic biography of Melville, and a bibliography. The criticism on this very American author makes almost no comparative thrusts, although one essay discusses Melville's reputation in England and another treats of *Moby Dick* as an epic. Nothing on Cervantes' influence on Melville or the Italian sources of his prose (*Pierre*) or poems on his travels. Yet this splendid format is most promising for future study of novels in comparative literature courses, for the critical apparatus can be selected to show the international involvements and repercussions of such a masterpiece.

Between the novel and the short story lies the novelette or short novel, sometimes called novella by American scholars with a disregard for European literary history. Collections of these are frequently comparative in scope. *Ten Modern Short Novels*

(Putnam), edited by Hamalian and Volpe, provides 700 pages of this genre by Tolstoy, James, Conrad, Andreyev, Unamuno, Gide, Mann, Faulkner, Camus, and Moravia. The value of such a text is explained by the editors.

> An anthology of the short novel permits the combination of intensive reading with a more general survey. The short novel offers a more representative expression of the writer's ideas and his means of shaping them than selected passages could ever do. . . . It has the singleness of theme, the limited number of characters, the quality of concentration which characterize the short story. But the modern novel, too, often has these same characteristics. A list of qualities of the short novel could be assembled, but only one of them would really serve to distinguish this form of fiction—length.

The short story collections, including those covering many literatures, are legion. How does a publisher or even an editor justify yet another one? The editors of *Short Fiction of the Masters*, Hamalian and Karl, explain their criteria of selection:

> First, we sought to include only the story which is continuous with the author's major work, not the isolated or the bizarre piece. The stories should thus provide an introduction to their longer and more involved fiction. . . . Second, it had to be as well one of the short masterpieces of that writer [although] avoiding the over-anthologized story. Third, we made our selections from authors whose work stands at the center of major Western literature.

The comparative nature of the selection (Musil, Beckett, Proust, Silone, Moravia) is thus guaranteed. A further paragraph of this introduction demonstrates that this economical form shares the substance of all great literature. It remains nonetheless true that the short story is difficult to accommodate to a comparative literature course—a course almost never offered—because of its narrow dimension and its resistance to generic definition. On the other hand, the interrelated mediaeval and Renaissance novellas, presented in collections, shared by many countries, defined by several Renaissance theorists, contained in cornices, assigned themes and motifs, unified by a long tradition going back to the

Orient, and dedicated to social and religious reform, constitute an excellent form for a comparative literature course (see p. 144). Such a college reader, *The Palace of Pleasure*, edited by Levtow and Valency, should be reprinted or replaced.

Fig. 4. *Checklist of Elements of Epic Poetry*

I. Aristotelian Elements

UNITY: "Clearly the story must be constructed as in tragedy, dramatically, round a single piece of action, whole and complete in itself, with a beginning, middle, and end. . . . A plot does not have unity simply because it deals with a single hero. . . . In drama the episodes are short, but it is by them that the epic gains its length; the *story* of the *Odyssey* is quite short."

UNITY OF TIME: "The epic is unlimited in point of time." Renaissance commentators arbitrarily created the unity of one year.

HISTORICITY: "In history what is required is not a single piece of action, but a single period of time . . . events have a merely casual relation to one another." Aristotle also points out that details of an epic may be unhistorical and fictional, but that the final historical outcome cannot be altered.

FOUR ELEMENTS OF EPIC: Of the six elements of tragedy—plot, character, diction, thought, spectacle, and melody—Aristotle says that epic shares all these except spectacle and melody.

METER: Epic is defined as "representation of life in hexameter verse." "Heroic hexameter is the right meter." "Hexameter is the most sedate and stately."

INVOLVEMENT OF AUTHOR: "The poet should speak as seldom as possible in his own person."

MARVELOUS: "The epic offers greater scope than tragedy 'for the inexplicable.'"

VERISIMILITUDE AND POETIC LICENSE: "What is convincing (plausible) though impossible is preferred to what is possible and unconvincing (implausible)." "To the charge 'That is not true' one may respond 'It ought to be.'"

CHARACTER (HAMARTIA): "There remains the mean between the thoroughly good and thoroughly bad man. . . . Through no badness of his own this man falls into misfortune through some fatal flaw."

KATHARSIS: "Fear, pity, and wonderment are best when they are aroused by the actual incidents themselves." This emphatic device is at the basis of Aristotle's justification of poetry and fine arts.

ANAGNORISIS: Recognition. A device for the heightening of suspense.

PERIPETEIA: An upturn or downturn of the plot line.

COMPLICATION AND DÉNOUEMENT: Try to chart the point or points where the plot begins its *desis* or unweaving.

II. Elements Drawn from Modern Scholarship and from Class Discussions

1. Invocation to gods or muses.

2. Extensive geographical traveling.

3. Visit to the underworld.

4. Exaltation of a dynasty, propaganda value.

5. Exaltation of a religion, messianic value.

6. Lofty style and Homeric similes.

7. Hero has fellows of equal stature.

8. Setting in a "heroic age."

9. Author or scribe keeps self totally absent from story.

10. Nature interludes between scenes of strife.

11. Supernatural events and interference by the gods.

12. Unusual birth or death of epic hero.

13. Epic meter (hexameter, golden octave).

14. Long interval between events recorded and the composition of epic poem.

15. Use of catalogs and lists.

16. Unity of one year (after Renaissance).

17. Final outcome of the epic conforms to historical truth.

18. Rationalizing the vanquishing of the invincible hero.

19. Physical properties making hero vulnerable or invulnerable to injury: Odysseus, Achilles, Siegfried, and others.

Fig. 5. *Checklist of Elements for Study of the Novella*

1. The cornice: situation holding the corpus of tales together

2. The days-nights unity: reason for given number of days; affects title?

3. Length of the novella; lengthening from Middle Ages to Elizabethan period

4. Classification of the groups of novella into themes, moral or otherwise

5. Novella as an unaccepted or unrecognized genre; theory by author on this?

6. Moralizing elements: present in stories or in cornice or both

7. Author's justification of the novella; the useful or the sweet

8. Degree of obscenity, psychological realism, picaresque, etc.

9. Insights into the thinking, prejudices, and daily living of period; scandals, contemporary events

10. Social criticism; against feudal system, wars, taxes, etc.

11. Religious criticism; indulgences, sacraments, mass, miracles, relics, infallibility of pope, free examination, vows of chastity, marriage without parental consent, confession, etc.; general religious position of author

12. Relationship to farces and fabliaux

13. Rivalry between form and content: between narrative in cornice and that of the novella

14. Public for whom novella written: tradition of writing for ladies

15. Stories in collection which have been traced to antiquity, East, or Near East

16. Stories in collection which have come down to modern times

17. Class struggle apparent in the novella: view of teller aristocratic, bourgeois, proletarian; stories dedicated to nobility, etc.

18. Outstanding characters or characterizations; names remembered;

strong characters in cornice as well as in novella; psychological depth

19. Presence of historical personages along with fictitious characters

20. Tales of a folkloric tradition; spoken or written; much dialogue; acknowledgment that stories are collected as by modern folklorist

21. Novella unified or episodic

22. Speech learned, popular, dialectal

FIG. 6. *Syllabus of Western Heritage Genre Course: Epic Poetry*

CLASS ASSIGNMENT	CLASS REPORT
1. Epic poetry, nature and definition. Theories of epic. Traditional elements. Folk vs. literary epic.	
2. Homer, *Odyssey* and *Iliad* (ca. 850 B.C.)	Kazantzakis, *Odyssey* (1938)
3. Vergil, *Aeneid* (29–19 B.C.)	Apollonius of Rhodes, *Argonautica* (3rd century B.C.)
4. *Beowulf* (ca. A.D. 725)	Forms of Arthurian epic up to Malory
5. *La Chanson de Roland* (11th century A.D.)	*The Edda Poems* (A.D. 900–1050)
6. *El Cantar de mío Cid* (ca. A.D. 1140)	Wagner and Mediaeval folk epic
7. *Nibelungenlied* (ca. A.D. 1200)	Petrarch, *Africa* (mid-14th century)
8. Dante, *La Divina Commedia* (ca. 1300–1321)	Vida, *La Cristiada* (1535)
9. *The Song of Igor* (early 13th century)	
10. Epics on the Crusades: Tasso, *Gerusalemme Liberata* (1575) Lope, *Jerusalén Conquistada* (1609)	Trissino, *L'Italia Liberata dai Gothi* (1547–1548)
11. Luis de Camoëns, *The Lusiads* (*Os Lusíadas*) (1572)	Ercilla, *La Araucana* (1569–1590) and Pedro de Oña, *Arauco Domado* (1596)

CLASS ASSIGNMENT	CLASS REPORT
12. Three Christian epics Reformational and post-Reformational: Du Bartas, *Les Semaines* (1578); D'Aubigné, *Les Tragiques* (1616); Milton, *Paradise Lost* (1667)	Ronsard, *La Franciade* (1572)
13. Voltaire, *La Henriade* (1728)	Jacinto Verdaguer, *La Atlántida* (Catalán) (1880s)

Students will be required to present a class report and a term paper. There will be no final examination. All books unavailable for purchase will be found on library shelves, as will foreign language versions of epics above.

Fig. 7. *Syllabus of Western Heritage Genre Course: European Novella*

JUNE 10   The novella in historical conspectus; anatomy of the novella

JUNE 12   Giovanni Boccaccio: *Il Decamerone* (ca. 1350)
REPORT TOPICS: Boccaccio and Shakespeare (*Cymbeline* and *All's Well*) / Franco Sacchetti, *Trecento novelle*

JUNE 17   Geoffrey Chaucer: *Canterbury Tales* (1387–1400)
REPORT TOPICS: Griselda in Boccaccio and Chaucer / *Les cent nouvelles nouvelles* (1450–60)

JUNE 19   Matteo Bandello: *Novelle* (1554)
REPORT TOPICS: Romeo and Juliet, development of a tale / John Rastell, *A Hundred Mery Tales* (1525) / Basile, *Il Pentamerone*

JUNE 24   Marguerite de Navarre: *L'Heptaméron* (1540–47; 1558)
REPORT TOPIC: Des Périers' *Récréations* and *Cymbalum mundi*

JUNE 26   Giraldi Cinthio: *The Hundred Myths* (*Ecatommithi*) (1565)
REPORT TOPICS: Othello in Cinthio and Shakespeare / Geoffrey Fenton, *Tragical Discourses* (1567)

JULY 1   William Painter: *The Palace of Pleasure* (1566, 1567)
REPORT TOPIC: *The Gesta Romanorum*

JULY 8   William Pettie: *The Petite Palace* (1576)
REPORT TOPIC: María de Zayas y Sotomayor, *Novelas amorosas y ejemplares* (influence on Scarron, Mérimée)

JULY 10   Miguel de Cervantes: *Novelas ejemplares* (1613)
           REPORT TOPIC: Tirso de Molina, *Cigarrales de Toledo*
JULY 15   Conclusions and summary
NOTES: Class reports are not to exceed 25 minutes in length.

There will be no final examination. Students are required to present a class report and a term paper. The term paper will consist of a careful anatomy of a given novella collection based on twenty-two elements characteristic of the novella. A list of these elements will be supplied at the beginning of the course, as well as a sheet of instructions for the styling of the anatomies.

The student will also receive a list of paperback editions in English of the titles listed above. Especially useful will be *The Palace of Pleasure, An Anthology of the Novella*, edited by Levtow and Valency (Capricorn Paperback, 1960, now out of print but still available in some bookstores). Background reading will be assigned in *Anatomy of the Novella* (New York University Press), by Clements and Gibaldi. Paperback edition available.

VII

Periods, Movements, Influence

Pour en finir, nous croyons que le Romantisme consiste à employer tous ces adjectifs, et non en autre chose.
ALFRED DE MUSSET, *Lettres de Dupuis et Cotonet*

Periods, Movements, Generations, Schools

Western literature is traditionally studied in the context of identifiable literary movements or periods, such as scholasticism, humanism, neoclassicism, romanticism, realism, symbolism, expressionism, and surrealism, which are characterized by specific themes, aesthetic canons, and stylistic practices. Some departments, like that of SUNY-Binghamton, offer a similar basic sequence of period courses: Mediaeval, Renaissance, Seventeenth-Century, Eighteenth-Century, Romanticism, Late Nineteenth-Century, and Modern Literature. Some historians distinguish literary movements by their dominant moods: joy has been claimed as the key mood of rococo, tragicity of baroque, equanimity of neoclassicism, and melancholy of romanticism. Hegel viewed such movements as the common denominator of literary study. They demonstrate how often, during the history of thought, literature becomes a unified, even international enterprise, with writers in different countries saying much the same things in much the same ways. Movements encourage international influences, as we shall see below. Thus, responding to the libertarian drive of romanticism, Schiller in Germany, Shelley in England, Hugo in France, and Pushkin in Russia wrote poems to liberty. Because of their common origin in the movement of romanticism, these hymns can be fruitfully compared in terms not only of their theme, but also of their mood and mode of expression. In this manner, movements form a convenient framework for the study of literature.

Literature may also be studied, with less precision, in terms of literary periods, ages, schools, and even generations. Some historians of English literature have considered the term "age" as a subdivision of the term "period." Thus, the Neoclassical Period (1660–1789), which started later in England than on the Continent, is subdivided into the Restoration, the Augustan Age, and the Age of Johnson. The earlier Renaissance Period (1500–1660) is subdivided even more, being composed of the Early Tudor Age (1500–57), Elizabethan Age (1558–1603), Jacobean Age (1603–25), Caroline Age (1625–49), and the Commonwealth Interregnum (1649–60). Even though Queen Elizabeth wrote passable poetry, the linking of literary ages with monarchies does not seem particularly fruitful, and one suspects that the literary historians could have found more appropriate solutions. A literary "school" implies a similar experience, training, or education on the part of the members, the same factors that tend to form a "generation."

Defining a Generation

According to Petersen's pioneer study *Literarische Generationen,* the members of a literary generation are drawn together by a common heredity, education, age, language, governing principles, and generational experience, as well as by a shared rejection of the preceding generation. The Cuban literary historian José Antonio Portuondo, leaning toward communism, logically accepts all these save heredity. Petersen's book dealt mainly with the closely knit Spanish group of the Generation of 1898, in which aesthetic and political motives joined the leading thinkers Ganivet, Azorín, Baroja, Valle Inclán, Machado, and Ortega y Gasset.

Malcolm Cowley has dissented from the traditional discussions of generation. "A generation is no more a matter of dates than it is one of ideology. It appears when writers of the same age join in a common revolt against the fathers and when, in the process of adopting a new life style, they find their own models and spokes-man." He is referring to and building his definition on the Lost Generation of Hemingway, Fitzgerald, Dos Passos, Cummings, and their expatriate group. A loosely formed generation was the Pre-Raphaelite Brotherhood, having in common mainly an anti-Academic attitude and a sense of the identity of poetry and art. Sometimes the "generation" functioned like a club or a circle, the *contertulianos* of the Generation of 1898 meeting in their cafés, and Dr. Johnson's Literary Club, which included Burke, Gold-smith, Garrick, Gibbon, Adam Smith, Bishop Percy, and Boswell. This circle rejected any narrow definition of generation, however, for its later membership extended to Scott, Macaulay, Hallam, and Tennyson.

The reason why the foregoing terms are less satisfactory than "movements" is precisely that they have temporal and national connotations that do not always correspond to transcendent liter-ary fluctuations. To take an obvious example, a literary movement and a literary generation can be dissimilar in duration. The movement of humanism, starting in Italy during the third quarter of the Quattrocento, did not sweep across to England and Portu-gal until a century had passed. It is impossible, then, to consider Politian and Shakespeare as belonging to the same generation—or even Michelangelo and Shakespeare, since Michelangelo died the year Shakespeare was born. Yet all three were fellow humanists. Similarly, Dryden and Pope, fellow neoclassicists, were born a half century apart. On the other hand, the ascendancy of a single literary generation usually remains national and even local. Spain's Generation of 1898 had little meaning or influence outside the frontiers of their country. The main limitation of studying Western literature in terms of "ages" is that the dates of a literary age, as we have noted above, are often based arbitrarily on non-literary factors. In contrast, a period may include more than one literary movement. During the Grand Siècle, France's seven-teenth century, both neoclassic and baroque writers existed side by side while representing irreconcilable positions. The baroque writers fed upon Christian subjects and miracles. Boileau was revolted by them. By studying international literature in the context of literary movements, however, one's attention is focused on major literary developments rather than on nonliterary or local events.

As they swept across frontiers, from *pays émetteurs* to *récepteurs*, making their way to Russia and the Americas, accommodating themselves in sometimes unpredictable ways to national conditions and languages, movements like romanticism, neoclassicism, and symbolism are of special interest to the student of comparative literature. For comparative literature seeks not only resemblances among the novels, let us say, of Scott, Hugo, and Manzoni, but also the gradations of difference within the general resemblances. Scott's novels are not essentially motivated by the political goals that impelled Shelley, William Godwin, and Blake (even though Soviet criticism following Lukács simplifies the Waverley novels as a chronicle of class struggle against mediaeval feudalism). Hugo's mature novels, on the other hand, are dedicated to sociopolitical reform and the destruction of the monarchist or imperial reigns, of which he had approved as a youth. *I promessi sposi*, modeled upon Scott, was nevertheless invoked to encourage Manzoni's countrymen to throw off the yoke of the Austrian occupants of Italy. And yet, the three novelists with their differing motivations shared many romantic traits in common (see checklist, p. 161). Indeed, when Scott met Manzoni and was embarrassed by the gracious Italian writer's insistence that *The Betrothed* owed everything to the Scotsman, he courteously acknowledged that the novel was then "my best work."

Spread and Duration of Movements

A literary movement will thus retain its essential identity as it crosses a continent; but it will undergo adaptations and modifications that tell us about the countries involved and even about the potential of the movement itself. The England of Dryden and Pope remained long captivated by French neoclassicism, while Spain, as Menéndez y Pelayo and other Spanish historians remind us, sought to impose upon playwrights until 1799 the practices of Boileau and Racine, representatives of the homeland of the imminent Napoleonic invaders. In the case of romanticism, each of its basic elements—rejection of the Aristotelian "rules" of neoclassicism, revival of Gothic Catholicism, cult of the individual, greater freedom of versification and expression, and others—had its own particular fortunes in the several literatures of Western Europe. France and England during romanticism revived many aspects of the Christian Middle Ages and made a cult of Gothic architecture whereas Italy, for centuries host to the papacy and idolator of Dante, had no need of such a revival, never having lost sight of the Middle Ages. Finally, the cult of the individual and the libertarian ideals of the romanticists, inherited from Rousseau and Goethe's antibourgeois *Werther*, contributed diversely to sociopolitical reform in each country. Yet, by the time of the convulsive year 1848, romanticism had set the stage for the great, sweeping rebellions against Metternich, Louis Philippe, and Friedrich Wilhelm IV. The great movements of literature then can never be adequately defined or even understood in terms of one or two nations or literatures. The necessity for the total view is the stimulus for studying literature comparatively.

The dates of the beginning and end of the major literary movements are not easily established. Rare is an official decision like the one accepted by the Mediaeval Academy and ratified by bookdealers everywhere (though not by the Renaissance Society) that the Middle Ages were succeeded by the Renaissance at midnight on December 31, 1500 (*not* 1499). Frequently, too, there are the so-called transitional periods, in themselves of interest to the student of literature, just as there are the transitional writers like Stendhal, the romantic-realist, and Goethe, whose romantic (to the Germanists, preromantic) *Werther* (1774) was followed only five years later by the first version of his neoclassical tragedy *Iphigenie*. Frequently the appearance of a basic text, such as Wordsworth and Coleridge's *Lyrical Ballads* of 1798, serves as the convenient tocsin announcing the arrival of an international movement within a given country. More difficult to pinpoint is the single text that unleashes an entire international movement. This is true even of dadaism, whose date of inception is definitely established as 1916. One historical fact of interest to the literary scholar is that there is almost never a moment or a year in the history of continental Europe that does not fall within a well-defined movement or at least an equally well-defined transitional period.

We have not until now paused over the lesser literary fluctuation called the trend. Since François Jost has defined it well in his excellent *Introduction to Comparative Literature*, his statement follows:

> A rather clear distinction can be made between a movement and a trend insofar as the movement refers to the characteristics of a much wider and varied group of works than a trend, which denotes a more particular phenomenon and often represents a temporary literary fashion. . . . A movement, therefore, is a general, widespread phenomenon, like the baroque or the enlightenment. Trends, on the other hand, may be observed within a movement; neo-hellenism, for example, is a trend within romanticism.

Similarly, mysticism is a trend within the baroque.

One-Man Movements: Individuals and Nonconformists

There is a special type of movement that does not always rise and fall in the same cadence as the others. Examples would be Neoplatonism and Petrarchism, movements that serve as catalysts to literature over several centuries. Unlike the more chronologically organic movements of romanticism and neoclassicism, which are not the product of a single founder, they represent the more gradual sweep of the influence of the founder of an intellectual tradition. Thus Petrarchism is a specific movement that dominated European poetry from Petrarch's own time, the fourteenth century, through the sixteenth, leaning on themes that eventually became commonplaces by the time they informed the poetry of Sir Thomas Wyatt. The bittersweet quality of love, the gentleness of one's enemy, the presence of an absent mistress— these motifs are supported by a group of characteristically Petrarchan stylistic elements: contradictions, paradoxes, oxymora (sweet enemy, agreeable poison, etc.). Petrarch was also the one man most responsible for the enduring popularity of the curious sonnet form, which with a few variants is still practiced (see p. 131) in our century.

The same demonstration can be undertaken for Plato and Neoplatonism, a movement that emanated from the Platonic

Academy founded in Florence in 1462 and spread over European literature for three or more centuries—indeed, even to Goethe and Shelley. This movement, too, had its favorite themes, adapted from the Platonic dialogues: the theory of prototypical ideas, the primordial unity of the sexes (the androgyne or hermaphrodite), the ladder of love, and so forth. Thus, a philosophical style resulted, bearing with it a series of stylistic clichés: "my other half," "the reunion of lovers," "the ascension to the True, the Good, and the Beautiful"—expressions reflected abundantly in the poets of Shakespeare's generation as well as that of Keats and Shelley (conspicuous by the capitalizing of these abstract nouns).

The category of special cases must include not only those movements that persist through several centuries, but also those writers who seem to discover themselves artistically only by rejecting very specific movements into which they are born. These, the mavericks of literary history, would include Shakespeare as dramatist (only), as well as the Spaniard Lope de Vega, both of whom consciously attempted to circumvent the Aristotelian norms of Renaissance tragedy. Sometimes an author's originality makes him hard to classify within a movement or even a generation. Such is the case of Milton, diversely styled neoclassical, baroque, or "Bartasian" (from Du Bartas). Such is also the case of the unclassifiable William Blake, despite the many social tenets he shares with the upcoming romanticists. While such writers seem to find their strength only by going against current canons of style, others have weakened themselves by subscribing blindly to the dictates of a literary movement, as is the case of Dryden in his attempt to vie with Shakespeare's *Antony and Cleopatra* by writing *All for Love*, a weak but very neoclassical version of the story (not at all a baroque version, despite Highet's claim).

Excepting these categories of conformist and nonconformist, it is probably true that most writers do benefit from participation in a contemporary literary movement, gaining from it guidance, inspiration, and motivation. As we have suggested, Manzoni's *Promessi sposi* might never have been written had he not been inspired by Scott. Often the members of a literary movement try out their writings on one another, like the Generation of 1898 in a corner table of the Café Gijón or the symbolist poets gathered once a week in the home of Mallarmé. Only Mallarmé himself

was loath to recite, waiting as he did during his lifetime to write
the poem.

Source Study, Influence, Plagiarism

Two interlocking areas of our literary activity are influence
study and source study. These are both facets of a similar activity, one emphasizing the *émetteurs*, or influential writers, and the
other the *récepteurs*, or writers who have undergone influences
and whose sources therefore become an inspiration for literary
detectivism. These two French substantives were long used in
France before being taken up by the current practitioners of
semiotics. M. Guyard correctly recalls that influence, or the alternative palliative of *succès*, constituted the first great thrust of
French comparatism. He notes that the older bibliographies will
be replete with studies on *Shakespeare en Serbie, Racine en
Bulgarie*, and *Paul de Kock en Russie*. Yet he readily admits the
importance of such early exercises in influence study as Brown's
Rabelais in English Literature, or multiple influence such as Van
Tieghem's *La découverte de Shakespeare sur le continent*. If
Americans tend to criticize source studies as a Germanic phe-
nomenon, it may be because the literary give-and-take between
France and Germany was much explored by both nations around
the turn of the century (*Heine en France* of Betz, *Goethe en
France* of Baldensperger, *Schiller et le romantisme français* of
Eggli).

Although we are including this brief discussion of influence,
success, and source study in a chapter on movements, where they
are most readily traceable along their *fil conducteur*, one could as
easily discuss them in the other contexts of comparative literature: themes and forms. That massive influences take place via
movements and even centuries is demonstrated by Guyard's
pages showing how France was influenced by Italy in the sixteenth century, by Italy and Spain in the seventeenth, by
England in the eighteenth, by Germany in the nineteenth, and
apparently by America in the twentieth. After discussing the
matter of influence, and the caution that must accompany claims
of influence, we shall conclude with some recent expressions of

dissatisfaction or reservation concerning influence and source study.

One of the most useful discussions of source study is found in a book written over a half century ago, André Morize's *Problems and Methods of Literary History*. The genial Morize was interested, like many of his generation, in eighteenth-century literary relations between France and England. He noted that establishing literary indebtedness did not mean merely "catching Chateaubriand or Hugo, let us say, 'in the act'—the relish of showing beyond the shadow of a doubt that some page of the *Voyage en Amérique* or some line in the *Légende des siècles* is nothing but a clever appropriation from the text of an obscure traveler or of a forgotten journalist." We are of course more discriminating now about source study, and look beyond the mere act of plagiarism whether conscious or unconscious, admitted or denied. In the twenties most of the source studies appearing in France involved major writers, in the old tradition of Stendhal's *Racine et Shakespeare* or the later tradition of *Diderot en Allemagne*, etc., leading Morize to comment:

> We are disposed to accept too readily the false theory that great writers read only great writers—that geniuses merely pass on the torch from one to the other. Nothing is more untrue. A certain celebrated page by Rousseau can be traced to his having read the *Journal encyclopédique*; a brilliant witticism of Voltaire was his reaction to a passage by an obscure and ignorant Jesuit father.

Morize then provides in detail several cautions against becoming a "source-maniac," reminding us of Musset's sarcasm, "C'est imiter quelqu'un que de planter des choux." Influences are so varied and so constant that their seeker must avoid what Morize calls "the hypnotism of the unique source." One must not lose his ability to distinguish between a resemblance and a direct dependence, and we must remember the existence of intermediaries. Thus, when Montaigne quoted from Calpurnius or Prudentius, whom he had never read, he was borrowing from the middleman Justus-Lipsius. Another compulsion we must recognize is "obsession for the written source," when none exists. For there are many types of source other than written or documentary. Indirect sources (oral, indefinite, inspirational) exist, but they simply cannot be pinpointed and proved.

Morize warns that the zeal for discovery of sources and influences has led to many false or unprovable claims:

> Too often the illusion of the author arises simply because he lacks a general acquaintance with the literary, intellectual, philosophic, or artistic background of the epoch in question. He acts very much like a student of geography who, perched on a mountaintop above an ocean of clouds and perceiving to the left and right of him a few isolated peaks, attempts to describe the mountain range they belong to. His work will amount to nothing until he sees the whole chain and studies not only the surface but the layers of subsoil.

Morize concludes his chapter with the obvious reminder that establishing a plagiarism or an influence is not an end in itself. It must lead us to conclusions about the author's thought, the evolution of his art, his working method, his character, and his originality. I recall an article of mine, published in the *Romanic Review*, that uncovered a number of new plagiarisms from Petrarch in the poetry of Desportes. A single final page explained the significance of this research in evaluating Philippe Desportes's role as the major Petrarchist of his time. The editor proposed dropping this page to save space. Fortunately I was able to persuade him that, in Morize's words, discovering plagiarisms was not an end in itself.

Perhaps Montaigne, that archplagiarist, knew best of all that mere borrowing was insignificant of itself.

> To distinguish in an author the worthiest parts, and those more strictly his own, the strength and beauty of his soul, we must know what is his and what is not; and, in the case of what is not his, how much we owe to him of the selection, arrangement, ornamentation, and language used therein.

Indeed, on the theory of Cyrano de Bergerac that plagiarism was the greatest of compliments, Montaigne would have been pleased to know how many, including Shakespeare, were to pillage him for ideas.

Influence studies are common in our profession, more appropriate for theses than for courses. Influence is often paired with the concept of success, although success is merely the inevitable ingredient necessary for literary influence, just as source study is merely one of several criteria certifying the existence and nature of the influence. Some authors, like the English metaphysical poets, enjoyed a brief popularity, were eclipsed, and then emerged when discovered by T. S. Eliot and his generation. Indeed, this curious and intriguing revival of a group of England's most individual poets not only is of itself an illustration of influence and of a movement, but parallels similar nineteenth-century resurgences at around the same time of the baroque, culteranist, and mannerist poets in France, Spain, Italy, and Germany, relatively forgotten and uninfluential for about the same period as Donne and Marvell. Góngora's resurgence occurred specifically in 1927. Influence then depends on a number of imponderables including taste, as well as a rejection of a reigning taste and a desire for something new. Comparatists are less concerned with intranational interests, such as Logau's debt to Lessing, than with those of an international dimension. There are many cases of a writer having a greater influence abroad than in his own homeland. Breuillac has shown that Hoffmann "had no vogue whatever in Germany" when all the French romantic writers were devouring him, partly because the normally logical French reading public had become "accustomed to the supernatural." The Roman proverb quoted in our Foreword, "books have their own destinies," applies to some novels or dramas appearing at the very moment when positivistic forces made them most welcome. The role of literary critics and book reviewers enters into the question, of course, and an article by Jules Lemaître is said to have killed the novelist Georges Ohnet just as the reviewer Croker was accused by Shelley of killing Keats. Sometimes a most colorful and influential writer will create an influence neither foreseen nor explainable. Wilde, Joyce, Shaw, Proust, Pirandello, Nabokov, Moravia, and others become such towering figures that their roles themselves make their works influential, out of the reach of quibbling critics.

As suggested earlier, there has been of late a change of feeling in both Europe and America about the values of source study. In Wellek's words, "Parallel-hunting has been widely discredited recently, especially when attempted by an inexperienced student." The same is of course to be said of establishing plagiarisms, unless analyzed and evaluated. It is often alleged that the influences of all the great writers have been worked over by now with nothing left to be done. This is patently a dubious conclusion, as is the argument that influences established are usually inconsequential. Croce, for example, warned after reading an "influence study" on the theme of Sophonisba against the lurking "dangers of these works of comparison." Haskell Block, too, warns of their "marginal or trivial" results, ridiculous mice spewed forth from trembling mountains. A recent thesis on Dante's influence on Rimbaud by Margherita Frankel has discovered in a nineteenth-century French translation of the *Divina Commedia* the key to much of Rimbaud's vivid and unusual language and metaphor— serving as a counterargument to Croce. Sometimes the anticipated results of source study differ from the actual discoveries. Thus, a study of mine on Rilke's *Geschichten vom lieben Gott* and Michelangelo's *Rime* disproved that it was Rodin who interested Rilke in Michelangelo and invalidated the accepted belief that it was Rodin who made Rilke view art as an artist rather than as a *littérateur*. Considering the stature of the three figures concerned, the conclusions were accepted as more than marginal or trivial. Étiemble's suspicion of influence studies as mere causes and effects leads him to conclude that comparatism can still exist "even where the possibility of direct influence is ruled out." As we have acknowledged elsewhere in this volume, comparative literature contrasts as well as compares. In any case, meaningful influences will always be plentifully available for exploration, and as Wellek has stated, whatever the abuses of the method, it is a legitimate one and cannot be dismissed, as some would now propose.

That *succès* and influence are two distinct concepts, however, was the conclusion of a much quoted article by Anna Balakian in the *YCGL* of 1962. In this carefully reasoned discussion on the equivocal function of the two areas of study, she concludes: "On the basis of results observed, it seems that when the scholar tries to establish at the same time literary fortune and influence, he gets lost in a Cartesian forest of many devious pathways and fails to reach any destination at all."

Conclusion

The great literary movements expand geographically and intellectually, transcending belles-lettres, moving beyond such conventional literary matters as aesthetics, structure, stylistics, and so on. Such movements as the baroque, neoclassical, romantic, and symbolist not only determine the development of music and the fine arts as well as literature, but also are constantly interrelated to politics and social thought. Humanism, with its insistence on *le libre examen* and its rejection of Scholasticism, made as important contributions to science and politics as it did to literature, replacing alchemy by chemistry, astrology by astronomy, numerology by mathematics, and so on. The neoclassicists' reliance on rules, authority, and restrictive canons in literature helped to sustain an authoritarian government in France, England, and even Spain, where, as suggested above, the government until 1799 fought an eventually losing battle to maintain and subsidize Racinian theater. Romanticism, on the other hand, with its exaltation of the individual and its acceptance of Rousseau's idea that man was innocent until corrupted by society and its prejudices, led to a radical rethinking on education, religion, and of course politics. François Jost has noted in his *Introduction to Comparative Literature* (III, 7) that the *Junges Deutschland* "movement" was paralleled by individual national "schools" elsewhere: La Giovine Italia, La Jeune France, and the Mloda Polska in Poland. Such consequences of the expanding potential of literature—not forgetting authoritarian literatures of left and right of course—sweep across national frontiers and heighten the interest of comparative literature study.

Textbooks on Periods and Movements

It is a rare major period or movement that could be served by one single classroom reader. Let us take the Middle Ages (Scholasticism) as a single, typical example. The most comprehensive single text at our disposition is probably Charles Jones's *Mediaeval Literature in Translation* (Longmans, Green). Its 1,004 pages encompass a vast area of mediaeval literary forms, necessarily abridged. Jones himself rationalizes the value of abridged anthologies, especially in the mediaeval field. "There are those to whom anthologies, abridgements, and scissors-and-paste are hateful. Sometimes I am of their humour; but not with respect to mediaeval literature. From the first, the mediaeval author wrote to have his book excerpted. Many of the authors represented here were themselves editors of *florilegia*." Such an anthology for the Renaissance, also published by Longmans and edited by Harold Blanchard, must condense works while "trying to give parts which leave the reader with a conception of the work as a whole." The basic anthology can be supplemented by readers presenting specific genres but in more complete form. Thus, the text of Charles Jones can be supported by the Modern Library *Mediaeval Epics*, the Loomis anthology *Mediaeval Romances* (also Modern Library), Willard Trask's *Mediaeval Lyrics* (World), Angel Flores' collection with the same title in the Modern Library, or parallel broad anthologies that will of necessity contain some duplication, such as the *Portable Mediaeval Reader* (Viking) or the entertaining *Dark and Middle Ages Reader* (Putnam, Capricorn). However, it is obvious that readings supplementing a basic extensive anthology would best serve our purposes by covering individual works in the foreign language.

In this textbook area, as well as for courses on genre and on theme, the paperback editions disappear with dismaying frequency. The instructor will have to consult periodically the inventory in *Books in Print*, or have a bookseller willing to do some research to come up with equivalent texts—a task that some private booksellers will undertake more willingly and efficiently than the clerks in the college bookstore or cooperative.

Fig. 8. *Checklist of Elements of European Baroque*

I. Collected from Buffum and others:

A. Energy:
    1. Spirit of propaganda
    2. Devices of emphasis and exaggeration (asyndeton; echo devices; verbs of violence and horror)

B. Spectacle:

    3. Theatricality
    4. Merveilleux chrétien (contact and union with God; mysticism)
    5. Terribilità

C. Incarnation:

    6. Concreteness of imagery
    7. Personification
    8. Redness and radiance
    9. Synesthesia (multiple sense imagery)
    10. Erotic-ecstatic: longing for union and death; flaming heart

D. Paradox and mutability:

    11. Oxymoron
    12. Puns and conceits
    13. Metaphoric antithesis
    14. The surprise climax
    15. Contrast; disguise; metamorphosis; illusion
    16. Doubt; contradiction; disenchantment; desengaño
    17. Tension; movement

II. After Wölfflin:

    18. Magnifying epithets
    19. Resounding words and syllable echoes
    20. Heavy repetitions
    21. Complicated structures
    22. Slow rhythms
    23. Imprecise unified images

III. From Jean Rousset:

    (15) La métamorphose; le déguisement; le trompe-l'œil; l'inconstance
    24. Le spectacle de la mort
    25. L'instabilité; la mobilité; la domination du décor

IV. Other sources:

    26. Lomazzo: "Frozen motion"
    27. Spitzer: "Chiaroscuro"
    28. Eugenio d'Ors: "Emancipation from the earth"

29. Ortega: "La visión lejana"
30. Casalduero: "Una forma confus-
    amente clara"
31. Hatzfeld: "Un beau désordre"

Fig. 9. *Checklist of Elements of European Romanticism*

(derived from course lectures and reading assignments)

1. Anti-intellectualism; emotion over intellect
2. Faith in instinct over reason
3. Interest in the individual over the universal
4. Tone, atmosphere; nervousness, frenzy reflected in style
5. Idealism, ideal world, remote in time and space; Middle Ages
6. Mystery, dream world, duality of worlds, supernatural, mystic; occult metaphysics
7. Unrestrained imagination; general lack of restraint
8. Nature love; irregular aspects of nature
9. Individual against society: rebel; *culte du moi*; egalitarianism; antibourgeois; society corrupts
10. Form: plots rapid and complex; mixed genre; variety of forms; freedom of form; form less important than content; antiunities
11. High characterization; fluctuation; lower classes of society, demophilia
12. Degree of selectivity: seeks the interesting and pleasing; high color
13. Quality of diction
14. Ruins, tombs, abbeys, cathedrals
15. Melancholy, unfulfilled love, pallor, inner conflict
16. Romantic irony
17. Suicide and death
18. Amorality: own standards
19. World weariness: flight; solitude
20. Inbreeding: mention of other romantics
21. Interruptions in narrative or poetry (*Harold* and *Onegin* poems to women)
22. Local color: exoticism
23. Patriotism
24. Innocence over experience

**Fig. 10. *Syllabus of Western Heritage Movement Course:*
*European Romanticism***

FEB. 3   Definitions and Elements of Romanticism; Romanticism in Relation to Other Movements

FEB. 10   Romanticism as Seen by the Romanticists; Exuberant and
           Satirical Definitions
           ASSIGNMENT: Read H. Hugo, *Portable Romantic Reader*
           (Viking paperback) or Karl Petit, *Le livre d'or du
           Romantisme* (Editions Gérard, Verviers)

FEB. 17   Romanticism in Germany
           ASSIGNMENT: Read Goethe's *Werthers Leiden* (Holt,
           Rinehart paper/Signet)
           REPORTS: Novalis:_____ Schiller:_____

FEB. 24   Romanticism in Italy
           ASSIGNMENT: Read Manzoni's *The Betrothed* (Dutton
           paperback)
           REPORT: Leopardi's verse:_____

MAR. 2   Romanticism in France
           ASSIGNMENT: Read Chateaubriand's *Atala* and *René*
           (University of California)
           REPORTS: Hugo as poet: _____ Hugo as drama-
           tist: _____

MAR. 9   Romanticism in France
           ASSIGNMENT: Read *The Romantic Influence* (Dell paper-
           back)
           REPORT: Lamartine:_____

MAR. 16   Romanticism in England
           ASSIGNMENT: Read Byron's *Childe Harold* (in *Selected
           Poetry of Lord Byron*, NAL)
           REPORTS: Ossian:_____ Scott's Waverley novels:
           _____

MAR. 23   No class: Spring recess

MAR. 30   Romanticism in England
           ASSIGNMENT: Read *Portable Romantic Poets* (Viking pa-
           perback)
           REPORTS: Shelley:_____ Wordsworth:_____

APR. 6   Romanticism in Spain
           ASSIGNMENT: Read Duke of Rivas, *Don Alvaro* (or libretto
           of derivative opera, *La forza del destino*)
           REPORTS: Larra:_____ Bécquer:_____

APR. 13   Romanticism in Russia
           ASSIGNMENT: Read Pushkin, *Evgen Onegin* (Nabokov
           trans., or Arndt, Dutton)
           REPORT: Lermontov:_____

APR. 27   Echoes of European Romanticism in America
           ASSIGNMENT: Read *Portable Romantic Poets* (Viking pa-
           perback)
           REPORTS: Irving:_____ Hawthorne:_____

MAY 4   Romanticism in Art (slide lecture)

MAY 11   Romanticism in Music; Politics, Transition, Decline, Im-
           pact
           REPORTS: Music:_____ Opera:_____

FIG. 11. *Syllabus of Western Heritage Movement Course: Symbolism*[a]

SEPT. 22   The Meaning of the Word; Symbolism and Literary Criti-
           cism

SEPT. 29   Swedenborg, the Theory of Correspondences and Its
           Impact on Romanticism

OCT. 6   The German Background: Novalis, Hölderlin, Jean-Paul,
           Tieck, Wagner

OCT. 13   Baudelaire (cf. Poe) as a Precursor of Symbolism: "Cor-
           respondances," "Harmonie du soir," "Le Cygne," and
           prose: "Le Poème du Haschisch," "L'Art Romantique"

OCT. 20   Verlaine, Rimbaud, Laforgue
           Cf. Verlaine: "L'Art Poétique," *Romances sans paroles*;
           Rimbaud: "Les Voyelles," "Le Bateau ivre," *Une Sai-
           son en enfer*; Laforgue: *Moralités légendaires*

OCT. 27   Mallarmé and the Symbolist Cénacle
           Cf. "Hérodiade," "L'Après-midi d'un Faune," and selected
           essays; Huret: *Enquête.* Manifestos of Moréas, Kahn,
           Ghil

NOV. 3   The International Coterie in Paris and the English Inter-
           mediaries
           Maeterlinck; Stuart Merrill; George Moore, *Confessions
           of a Young Man*; Edmund Gosse, *Leaves and Fruit.* Cf.

[a] This syllabus was kindly supplied by Professor Anna Balakian of New York
University.

Temple, *Critic's Alchemy*; Symons, *The Symbolist Movement in Literature*

NOV. 10 The International Coterie (*continued*)
Stefan George (selections) and his followers

NOV. 17 The Literary Conventions of Symbolism in the Romance Literatures
Rubén Darío, Manuel Machado, etc.

NOV. 24 The Heritage of Symbolism
T. S. Eliot and W. B. Yeats

DEC. 1 The Heritage of Symbolism
Valéry, Rilke, Stevens

DEC. 8 The Heritage of Symbolism
Lorca, Jiménez, Blok, Biely

DEC. 15 The Symbolist Theater
Maeterlinck, Hofmannsthal, and others

JAN. 5 The Symbolist Theater
Summing up of the course

VIII

Themes and Myths

Erzählen wird man von dem Schützen Tell,
Solang' die Berge stehn auf ihrem Grunde.
FRIEDRICH SCHILLER, *Wilhelm Tell*

Themes, Myths, Motifs, Stoffgeschichte

A third logical and traditional way to approach the comparison of authors and literatures is the thematic one or, in the German popular term, through *Stoffgeschichte*, narrative material, the "stuff" of prose and poetry. Obviously, since the matter of literature may involve themes, topics, myths, rituals, motifs, metaphors, plots, or even theses, this is a very broad approach indeed. Its breadth is further indicated in Wellek's statement, "'Myth,' a favorite term of modern criticism, points to, hovers over, an important area of meaning, shared by religion, folklore, anthropology, sociology, psychoanalysis, and the fine arts. In some of its habitual oppositions, it is contraposed to 'history,' or to 'science,' or to 'philosophy,' or to 'allegory' or to 'truth.'"

Because the study of mythic heroes is so dominant in this field, let us look first at their role in comparative literature. The psychologist Otto Rank summarizes the archetype of mythical hero, to be found in the oldest literatures of the Occident, Near East, and Orient:

The hero is the child of distinguished parents, usually the son of a king. His origin is preceded by difficulties, such as continence or prolonged barrenness or secret intercourse of the parents due to external prohibition or obstacles. During or before the pregnancy there is a prophecy, in the form of a dream or oracle, cautioning against his birth, and usually threatening danger to the father (or his representative). As a rule he is surrendered to the water, in a box. He is then saved by animals, or by lowly people (shepherds), and is suckled by a female animal or an humble woman. After he has grown up, he finds his distinguished parents in a highly versatile fashion. He takes revenge on his father, on the one hand, and is acknowledged, on the other. Finally he achieves rank and honors.

Among folk heroes whose lives conformed more or less to this pattern were Sargon of Babylonia, Moses, Karna of India, Oedipus, Jesus, Cyrus, Hercules, Romulus, Siegfried, Lohengrin, and Tristan. The spread of this mythical pattern from Wales to India is an astonishing testimonial to the vitality of themes and legends. Rank's examples correspond to Thrall and Hibbard's widely accepted definition of myths as

anonymous stories having their roots in the primitive folk beliefs of races or nations in an effort to make concrete and particular a special perception of man or a cosmic view. Myths differ from legends in that they have less of historical background and more of the supernatural. They differ from the fable in that they are less concerned with moral didacticism and are the product of an ethnic group rather than the creation of an individual.

Primitive myths are nowhere more abundantly illustrated than in the eighteen books of the Chinese *Book of the Mountains and Seas.* The very names of many mythical protagonists to whom comparative literature courses or theses are now dedicated— Uranus, Oedipus, Electra, Narcissus, Prometheus—acquired allegorical meanings, as Jan Brandt Corstius has stated, before investing themselves with the rich meanings with which psychology has endowed them. The popularity of this specific, ancient *Stoffgeschichte* is explained as follows by Raymond Trousson:

Why do we ceaselessly feel the need to set up inventories of these ancestral legends? The reason is that to study their history, to pause over the secret of their infinite mutations, is also to learn to know one's own odyssey in its most elevated and often most tragic aspect. In every conscience enamored of justice there is an

Antigone, in every revolt a Prometheus, in every quest an Orpheus. We shudder before Medea, dream before Tristan, tremble before Oedipus. . . . Our myths and our legendary heroes are our polyvalence. They are the exponents of humanity, the ideal forces of tragic destiny, of the human condition.

By the Renaissance the eternal values of symbol had been assured for the heroes of Greco-Roman myth. Renaissance writers lent them enhanced meaning and potential. The same held true for the great figures of the Bible of course. Michelangelo likened himself in his love poetry to the unhappy Phoebus and Tityus, even as he gave allegorical qualities to the Old Testament prophets on his Sistine ceiling. Other ancient heroes like Phaeton and Icarus who suffered equally harsh punishments are the Satan of Carducci, the Cain of Leconte de Lisle, the Prometheus of Shelley. Since, as Van Tieghem reminds us, they were all rebelling against an oppressive religion, they were basically the same symbol under three names.

Improvisation on Themes and Myths

In modern times writers seem less willing to accept the mythical figures as static symbols and tend to improvise more on the central figure of the myth as well as the myth itself. This becomes apparent as one reads the several variants of the Oedipus legend in the hands of Hofmannsthal, Gide, and Cocteau. The modern author takes pleasure in manipulating the myth, classical or biblical, contradicting the meanings or values that it previously embodied, endowing it with more sophisticated interpretations. Judas, fallen into the hands of the Greek novelist Nikos Kazantzakis, announces to Christ that he cannot betray Him for a handful of silver. Christ, however, insists on the betrayal, lest the lesson of the entire New Testament collapse. Or again, in Max Frisch's revolutionary handling of the Don Juan figure, the Spanish scapegrace insists to the Bishop on his own sacrifice, so that he may stand for future centuries as symbol of the punished sinner. In the final act, Don Juan is condemned not to the flames of hell but, apparently even worse, to marriage and family life. Studying and pondering on these variants is a more fruitful exercise than the traditional search for identical elements to establish sources or to measure influences.

When much play is left to creativity and imagination, exciting and meaningful topics can be pursued through several literatures. Disasters such as the destruction of Troy, the Fall of Man, and so on are philosophically and allegorically stimulating. A thesis on the plague in literature would seek the social, moral, psychological, and allegorical values attached to pestilence in the works of Boccaccio, Defoe, Manzoni, Camus, and many others. Geographical areas, as well as periods of time, find different values in myth and mythical characters. Gendarme de Bévotte's classic study showed Don Juan condemned as a woman chaser in northern Europe and as a scofflaw in the Mediterranean area.

Another curious type of improvisation on legendary characters arises in the recent revival of the early biblical exegetes' notion that one Old Testament figure prefigures a later legend or figure. It was believed, for example, that the sacrifice of Isaac prefigured the crucifixion of Christ. The Old Testament was viewed in entirety as an anticipation of the New. If one accepts the notion of prefiguration, recently elaborated by Auerbach, it would be possible to apply it to the Renaissance writers. Even while they were writing tragedies on legendary Greek and Roman heroes, they established a repertory of their own generational heroes to correspond, including Faustus, Don Carlos, Wilhelm Tell, Hamlet, Inés de Castro, Maria Stuart, among others. Imaginative scholarship could establish this parallel panoply of ancient and Renaissance pre- and postfigurations. Orestes prefigured Hamlet, Antigone prefigured Mary Stuart, Sophonisba prefigured Inés de Castro, and so on. If this were not the case, the question remains to be probed why the Renaissance found a need to create these mythical *figurae* of its own.

Types and Stereotypes

As Owen Aldridge reminds us in the third chapter of his *Comparative Literature: Matter and Method*, classical literature, the Bible, and mythology supply us with great mythical figures, but lesser literature provides types, or social and historical character abstractions, such as the lover, farmer, bureaucrat, proletarian, indolent servant, or alienated man. These types or stereotypes abound in comic or bourgeois literature, and have an ancient antecedence in Aristophanes and Plautus. In comedy they sometimes had masks denoting their identity. Most familiar are the miser, the pedant, the boastful soldier, the bohemian, the expendable man, the rebel, and of course the cuckold. Since their characters are established through situations, theme and plot regain their full importance, whether in comedy or the novella. Indeed, in the vast collection of novellas following the path of the *Decameron*, stories are often grouped under specific themes: the magnanimity of love, the trickster tricked, wives' stratagems against husbands, husbands' against wives, etc.

Although several distinguished names are associated with the tracing of literary motifs and plots to various parts of the world, such as that of Sir James G. Frazer, it was the American professor Stith Thompson of Indiana who attained world fame through his painstaking *Motif-Index of Folk Literature*. It is no problem for Thompson to take some of the popular stories of, for example, Hans Christian Andersen and, fitting them into his catalog of themes, discover immediately Andersen's debt to many older literatures. Thus, he finds that Andersen's tale "The Traveling Companion" fits into Type 507-A (The Monster's Bride). "The Tinder Box" belongs to Type 562 (The Spirit in the Blue Light). He finds that Andersen's beloved "Big Claus and Little Claus" has appeared in 874 recorded versions, including several in American Indian tongues.

Themes of course overlap, as Professor Thompson's *Index* shows clearly, and even such a historically identifiable theme as Utopia becomes easily involved with such kindred topics as the Golden Age, the primordial Innocence of Man, Arcadia, the Voyage to Cytherea, etc. It is difficult to restrict this Protean subject, for it strays easily to such subjective and almost indefinable matters as man's longing for a better world, pacifism, the definition of happiness, and the like.

Sometimes a theme or topic is so vehemently and convincingly advanced that it becomes a thesis. The thesis, proposition, or message may be clearly propounded as the emancipation of women in Ibsen's *Doll's House*, the evil of capital punishment in

An American Tragedy, etc. Or the message may be clouded or indirect, as we seek the ambiguous moral of Captain Ahab's violent death.

Chapter discussions of thematology that deserve the attention of all are found in Ulrich Weisstein's *Comparative Literature and Literary Theory* and François Jost's *Introduction to Comparative Literature*. Jost illustrates thematology by including three essays on Thomas à Becket in fiction and drama, on Wilhelm Tell, and on the motif of suicide. An interesting, traditionalist treatment of theme and myth is found in Guyard's *La littérature comparée*, which encourages study of this still rewarding field. R. Trousson's *Les Études de Thèmes: Essai de Méthodologie* (1965), on the other hand, warns against thematic influence studies in the old Germanic tradition, source studies that run the risk of sterile and perfunctory researches. Otherwise, he finds thematology rewarding. René Étiemble's two-page remarks in *Comparaison n'est pas raison*, briefly discoursing "for and against *Stoffgeschichte*," are hasty and trivial.

Several excellent books on this topic have appeared recently in America. One of the best is *Myth and Mythmaking* (Braziller), an anthology of essays by several important scholars, edited by Henry Murray. The variety of approach is clear from several authors' names: Joseph Campbell, Clyde Kluckhohn, Harry Levin, Jerome Bruner, and Thomas Mann. Students find provocative John Vickery's *Myth and Literature: Contemporary Theory and Practice* (Nebraska), an anthology of "myth criticism." As the editor states, "myth criticism is a committed point of view and so cantankerous, obstreperous, irritating, wrong on details, and dictatorial, but it is passionate and live and has something to say." The most interesting section of the book is Part III, which sets myth critics loose upon such attractive prey as Homer, Shakespeare, Milton, Melville, Stephen Crane, Dickens, Conrad, Kafka, Mann, Joyce, and others. The reviews of this useful volume were favorable, even though accusing some "myth critics" of "straining at gnats."

There are so many studies on the various thrusts of myth important to comparative literature that it is difficult to sift among them. However, a minimal list would include *Myth and Christianity* of Jaspers, *Myth and Guilt* of Reich, *Myth and Reality* of Eliade, *Myth and Symbol* of Frye, *Myth of the Birth of the Hero* of Rank (see above, p. 165), *Myth of the State* of Cassirer, *Mythologies* of Lévi-Strauss, *Mythology* of Hamilton, *The Age of Fable* of Bulfinch, *Myths, Dreams, and Religion* of Campbell, and *Myths of the Hindus and Buddhists* of Coomaraswamy.

We have suggested above that Trousson's *Études de Thèmes*, while unenthusiastic about source and influence studies, finds thematology still a fruitful field of research. Indeed, his rotund summation goes considerably further, convincing us to let his conclusion serve as our own:

> In brief, thematology will be defined, we trust, not as an auxiliary or secondary discipline, not as an amusement of the mind, nor yet a collation of uneven passages gathered together. Let the study of themes be a genre in itself, one which is obviously lodged in the framework of comparative literature, but contains however its particular demands and claims to autonomy. . . . Theme is the conducting wire, eternal through the years, which is charged over the centuries by all the philosophic and artistic booty gathered along the way by that adventurer, man. That is why it preserves and gives back through its innumerable transmutations a few constant, a few fundamental concerns—in a word, something of the essentiality of human nature.

A Sampling of Textbooks on Themes and Myths

We found in Chapter vi that editors of textbooks on genres and forms not only defined their subject matter, but explained their value for didactic purposes. Editors of thematic anthologies do no less. Bens and Baugh, editors of the thought-provoking *Icarus, An Anthology of Literature* (Macmillan), have chosen texts that more subtly, even more indirectly, present the myth of Icarus. They assure students that nevertheless

> all of the materials can be either directly or indirectly related to the Icarus theme. . . . What one stresses in the myth will determine whether Icarus' story symbolizes man's aspirations or his foolhardiness, whether his fall expresses the cruelty of fate crushing the hopes of man or whether it brings to mind the relative position that man occupies in the greater framework of nature. Men have identified many feelings and thoughts with this myth.

A youth winging to the sun is an image which suggests thoughts of daring and adventure, perhaps even pride that man can approach to the level of the gods. But Icarus falling expresses imminent loss and the failure to gain wisdom until too late. Seen as admonition, however, this image is not necessarily defeatist.

The editors exert themselves to tie the Icarus myth with such disparate works as Hemingway's "The Killers," Keats's "Ode on a Grecian Urn," and Marvell's "To His Coy Mistress."

The theme of Oedipus could of course be extended or extrapolated in this way just as easily, but the Kallich et al. anthology, *Oedipus, Myth and Drama* (Odyssey), offers a simpler challenge to the student:

> This book has three general aims—to provide a basis for the understanding of perhaps the most important myth of ancient and modern civilizations . . . , to stimulate an awareness of the significant ways in which this myth is reflected in man's unconscious life. And last of all, to encourage investigation of changing ideas about the content of tragedy and its form in various ages.

If only the versions of Sophocles, Dryden, and Hofmannsthal are included, this leaves many pages for explanatory essays on the theme by Gilbert Murray, Maurice Bowra, H. D. F. Kitto, and others. A similar anthology of plays on this same tragic figure is Sanderson and Zimmerman's *Oedipus* (Houghton Mifflin), which complements the choice of plays in the previous volume, for it fills out the picture by the versions (after Sophocles) of Seneca, Voltaire, Gide, and Cocteau. The two collections together, currently available in paperback and reasonably priced, make a convenient adoption for a course on this basic myth. Furthermore, the second volume includes further commentary by Aristotle, Freud, Lattimore, Fergusson, and others. The editors characteristically write a preface on myth:

> The word *myth* has become a familiar term in the vocabularies of a number of disciplines, including classics, art, literature, religion, anthropology, sociology, and political science. The resulting proliferation and the broadened spectrum of its meanings from, in Francis Fergusson's words, "nonsense or willful obscurantism" to the "deepest wisdom of man" make it a difficult word to use with precision.

They are content with Philip Wheelright's definition: "A story or complex of story elements taken as expressing, and therefore as implicitly symbolizing, certain deep-lying aspects of human and transhuman experience."

We have given high praise to the Norton Critical Edition of *Moby Dick* in Chapter vi. Let us merely add that the Norton *Oedipus* in this series, while containing only the Sophocles tragedy in translation, is rich in critical materials ancient and modern.

No publisher would seem more active in making thematic paperback textbooks available to university students than Houghton Mifflin. In the same structure and format as the *Oedipus* anthology mentioned above are *Phaedra and Hippolytus, Myth and Dramatic Form; Orestes and Electra, Myth and Dramatic Form;* and *Medea, Myth and Dramatic Form.* All these carry a similar preface acknowledging Wheelwright's definition of myth (see above) as well as a rich appendix of critical essays.

One further legendary figure often appearing in comparative literature courses is the irrepressible rake Don Juan. There is a popular anthology of Oscar Mandel, mentioned earlier, *The Theater of Don Juan* (Nebraska), which includes all major dramatic versions—Tirso, Molière, Shadwell, Mozart–Da Ponte, Grabbe, Moncrieff, and Zorrilla—along with important essays on the legend by Rank, Camus, Shaw, and others. It has been prepared with much imagination, and can be faulted only for certain excisions in the early texts. Finally, one must mention John Yohannan's truly international anthology *Joseph and Potiphar's Wife* (New Directions), treating of the lustful stepmother, also known as Phaedra, Zulaikha (Muslim), Tishya-rakshita (India), Anpu's Wife (Egypt), and eight other named or unnamed adulteresses. This is indeed an anthology adaptable to a world literature course.

A cursory reading of college catalogs leads me to conclude that perhaps the four most popular thematic courses deal with Oedipus, Faust, Don Juan, and Utopia. Since there is no Faust anthology comparable to the collections above (see p. 177), we conclude this sampling of thematic textbooks with comments on J. W. Johnson's *Utopian Literature* (Modern Library). As in every quality textbook on myth, the editor comes at once to grips with the importance of his vast theme. Tailoring his collection to a view of the past and the future alike, he writes:

The very nature of the human mind is such as to foster Utopian speculation. Human beings possess both hindsight and foresight: the ability to remember the past and to anticipate the future. As a result, none of us lives solely in the present, in his sensations and emotions of the moment. Our recollections, accurate or inaccurate, mingle with our thoughts of the present and our presentiments of what is to come. Almost always, today is somehow lacking in whatever would make us completely free from worry. . . . The readings in the present anthology were selected to show the linear development of the Utopian concept from past to present and future, to indicate the chief variations of the idea and relate these to other significant concepts, and to open up some lines of reflection. To see the mutation of the Utopian dream through the centuries not only permits us to understand the intellectual tradition that has formed our own world. It reveals to us some of the deepest and more desperate needs of the human race and, in doing this, discloses the basic human drives that lie in our own hearts.

If *Utopian Literature* traces its noble theme from such prehistoric beginnings as Adam and Eve, Prometheus, Saturn and the Saturnalia, it carries it into the far future of Ray Bradbury's *Martian Chronicles*, when the consequences of the scientific Utopia early dreamed by Francis Bacon will have created the ultimate havoc: a well-ordered earth no longer burdened by mankind.

Fig. 12. *Checklist of Elements of Don Juanism*

To understand the "plurality" or many-sidedness of the mythical Don Juan, and to distinguish between the variant characters in the several versions you will read this semester, keep in mind the following topics and issues. Use them as a checklist for class reports and for term paper and/or examination.

1. THE DON JUAN CHARACTER

Perverse sexuality: needs excitement of first encounter to be stimulated

Satyriasis, "triumph of sensuality" (Oscar Mandel)

A physical drive: "from the bull country" (Madariaga)

Inverse sadism: "the sadist overpowers through pain, Juan through pleasure" (Francisco Umbral)

Overcompensation for a fear of impotence

Narcissism: to give and receive love (Unamuno)

Latent homosexuality, sometimes "tied to sister or mother" (Lucas)

Hatred of mother, transferred to other women; mother dominant

Hatred of unfaithful mother; her infidelities become his (Von Gebsattel)

Oedipal love of mother, incest quest (Otto Fenichel, Otto Rank)

Oedipal resentment of father, the "unconquerable mortal enemy" (Rank)

Egotism and self-centered nature

Destined to Don Juanism by fate

A heightening of tendencies in every man

Routine activity induced by an idle, leisured life; economic status

Privilege of a noble class; *droit du seigneur*

The *démon du midi*, heightened sexual activity in maturity, sense of urgency

Don Juanism as a Mediterranean phenomenon ("an innate, national Spanish soul"—Victor Said Armesto)

2. WOMEN

Personal charisma, beauty, attractiveness to women

Women exaggerating Juan's offenses

Women seducing him, the female Don Juan: Donna Julia and Catherine the Great in Byron's *Don Juan*; the goose must chase the gander (Shaw)

Techniques of seduction, or do his mere desires tumble women? (Rougemont)

Is Juan really bored by women? Excited?

Any code of conduct, even demoniacal?

The Androgynous Quest or screening process (1,003 women tried by Rostand's, who failed to recognize the right one)

Mendacity, misrepresentation, deception

Promises of fidelity or marriage as bait

Recognition of paternalism in the act of seduction

3. GUILT, REBELLION, PUNISHMENT

Southern European theory: Don Juan as scofflaw; legal penalties for Don Juanism; essentially a rebel against law and society and religion; blasphemer against God; immorality, amorality; atheism

Juan on deviationism, organized vice, social crime; "guilt and punishment complex" (Rank); does punishment fit crimes? other worse fates? the Stone Commander: compassionate or intransigent judge; at what point is Don Juan damned?

Do circumstances create Don Juans? (sea voyages, channel fever, spas as in Pushkin and Lermontov)

"Why must Don Juan love only once to love well?" (Camus)

Fig. 13. *Syllabus of Western Heritage Theme Course: Don Juan*

JUNE 9 The Issues: Don Juan scofflaw or seducer. Psychiatric or psychological diagnoses. Don Juanism as mother fixation; Oedipal resentment of father; fear of impotence; latent homosexuality; woman hatred.
The Background: Paris of Troy. Ovid's chapbook for Don Juans. *Le Roman de la Rose* and female Don Juans. *El libro de buen amor.* Chaucer's *Shipman's Tale.* Callimaco in Machiavelli's *Mandragola.*

JUNE 11 Tirso de Molina, *El Burlador de Sevilla* (1616?)
ASSIGNMENT: *El Burlador de Sevilla*

JUNE 16 Molière, *Dom Juan, ou Le Festin de Pierre* (1665)
ASSIGNMENT: *Dom Juan*
REPORT TOPICS: Jacques de Casanova as a Don Juan / Macheath in Gay's *Beggar's Opera* as a Don Juan

JUNE 18 Mozart–Da Ponte, *Don Giovanni, o Il Dissoluto Punito* (1787)
ASSIGNMENT: *Don Giovanni*
REPORT TOPICS: Goldoni, *Don Giovanni Tenorio* / Valmont in *Les Liaisons dangereuses* as a Don Juan

JUNE 23 Lord Byron, *Don Juan* (1834)
ASSIGNMENT: *Don Juan*
REPORT TOPICS: Alexander Pushkin, *Kamenyi Gost* (*Stone Guest*) / Stendhal's *De l'amour* applied to Don Juanism

JUNE 25 José Zorrilla, *Don Juan Tenorio* (1844)
ASSIGNMENT: *Don Juan Tenorio*
REPORT TOPICS: Christian Dietrich Grabbe, *Don Juan and Faust* / William Moncrieff, *Giovanni in London*

JUNE 30 George Bernard Shaw, *Man and Superman* (1903)
ASSIGNMENT: *Man and Superman*
REPORT TOPICS: G. B. Shaw, *Don Giovanni Explains* / Arthur Schnitzler's *Anatol* (Viennese Don Juanism)

JULY 7 Edmond Rostand, *La Dernière nuit de Don Juan* (1921)
ASSIGNMENT: *La Dernière nuit de Don Juan*
REPORT TOPICS: A. Figueiredo, *Dom João* / Lenormand, *L'Homme et ses fantômes* _____

JULY 9 Michel de Ghelderode, *Don Juan* (1928)
ASSIGNMENT: *Don Juan*
REPORT TOPIC: Albert Camus, *Le Mythe de Sisyphe*

_____

JULY 14 Henry de Montherlant, *Don Juan* (1956)
ASSIGNMENT: *Don Juan*
REPORT TOPIC: Ramón Sender, *Don Juan en la mancebía* (1972) _____

JULY 16 Max Frisch, *Don Juan oder Die Liebe zur Geometrie* (1962)
ASSIGNMENT: *Don Juan*
Summary discussion

The student will be supplied with a bibliography for background reading on the Don Juan theme, a list of paperback editions of the titles above, and a checklist of elements of Don Juanism for analysis and study. A term paper will replace a final examination.

FIG. 14. *Syllabus of Western Heritage Theme Course: Faustus*[a]

FEB. 3 Introduction to Faust in historic and literary tradition and criticism

FEB. 10 Early Faust books on the Continent and in English tradition in sixteenth and seventeenth centuries and Marlowe's *Dr. Faustus*

FEB. 17 ASSIGNMENT: H. C. Haile, ed., *The History of Doctor Johann Faustus* (Illinois Books)

FEB. 24 Christopher Marlowe, *Doctor Faustus* (Odyssey Press)
The Faust theme in Spanish literature
ASSIGNMENT: Pedro Calderón de la Barca, *El mágico prodigioso*

MAR. 3 German popular plays of Faust: Dutch, Bohemian, and Austrian puppet plays from 1700 to 1800

[a] This syllabus was kindly supplied by Professor D. Starr Guilloton of New York University.

Faust creations of Enlightenment and Sturm und Drang periods

ASSIGNMENT: Lessing, *Faust Fragment* [Reclam: in German; or in Lessing, Collected Works: *Letters on Literature* (#17)]

MAR. 10   Goethe's *Faust I.* Adaptations in music and paintings
ASSIGNMENT: J. W. v. Goethe, *Faust, Part I* (tr. Wayne)

MAR. 17   Goethe's *Faust II.* Interpretations and criticism
ASSIGNMENT: J. W. v. Goethe, *Faust, Part II* (tr. Wayne)

MAR. 31   The reception of Goethe's *Faust* in Europe, cross-currents, influences, translations in England, etc.
ASSIGNMENT: comparative criticism (see supplementary list)

APR. 7   Romantic Fausts in England, Germany, and Russia and successors.
ASSIGNMENT: Byron, *Manfred* in *Selected Poems and Letters* (Riverside edition)
Carlyle, *Sartor Resartus*
Chamisso, *Peter Schlemihl*
Pushkin, *Faust* (fragment)

APR. 14   Faust tradition continued into the nineteenth century: themes in French, American, Spanish, and Russian literature
ASSIGNMENT: Honoré de Balzac, *Le père Goriot*; *Louis Lambert*
Nathaniel Hawthorne, *The Scarlet Letter* (Perennial Classic)
Herman Melville, *Moby Dick* (Pocket Book)
José Espronceda Delgado, *El diablo mundo*
Juan Valera, *Las ilusiones del doctor Faustino*
Dostoevsky, chapters in *The Brothers Karamazov*

APR. 21   Faust works in the early twentieth century
ASSIGNMENT: Michel de Ghelderode, *Plays*, vol. 2 (Mermaid Drama Book)
M. Bulgakov, *The Master and Margarita* (New American Library)

APR. 28   Mid-twentieth-century Faust creations in France and Germany

ASSIGNMENT: Paul Valéry, *Mon Faust*
Thomas Mann, *Dr. Faustus*

MAY 5   Thomas Mann, *Dr. Faustus*, continued. Other contemporary Faust works.
Interpretations and controversy in East and West (Brecht: Hanns Eisler, *Johann Faust*, etc.)
ASSIGNMENT: Lawrence Durrell, *An Irish Faustus*

MAY 12   Cinematic adaptations. *The Faustian. Faust III.*

IX

Interrelations of Literature

Ut pictura poesis; erit quae, si propius stes,
Te capiat magis, et quaedam, si longius abstes;
Haec amat obscurum; volet haec sub luce videri,
Judicis argutum quae non formidat acumen.
                                HORACE, *De arte poetica*

The Approach through Interrelations

One of the fascinations of literature is its gregarious nature.
Literature associates as intimately with other arts and with the
sciences as did the Muses Calliope (epic poetry), Erato (lyric
poetry), Melpomene (tragedy), and Thalia (comedy) with their
sisters Clio (history), Euterpe (music), Polyhymnia (religious
music), Terpsichore (dance), and Urania (astronomy). Literature combines with history to produce epic poetry, historical
novels, and fictionalized biography; with music to produce opera,
odes, and ballads; with religious music to create oratorios and
hymns; with dance to produce programmatic ballets; and with
astronomy to produce science fiction from Ariosto and Cyrano to
the present.

So great is the centrifugal drive of literature that the poets
have long infiltrated the camps of their traditional opponents, the
philosophers, historians, churchmen, and pedants. By the Renaissance literature had gained a foothold in all these fields, while
literature departments today are teaching the writings of masters
in these four camps, Montaigne, Machiavelli, More, and Alberti.

We have read earlier that Henry Remak defines our discipline
as the comparison of literature with others or with other spheres

of human expression. That this thrust, recognized by both reports of the ACLA Committee on Professional Standards, has gathered great force is acknowledged in a recent address by Haskell Block: "Today we are witnessing a dramatic enlargement of the plane of humanistic learning. The frontiers would seem to lie not so much at the center of the traditional subject-matters as at their boundaries, where they intersect with other disciplines. The French term, *sciences humaines*, may convey some notion of this enlargement."

ACLA Report II does, however, voice a demurrer once having approved the new cross-disciplinary trends:

> They have a salutary role to play in reorganizing our patterns of knowledge: we should be able to learn from them as well as contribute our own perspectives. But we must also be alert lest the crossing of disciplines involve a relaxing of discipline. Misty formulations, invisible comparisons, useless ingenuities, wobbly historiography plague all fields in the Humanities including our own: cross-disciplinary programs are not immune from them. As participants, we need to muster the theoretical sophistication, the methodological rigor, the peculiar awareness of historical complexities our special training affords us.

Ex rugitu leonem: One discerns the cautious tone of Committee chairman Thomas Greene.

These cautions about interrelating literature and other disciplines may be traced to Curtius and especially Cornelis de Deugd's *De Eenheid van het Comparatisme*, which worries that such studies are not literary studies and that comparative literature, already an extensive discipline, should not be extended even further, lest it become dilettantism. Like some French critics he characterizes interrelating as typical of the "American" school of comparatism. We are trifling with logic here, of course, for a study on, let us say, incest in European literature would be vastly more extensive than an interdisciplinary study on incest as adapted to romantic opera.

In the late 1960s James Thorpe edited for the Modern Language Association a most useful anthology, *Relations of Literary Study*, containing essays on the interdisciplinary contributions to literature of history, myth, biography, psychology, sociology, religion, and music. Although the prevailing context of the essays is English and American literature, they constitute a useful breviary on methodology in our field. A similar, if briefer, symposium is contained in the *YCGL* of 1975.

The study of literature is enriched and deepened by this binary approach to a large roster of other disciplines, but we should be wrong to associate this trend with only our own century. By the end of the fifteenth century, literary theorists and literary practitioners (often one and the same individual, unlike the present) preached the goal of broad learning, both from books and from experience. The Renaissance ideal of universal learning and the so-called Renaissance mind helped to achieve the rapprochement of literature with all other disciplines. Rabelais's letter of Gargantua, demanding the study of languages, letters, sciences, and social sciences, was not satire and exaggeration as some might accept it today. The contemporary treatises on poetic theory were making the same demands. In a hymn to Wisdom, Ronsard prescribes for the poet the study of natural sciences, astronomy, geography, civil law, morals, medicine, and magic, along with languages and letters.

Yet even before the Renaissance the interrelating of poetry with other disciplines was often initiated by the nonpoet. Indeed, sometimes even by the antipoet. Among the Sunday poets of antiquity one finds Plato himself, the archbaiter of poets in the *Republic*. Other philosophers of Plato's time who also indulged in poetry were Theophrastus, Herakleides, and Krates the Cynic, who wrote tragedy. In both Greece and Rome, poetry was written by historians, physicians, scientists (e.g., Lucretius), lawgivers (e.g., Solon), and statesmen. Even the soldier-statesman Julius Caesar wrote a tragedy on the Oedipus theme. In modern times the situation persists. Many scientists and social scientists have had a hand in literature. The novelist Somerset Maugham and the poet William Carlos Williams, as you will recall, were both practicing physicians. Even the prestigious French novelist Alain Robbe-Grillet is by training a specialist on tropical agronomy. Wallace Stevens wrote his sensitive poetry between his duties as vice-president of a major insurance company in Hartford, Connecticut.

Three interrelations among those most widely explored are the results of movements identified principally with three social scientists: literature and science (after Darwin), literature and psychology (after Freud), and literature and politics (after Marx). This trio not only affected literature, of course, but many areas of contemporary thought. One is tempted to add the name of Frazer, for the area of literature and mythology we have characterized as one of the earliest interrelationships explored by the European comparatists.

The Relations with Music and Cinema

Yet the most inevitable and traditional wedding of the arts is between music and literature. It is a more complicated matter than it would appear on the surface. Poetry, with its rhythmic nature, has never of course been dissociated from music. The earliest poetry was written to be sung to musical accompaniment; the very names of a large variety of poetic forms imply a musical source. While already in the ancient world some poetry was being written to be read rather than sung, later poetry and music have had a number of successful reunions, from the simplest level—for example, the Lutherans during the Reformation set Bible verses to tavern songs to arrive at their great hymns—to more sophisticated levels: the revival, after Palestrina, of the musical ode, with its splendid settings deriving from the new polyphony; the invention of opera by the humanist playwrights of Florence who mistakenly interpreted Aristotle as claiming that Greek tragedy was sung; the efforts of some symbolists after Verlaine's "Art of Poetry" to create poems approximating pure music; the attempts of the dadaists to reduce words to punctuation for bongo drum beats; T. S. Eliot's experiments in musical structure and resonance in his *Four Quartets*. After analyzing the content of all reported courses on literature and music in our comparative literature departments, Jean-Pierre Barricelli reported in the *ACLA Newsletter*, "A primary focus seems to be in relating the theory of measure and rhythm to poetic expression—what one might call the music of verse, as well as in bringing together writers and composers on the basis of those elements of musical structure which often inform literary expression (leitmotiv, idée fixe, fugue, repetition, etc.)."

The affinity of literature and music is apparent from a reading of some of the basic histories of music, such as Paul Henry Lang's *Music in the Western World* or Gustave Reese's *Music in the Renaissance*, which constantly trace parallel movements and even parallel forms between literature and music. Calvin Brown's pioneer *Music and Literature: A Comparison of the Arts* treats the influence of musical forms and techniques on poetry and conversely the influences of literature on music. The technicalities presented by this interdisciplinary study, which rule out the amateurism against which Thomas Greene warned above, may be illustrated by the book's chapter headings: "Rhythm and Pitch," "Timbre," "Harmony and Counterpoint," "Theme and Variations," "Balance and Contrast," "Repetition and Variation," "The Fugue," and "Fiction and the Leitmotiv." Brown finds in De Quincy, Browning, Whitman, D'Annunzio, and Conrad Aiken consistent endeavors to adopt musical forms and techniques. A few schools have gone so far as to teach opera libretti as literature. Many a thesis has been written on Wagner's "music drama" as literature.

Since the invention of cinema, this art has over the decades moved into an ever closer association with literature, despite attacks on Hollywood in the novels of Van Vechten, Fitzgerald, O'Flaherty, John O'Hara, Nathaniel West, and Isherwood, most of them film writers themselves. While films may be viewed historically as a development from the legitimate theater, most movies are now based on novels rather than plays. For a number of years there was a happy reciprocity of talent and ideals between the novel and film, with such novelists as Dreiser, Faulkner, Fitzgerald, and Bromfield moving to Hollywood to write films; with Moravia more recently claiming to the present writer that he finds writing for films more exciting than writing novels; with Sartre, Pasolini, and Robbe-Grillet creating fiction that lies somewhere between film scenario and novel, the *cinéroman*. The course Cinema as Literature, which Robbe-Grillet taught one semester at NYU, is offered now by both comparative literature and cinema departments.

Meanwhile, many of those who have stayed with the novel, like the Mexican Carlos Fuentes, consciously adopt cinematic techniques in their narratives. Alain Robbe-Grillet's novel *Projet pour une Révolution à New York* was surely more loaded with frozen frames, zooms, fade-outs, and other cinematic devices than any other novel written. Many writers now, hoping to see their novels bought for filming, have made their narrative more visual, episodic, and kinetic—more easily convertible. Many studies on this interrelationship have been undertaken, with the increase of departments of film in our universities and more frequent congresses on film as an art form. Literature, film, and televised film will be the object of more and more investigation and speculation in the future. The adaptability of literature to what used to be called the "silver screen" is carefully studied by Fred H. Marcus in *Film from Literature: Contrasts in Media* (Chandler). The basic study on this issue is George Bluestone's *Novels into Film* (University of California Press).

Several types of textbook are usable in a course on film and literature, although I know of no dual-media text allowing for "source study" by confronting a narrative or drama with its cinematic reworking. There are numerous scenarios worthy of being read as literature, one of the first being Sartre's *Les jeux sont faits*, which appeared in the late forties as a textbook adopted for French courses. Samuel Beckett has provided such a text in *Film, A Film Script* (Grove). New York University Press published in English the scenario of Cocteau's *Orphée*, and Penguin published the pioneer script *Sang d'un poète*. Simon and Schuster has made available for classes sixteen "Classic Film Scripts" (including *Ivan the Terrible, The Cabinet of Doctor Caligari, À nous la liberté, Un chien andalou*, etc.) and fifteen "Modern Film Scripts" (*The Third Man, Jules et Jim, Alphaville*, etc.). The converting of great narratives to film is an intriguing if complex field of endeavor, and one annual congress of Les Amis de Marcel Proust devoted two days to this specific problem. It is becoming more difficult to deny to a brilliant scenario any less a place in literature than that offered theatrical scripts. An enthusiastic younger generation of converts who, like comparatists themselves, improved their language facility by seeing undubbed all the greatest foreign films, are easily convinced that Sergei Eisenstein's *Ivan the Terrible* is much closer to Shakespeare's *Lear* than is any hero of prose narrative or myth, including Saul.

Literature and the Fine Arts

The special sibling relationship of literature to the fine arts was already apparent to the ancient Greeks. It was Simonides who first defined painting as "silent poesy" and poetry itself as "spoken painting." By the sixth century B.C. the painters were transferring dramatic scenes from the *Iliad* and *Odyssey* to walls and vases. Unknowingly Horace contributed a slogan to the eternal confrontation of poetry in his epistle to the Pisos (see incipit lines above). These verses paralleling the two major arts were picked up, in and out of context, and by the Renaissance and age of neoclassicism theorists were pointing out all sorts of parallels between poetry and the visual arts. In the celebrated words of the painter-theorist Giovan Paolo Lomazzo, poetry and painting are sister arts. "For we see that Leonardo da Vinci has expressed the movement and decorousness of Homer, Michelangelo the deep obscurity of Dante, Raphael the pure majesty of Petrarch, Titian the variety of Ariosto, etc." Shakespeare added to the paragon of the arts when his painter in *Timon of Athens*, hearing a philosophical lesson on the vicissitudes of fortune declaimed in verse, cries out:

> A thousand paintings I can show
> That shall demonstrate these quick blows of Fortune's
> More pregnantly than words . . .

Fine arts continued to inspire great literature in various ways. In Hawthorne's *Marble Faun* a statue allegedly by Praxiteles prefigures the development of one of the book's principal characters (named Donatello). Vermeer's *View of Delft* teaches to Bergotte—too late—in Proust's *La Prisonnière* the values of highlighting in painting. An ancient torso from Miletus in the Louvre inspired Rilke to write an imaginative sonnet, and the *Saltimbanques* of Picasso to undertake his fifth "Duino Elegy." Often it is the poem that inspires a work of art, a notable case being Politian's "Stanzas for the Joust," which led Botticelli to execute his famous *Birth of Venus* (known affectionately to college students as *Venus on the Half-Shell*). The romantic painters plundered the great authors before them; Blake created his own impressions of scenes from the Bible, Dante, and Milton. Delacroix, a poet himself, borrowed heavily from Dante, Shakespeare, Cervantes, Walter Scott, and Goethe in his paintings and drawings. Some poets felt that they were working in the same media as artists. Stefan George wove "tapestries," Rubén Darío struck "medallions," Ezra Pound painted "portraits," and Robert Penn Warren engraved "vignettes." The paragon of writer and artist becomes absolute in the case of the Apollo-Apelles like Michelangelo, Raphael, Blake, Pushkin, Gogol, Thackeray, Cocteau, Degas, Lorca, Valéry, and so many others.

One fruitful field of investigation is the common development of art and literature through the successive aesthetic movements in Europe from humanism to Dada. There is a constant parallel of the evolving theory. Thus, shortly after the neoclassicist Boileau has demanded of the writer in his *ars poetica*, "Avant donc que d'écrire, apprenez à penser," Coypel, the theoretician of the newly founded Academy of Painting and Sculpture, counsels in his *ars pictoria*: "Avant donc que de peindre, apprenez à penser." The realist Degas was the appropriate painter to illustrate the sweatshop scene from Zola's *Dram Shop*. Wallace Stevens' *Man with the Blue Guitar* weds his talent as a postsymbolist to that of Picasso in the latter's postimpressionist period. However, by the time Picasso has done his semicubist *Guernica*, he influences the surrealist poet Éluard to adopt an equally fragmentary kind of expression in his poem on the bombardment of that victimized town in the Pyrenees.

Another field of research is the multitude of novels centered on art or artists. Among the more successful are Hawthorne's *Marble Faun*, Balzac's *The Unknown Masterpiece*, Tieck's *Sternbald's Wandering*, Thackeray's *Newcomes*, The Goncourts' *Manette Salomon*, Zola's *L'Œuvre*, Cary's *Horse's Mouth*, Maugham's *Moon and Sixpence*, Wilde's *Dorian Gray*, and Unamuno's *Abel Sánchez*. Sometimes, unfortunately, the novelist never comes to grips with the problems or issues involved in the art he presumes to treat. Thackeray, although he had himself studied painting, does not exploit the rich possibilities of the creation of art in his feuilleton-novel about Clive Newcome. On the other hand, when Proust introduces the painter Elstir in his saga, everything we are told of Elstir situates him squarely in the impressionist and postimpressionist movement.

The fine arts thus serve as a very real seasoning for the study of literature. Haskell Block has written, "It would be easy to dwell on the dangers of amateurism—the literary scholar equipped with a slide projector is no match for the trained art historian; yet, there is no reason why scholars may not in time develop a high degree of competence in related disciplines." There are challenging methodological problems, of course. Helmut Hatzfeld has enumerated the following areas of investigation: history of ideas, cultural psychology, the problem of the generation, literary or artistic schools, and the network of individual, epochal, or national stylistic elements. Another question that must be answered prior to the course on literature and art is one of definition. Munro in his *Interrelations of the Arts* lists a hundred currently accepted forms of the fine arts. Even the definition of literature is not firmly fixed in an age when books are being replaced by film and television scripts, talking records and tapes, propaganda, public relations, and advertising in book form.

Nevertheless, as Ulrich Weisstein reminds us, J.-F. Sobry's *Cours de peinture et littérature comparées* of 1810 complains that the relations of literature and painting "remain scarcely explored. France has made the study of them a branch of aesthetics and smothers it with abstractions." This danger still exists, for just as some schools of criticism exile the textual *morceau*, so can aesthetics become so self-involved as to exile the painted canvas. A graduate student recently designed a course syllabus on literature and art in which no provision was made for the student to see reproductions of pictures and statuary or to read a single page of literary text. The classes and assignments were limited to discussions of aesthetic movements. This writer's solution in a course given biennially for twenty years is to assign simultaneously basic texts on evolving literary and art theory chronologically from the ancient Greeks to the present. During each class some thirty slides are projected. It is explained how each slide fits into its chronological aesthetic movement. As the slide is on the screen, the instructor reads a pertinent text which in itself also illustrates that movement. Thus, while the slide of Girodet-Triason's *Enterrement d'Atala* is on the screen, the corresponding paragraph by Chateaubriand is read, interrupted by comments on the common elements of romanticism that the painting shares with the novel. The same procedure follows projection of Degas's

Les repasseuses to the reading of the sweatshop scene of the *Assommoir*, both equally powerful in their realism. So rich and abundant is the material that there is no time for class reports, although class comments are solicited. Sometimes the emphasis is not to stress the common aesthetic character of text and slide, but to explore other areas of the comparison, or what Renaissance theorists called the *paragone*. Thus, while Breughel's *Return from the Hunt* is on the screen, students hear read poems in two or more languages that explicate the work (including our own Joseph Langland, William Carlos Williams, or Berryman) and evaluate each poet's success in penetrating the meaning and spirit of the painting. In the case of the poet-artists, one looks for keys to the painting or sculpture in the poetry itself, just as two poetic imprecations to Christ in Michelangelo's *Rime* explain auto-biographically the wrath and upraised arm of the Christus Iudex in the *Giudizio Universale*. The students must write a final term paper and find twenty such interrelationships of their own (see Fig. 15), which I obviously add with gratitude to my collection of over two thousand. Sometimes, five years after the course, a student will mail from afar a newly discovered parallel, attesting to a lasting consciousness of this challenging interrelationship.

FIG. 15. *Sample of Interrelation of Literature and Art*

ART: Velázquez, *The Surrender of Breda* (Prado Museum) (1639–41)
LIT:　Faria y Sousa, "Soneto a Diego de Velázquez" (1646)
　　Category: I-A
　　This painting pictures the end of the Spanish siege of the city of Breda in the Lowlands on 5 June 1625. The siege has lasted eight months. Philip II's continuous troubles with the Flemish and Dutch populations in that territory, especially with the Protestants, had drained the Spanish treasury. As seen in the painting, the Spanish commander (he was actually the Genoese captain Spinola) allowed his defeated rival, Justin of Nassau, to march out with his troops for a formal surrender. This painting was ordered by Philip IV. It is also known as *Las Lanzas* (The Lances).
　　It was executed in 1639 or 1641. "The artist has massed clear, warm colors and varying textures against cool blue-greens with a decorative, tapestry-like effect," as one art historian puts it. In the dense organization Velázquez has not forgotten to include one of his favorite broad horses.
　　Faria y Sousa commemorates both the incident and the painting in

a sonnet rich with meaning, even though it is not familiar enough to appear in the anthologies of Spanish poetry. Two decades after the victory and roughly six years after the execution of the painting, the poet points out the continuing meaning of the victory in Catholic Spain. His sonnet reads:

> Copiaste a España invicta recogiendo
> A Breda, con pinceles tan subidos,
> Que con los brazos de piedad tendidos,
> Venciste al fin: parece está diciendo.
> Los ojos cuando menos, presumiendo
> Están que da cuidado a los oídos;
> y estos sospechan, de esos suspendidos
> Que el oficio de oír está diciendo.
> El Júpiter hispano en acción propia
> Que de infanda invasión la Iglesia libre
> En este hablar visible (o Diego) copia.
> Palas le dé los rayos, El los vibre.
> Y al oír su rumor, y ver tu copia
> Gima el Rin, tema el Indo, aplauda el Tibre.

(Source: Miguel Herrero García, *Contribución de la literatura a la historia del arte*, Madrid, 1943, p. 41.)

The importance of this sonnet is that it contains not only a statement of the importance of Spinola's victory (that he was an Italian is conveniently forgotten), but that there is an explicit explication of the *ut pictura poesis* theme.

The historical message is that Spain alone is the defender of the Church Militant. The German Protestants along the Rhine are told to moan over this proof of Spanish might; Rome on the Tiber should applaud; the land of the Indus is to fear. There is a curious classical veneer to this intensely Catholic poem in that Pallas and Jupiter are on the side of Spain.

The panegyric to Velázquez is strongly stated. His style is abundant (*copia*). The painting, says the poet, seems to be speaking its message. The eyes seem to give way to the ears, and painting is more than silent poetry, as Simonides had put it.

Another interrelationship has been convincingly presented by Professor Hesse in *Hispania* (1952). He suggests that Calderón's play *El sitio de Breda*, also undertaken at the order of Philip iv, strongly influenced Velázquez. He points out that the surrender scene is vividly similar in both play and painting, and adduces several verses to support his claim. Since the drama (1625) preceded the painting by ten years, Hesse is able to conclude that "it is virtually beyond doubt that Velásquez was acquainted with Calderón's text."

Literature and Psychology

Freudian psychology is a relatively recent science, its founder having died in 1939. Literature of the West goes back to the sixth century B.C., but psychology and literature have been inevitably interrelated from the outset. Writers have been fascinated by the stirrings of man's psyche ever since the sibling rivalry of the sons of Oedipus, since the sadism of Odysseus on his return to Ithaca, since the infanticide of the psychotic Medea. Socrates had the same suspicions of creative writers as did Freud, who found them neurotics unable to come to terms with reality and inclined to "mould their fantasies into a new reality." Psychology has found that its very existence was sustained by the vast body of Western literature. The characteristics or crises of archetypes in Greek literature gave it the very names it needed to describe types or complexes: Prometheus, Uranus, Electra, Narcissus, and so on. Literature gave it recognizable material for comparison and stereotyping.

It might not be far from the truth to declare that until the coming of age of this science, writers themselves were unknowingly mankind's psychologists. Often when this idea has been alleged, someone has claimed that writers described psychological types correctly but without really understanding them scientifically. Yet when the modern psychologist studies the great literary prototypes, he usually finds an accurate if intuitive analysis of motivations, behavioral responses, and so on. Whatever questions are raised about Hamlet's indecisions, delays, sexuality, and the rest, Shakespeare's psychology comes off unassailed. The English psychologist F. L. Lucas concedes, "Modern psychology may know more of Madame Bovary than Flaubert knew himself, more of Hedda Gabler than Ibsen; but it also reveals how amazingly true the intuitions of these writers were; and with such artistry its own case histories cannot compete."

The services of literature and psychology are reciprocated, for psychology can aid considerably in clarifying fiction, poetry, and drama. Vernon Hall observes that the "insights of Dostoyevsky, for instance, anticipated so many of Freud's that one could almost construct Freudian theories from this one novelist alone." The same can be said for Shakespeare, of course. Psychology affords challenging theories for the understanding of the complex figure of Hamlet. Ernest Jones explains in a familiar passage why the prince failed to kill Claudius when he found him defenseless at prayer, since he had every intention of doing so. Hamlet, writes Jones, cannot, for he unconsciously identifies himself with Claudius. Claudius has been able to fulfill the most subconscious of desires within Hamlet: he has killed Hamlet's father and taken his mother to bed, two stock velleities of the Oedipus complex. Thus in killing Claudius Hamlet would be psychically killing himself.

In Stallknecht and Frenz's *Comparative Literature* Leon Edel supports this view of the interrelationship:

> Literature and psychology—and in particular psychoanalysis—have come to recognize in our century that they stand on common ground. Both are concerned with human motivations and behavior and with man's capacity to create and use symbols. In this process, both have become involved in the study of the subjective side of man. With the incorporation of psychoanalysis into psychology, that is the study of the unconscious from the symbols it projects, literature has found itself calling increasingly upon the knowledge derived from Freud's explorations of the psyche. . . .

Indeed, the case studies of not only Freud, but latterly Jung and Rank allow one to analyze retroactively such types as Oedipus, Faust, or Don Juan. To measure the considerable "psychological criticism" that mushroomed since Freud, one would do well to read Professor Hoffman's *Freudianism and the Literary Mind* and Lucas' *Literature and Psychology.*

In the MLA publication *Relations of Literary Study*, mentioned earlier, Frederick Crews discusses particularly the relationship of psychoanalysis. Despite its "weaker empirical credentials," he feels that psychoanalysis has more seriously altered our way of reading literature than have physiological psychology, cognition psychology, or especially Gestalt psychology, which "has told us virtually nothing about literature." He agrees that there are many objections to psychoanalysis. It should

not be called a science at all, but rather a technique of therapy or
a system of metaphors. The psychoanalytic view of the writer as a
neurotic is presumptuous and condescending. Psychoanalytic
criticism neglects literary form and supposes an unconscious
intention on the part of the author. It is unable to evaluate
(psychoanalyze) dead writers. It identifies unconscious content
with literary value. He concludes on a tone of moderation:
"While psychoanalytic ideas have permeated our intellectual life,
attempts at relating psychoanalysis to literature in a programmatic way have been handicapped by the need for cumbersome
explanations of theory and for rapid passage from one example to
the next. Our most respected critics have neither ignored
Freudianism nor made it a battle-cry." Veteran admirers of Professor Crews's satires on critical battle cries, *The Pooh Perplex*,
centered on A. A. Milne's tales for children, will never forget the
article by Karl Anschauung, M.D., "one of the last survivors of
Freud's original circle of Viennese followers," contained therein.
It is entitled "A. A. Milne's Honey-Balloon-Pit-Gun-Tail-Bathtub-
complex," and is an astonishing example of psychoanalytic literary analysis:

> A. A. Milne's case is a relatively simple one of advanced animal-
> phobia and obsessional defense, somewhat complicated it is true
> by anal-sadistic and oral-helpful phantasies, skoptophilia and
> secondary exhibitionism, latently homosexual trends in identifica-
> tion with the mother, severe castration anxiety and compensatory
> assertiveness, and persistence of infantile misconstructions of
> birth, intercourse, and excretion. Doubtless when he appears in
> my office Milne's further little symptoms will reveal, such as nail-
> biting, fascination with the analyst's foot, excessive squabbling
> over fees *und so weiter.*

The greatest satire on psychoanalysis, however, is found in Italo
Svevo's *Coscienza di Zeno* (English translation, *The Confessions
of Zeno*) in the form of an autobiography written at the insistence
of Zeno's doctor-analyst. Zeno is ridden with neuroses, with
fetishes, with Oedipal resentment of his father, with an inferiority
complex, etc. He plays a cat-and-mouse game with his analyst,
prevaricating during his psychiatric interviews, and is obviously
one of psychoanalysis' greatest failures. Written in 1923, this is

the first psychoanalytical novel in the accepted sense, and surely the most amusing. For those unfamiliar with Svevo, it must be added that he is now recognized as the prototype of Leopold Bloom in his friend Joyce's *Ulysses*.

Literature and Politics

The inevitable interrelations, even interactions, between literature and politics are attested, among so many evidences, by the long list of creative writers imprisoned, exiled, destituted, or censured by their governments. Examples abound from past to present. Plato fled Athens as a political refugee. Socrates, still protesting after the age of seventy that he was not a political activist, was condemned to death for corrupting the youth of Athens by his ideas. Horace, after seeing his family property confiscated as a punishment for his political and military activity, could well express "grave concern" over the foundering of the ship of state. Machiavelli was "broken" by the Medici rulers of Florence. Voltaire, already having sampled life in the Bastille prison, cautiously moved closer to the border between France and Switzerland. Pushkin was exiled for his liberal words to the South of Russia during 1820 and 1824. Silone fled from Italian fascism, while Bertolt Brecht safely escaped from the Germany of Hitler. Yevgenyi Yevtushenko was harassed for his poem "Babii Yar," deploring persecution of Jews, while his fellow-poet Andrei Vosnesensky summarized persecution of writers in a famous poem: "Dear Russian Poesy, how do you do? Would you prefer a knife, or a .22?". Indices of forbidden books are drawn up, whether it be the famous Index of 1564 or the blacklist compiled by the military dictators of Greece in 1968, forbidding the playing or printing of Aristophanes or Sophocles.

If politics has thus shaped the course of Western literature, prose, poetry, and drama have exercised a reciprocal influence on politics. The epic poem has been the most effective armament. Epics, from Homer's to Voltaire's, created the heroes and myths on which nationalism must rely. The stanzas of an early version of the *Song of Roland* were sung to whip up a battle spirit among William the Conqueror's troops about to invade England in 1066. The role of literature in this century's three-sided struggle for men's minds has offered an unusual spectacle. Communism and fascism controlled literature totally. In *Revolution in Writing* C. D. Lewis wrote typically, "Poetry is of its nature more personal than 'straight' propaganda: the latter is heavy artillery, the former is hand-to-hand fighting."

Without the space here to deal adequately with this vast topic, let us note that the interrelationship of literature and politics is of interest at two levels. A work of literature, even a humble one such as *Uncle Tom's Cabin,* may actually change national attitudes or even policy. At another level, a work like Graham Greene's *Quiet American* merely borrows or exploits the subject matter of politics to express a bias or viewpoint without changing the political climate. For this reason *The Ugly American,* unlike *The Quiet American*—both treating of Americans enmeshed in Southeast Asian politics and local warfare—created a much deeper impact on American thinking at its time, even while admittedly a novel of much less literary skill. Novels, plays, and even poetry (see p. 46) will either utilize politics merely as a theme or will seek the more difficult goal of influencing the political climate or even arousing the populace. Even literary criticism, as we observe from the writings of Gorki, Lukács, Sartre, and others will try to interpret or manipulate creative literature to political ends. None of course exceeds the Chinese in such interpretation, voiced in their columns of "criticism and repudiation" (see p. 37).

Literature and Theology

Before this chapter on interrelations is concluded, perhaps a few words might be said on theology and literature. This is a special case since literature seems to have grown out of religion and in a sense can never be totally separated from it. In many literatures of the world, as Edward Dimock alleges for the Indo-Pakistan subcontinent, it was until recently difficult to distinguish literature from religious documentation. Archaic tragedies were based on the ritual sacrifices to a god. In the Homeric epics gods share the stage with men. The Bible itself has for centuries been studied as literature and has given writers and painters their greatest fund of myth and imagery. Although twentieth-century literature often seems as remote as possible from religion, newly developed courses on literature and theology are now offered in several American seminaries and universities. One theologian involved in such a program claims that much of modern literature is a

> repository of an enormously profound insight into what it means to be human. It is through the study of literature that some of the most genuine and revealing points of contact between religion and art are likely to be found in our time. Thus, new meanings are found in seemingly unlikely works, such as Faulkner's *The Sound and the Fury*, superficially a sordid family chronicle narrated in part by an idiot, Benjy.

To a theologian at the University of Chicago, there is behind the novel's secular facade "a poetic expression of what theology called *kairos*—the divine gift of the time span in which man exists on earth." (At the time of the narration, Benjy is thirty-three years old, the age of Christ at the Crucifixion.) The journal *Comparative Literature Studies* has published issues devoted to literature and religion, as well as literature and philosophy and literature and art.

Other rewarding interrelationships of literature that we may merely mention in conclusion are with history, biography, sociology, anthropology, law (see p. 200), and dance. These interrelationships are often established with a single national literature, as the ACLA Report II reminds us. It is when the confrontation includes two or more literatures that it is truly enriched, and only then defined as comparative literature.

FIG. 16. *Syllabus of Western Heritage Interdisciplinary Course:*
Literature and Art

I. First Semester

OCT. 2   Introductory Lecture

OCT. 9   Prehistoric, Egyptian, and Hebrew Literature and Art (slides)
         READ: Adolf Erman, *The Ancient Egyptians: A Source Book of Their Writings* (Harper Torchbook)

OCT. 16   Greek, Etruscan, and Roman Literature and Art (slides)

READ: The *Poetics* of Aristotle, Longinus, and Horace (Penguin paperback)

OCT. 23   Medieval Literature and Art, including Early Christian and Byzantine (slides)
READ: Émile Mâle, *The Gothic Image* (Harper paperback)
(Giotto, Domenico di Michelino, Lorenzetti, Fouquet, Selestat, Martini, etc.)

OCT. 30   The Counter-Renaissance, with Its Medieval Survivals (slides)
READ: R. J. Clements, *The Peregrine Muse*, chap. I: "The Identity of Literary and Artistic Theory in the Renaissance." Use library copy.
(Breughel, Donatello, Mantegna, Murillo, Del Sarto, Juanes, Grunewald, Bosch, etc.)

NOV. 6   Renaissance Literature and Art: High Renaissance and Humanism (slides)
READ: J. A. Symonds, *Renaissance in Italy*, "The Revival of Learning" and "The Fine Arts." Use library copy or Peter Smith reprint
(Raphael, Botticelli, Veronese, Titian, Cranach, Pilon, Velázquez, Clouet, etc.)

NOV. 13   Reformational and Counter-Reformational Literature and Art (slides)
READ: J. A. Symonds, *Renaissance in Italy*, "The Catholic Reaction."
(Veronese, Berruguete, Brunelleschi, Holbein, Leonardo, Fra Angelico, Schongauer, etc.)

NOV. 20   Michelangelo's Poetry and Art (slides)
READ: R. J. Clements, *The Poetry of Michelangelo* (Gotham Library paperback)
(Opera omnia)

NOV. 27   Mannerism in Literature and Art (slides)
READ: John Shearman, *Mannerism* (Penguin Illustrated paperback)
(Cellini, Pontormo, Parmigianino, School of Fontainebleau, Wtewael, Leal, etc.)

DEC. 4   Baroque Literature and Art (slides)
READ: H. B. Segel, *The Baroque Poem* (Dutton paperback)

(El Greco, Veronese, Bernini, Tintoretto, Tiepolo, Palladio, Rembrandt, etc.)

DEC. 11   Neoclassicism in Literature and Art (slides)
READ: Gilbert Highet, *The Classical Tradition* (Oxford paperback)
(Rigault, Champaigne, Le Nôtre, Poussin, Wren, Le Nain, Lorrain, Cuyp, etc.)

DEC. 18   Literature and Art of Late Classicism and the Enlightenment (slides)
READ: G. E. Lessing, *Laocoon* (Bobbs-Merrill paperback)
(Watteau, Boucher, Pannini, Piranesi, Ingres, David, Fragonard, Hogarth, Prudhon, Tiepolo, etc.)

JAN. 8   Reading Period

1. The student may choose between writing a term paper on some interrelationship of literature and art (no restriction on period), due by noon of the date assigned for the final examination, or taking a final examination in the course.

2. A list of twenty interrelationships between literature and art is due by the last day of the semester, to be submitted to the departmental office. Each interrelationship must be entered on a separate sheet and conform strictly to the model sheet provided.

II. Second Semester

FEB. 7   Recapitulation of First Semester, Introduction to Second Semester

FEB. 14   Romanticism (Sentimental and Aesthetic) (slides)
READ: Irving Babbitt, *Rousseau and Romanticism* (Meridian paperback)
(Delacroix, Géricault, Girodet-Triason, Turner, Fuseli, Gros, Goya, Hicks, etc.)

FEB. 21   Romanticism (Social and Political) (slides)
READ: C. M. Bowra, *The Romantic Image* (Galaxy paperback)
(Same as above)

FEB. 28   Blake, Rossetti, and the Pre-Raphaelites (slides)
READ: *The Poetical Works of Blake* (Oxford Standard Authors paperback) (Blake, Rossetti, Holman Hunt, Burne-Jones, Deverell)

MAR. 7   Realism and Naturalism (slides)
READ: René Dumesnil, *Le Réalisme et le naturalisme* (Paris, 1955)
(Daumier, Courbet, Goya, Chasseriau, Rodin, Ryder, Millet, Degas, Repin, etc.)

MAR. 14   Nineteenth-Century Greek Revival and the Victorians (slides)
READ: Stephen Larabee, *English Bards and Grecian Marbles*
(Elgin Marbles controversy, Latour, Whistler, Sargent, Beardsley, etc.)

MAR. 21   Symbolism and Impressionism (slides)
READ: Arthur Symons, *The Symbolist Movement in Literature* (Dutton paperback)
(Manet, Monet, Pissarro, Sisley, Degas, Renoir, Morisot, Moreau, Valéry, etc.)

APR. 4   Postimpressionism (slides)
READ: Leo Tolstoy, *What Is Art?*
(Cézanne, Gauguin, Van Gogh, Seurat, Toulouse-Lautrec, Matisse, Rouault, etc.)

APR. 11   Surrealism and Dada (slides)
READ: Anna Balakian, *Surrealism, Road to the Absolute* (Dutton, 1970)
(Mondrian, Klee, Picasso, Duchamp, Schwitters, Arp, Ernst, Di Chirico, Lorca, Dalí, etc.)

APR. 18   Literature, Art, and Psychology (slides)
READ: Leon Edel, *The Modern Psychological Novel* (Evergreen paperback)
(Ensor, Masson, Munch, Dalí, Picabia, Magritte, Lorca, Picasso, Redon, Bacon, etc.)

MAY 2   Literature, Art, and Politics (slides)
READ: F. D. Klingender, *Marxism and Modern Art* (London, 1943)
(Diego Rivera, Grant Wood, Chagall, Beckmann, Ben Shahn, Curry, Serov, etc.)

MAY 9   Discussion of Novels Centered on Art and Artists
ASSIGNMENT: Prepare five-minute statement on one such novel.

MAY 16   Conclusion and Summary of Course

FIG. 17. *Syllabus of Western Heritage Interdisciplinary Course:*
Literature and Law. Professors London and Clements.

TEXTBOOK: Ephraim London, *The World of Law: Literature and Law*
(vol. I); *The Law as Literature* (vol. II). Reading assignments, unless
otherwise specified, will be from the anthology. Books chosen for class
reports are all available in paperback editions. Class reports on novels
will be shared by two literature and two law students. Assignments
and recommended reading will be furnished in advance of each lecture.

JUNE 15   Introduction to Course: Concepts of Law
           A discussion of the concepts of law of the major writers
           on jurisprudence

JUNE 18   Concepts of Law (continued)
           Discussion of theories of law advanced in the writings of
           major legal philosophers and discussion of assigned
           reading

JUNE 22   Canon Law
           Mediaeval literature sustaining Canon Law and the
           Renaissance literature attacking it. The Index of For-
           bidden Books. Dante and Rabelais on law. Satires on
           law in the Renaissance
           CLASS REPORT: Dostoevsky, *Crime and Punishment*

JUNE 25   Conflicts between Law and Literature
           Law's regulation of literature; the law of privacy; libel;
           obscenity. Discussion of major cases and their effects
           on literature

JUNE 29   Literature Serving the Ends of Law
           Hugo, Dickens, Anatole France, Zola. Discussion of
           assigned texts

JULY 1   The Raw Material and the Work of Art
           Law as a theme of literature; the *Yellow Book* and
           Browning's *The Ring and the Book*; Shaw's *Saint Joan*
           and *The Trial of St. Joan.*
           CLASS REPORT: Kafka, *The Trial* (Urteil)

JULY 6   The Raw Material and the Work of Art
           The Loeb-Leopold case and *Compulsion*; *The Black-*
           board Jungle; *The Paper Dragon*

JULY 8   Law as a Theme of Literature
           Sacco and Vanzetti case, Dos Passos, Upton Sinclair,

Robert Sherwood, Edna St. Vincent Millay, European
dramatists
CLASS REPORT: Dreiser, *An American Tragedy*

JULY 13   Law as the Theme of Literature
Vassili Vassilikos, Z; Faulkner, *Intruder in the Dust*

JULY 15   Legal Writing as Literature
Sheridan's defense against the charge of bribery; speeches
on the charges against Hastings. Discussion of assignments
CLASS REPORT: Camus, *L'Étranger*

JULY 20   Great Reporting of Trials and Legal Issues
Discussion of assigned reading
CLASS DISCUSSION: Harper Lee, *To Kill a Mockingbird*

JULY 22   Summation

There will be no final examination. Grades will be determined largely
by term papers. Term papers will discuss issues in three great novels
not included in the course. Term papers are due at the end of the sixth
week of the course.

Class discussions are not to exceed 25 minutes. Students should de-
cide with fellow participant(s) what major literary *and* legal issues are
to be covered in that time.

X

Literary History and Criticism

Es ist das Herz, das den Kritiker macht, nicht die Nase.
MAX MÜLLER

Literary History and Literary Criticism

Both literary history and literary criticism have ancient origins. Literary history and philology in antiquity met its greatest challenge in establishing the texts of the Old and New Testaments from the thousands of variant manuscripts. The confused state of the Septuagint texts and the contradictory passages of the New Testament (does Romans v.1 read "We have peace with God" or "Let us have peace with God"?) have kept philologists, linguists, and literary historians persevering until the present day. Dealing with ancient Hebrew, the linguists had to cope with an alphabet of consonants only. Dealing with hierarchical texts, the historians were not asked to give critical evaluation of their content. On the other hand, Aristotle, approaching drama and epic as a scientist and logician, did occasionally slip into literary appraisal or value judgment as, for example, when he praised Homer (e.g., that the Homeric poems surpass all others in diction, thought, scenes of suffering, and so on), not realizing that by the Renaissance literary critics would convert his *Poetics* and the very mention of his name into mechanisms of literary censure. In his *Republic*, the *Ion*, the *Phaedrus*, and elsewhere Plato became one of history's most dogmatic assailants of poetry, a literary critic with dubious criteria of judgment.

In the Renaissance Erasmus and the humanists indulged in literary evaluations of ancient and contemporary writers, but most of them were more active in classifying and analyzing genres and movements, discovering and establishing texts, translating, writing commentaries, and disseminating literature through the new medium of printing. The bases for philological study of literature were laid, congenial to such later refinements as the scientism of Taine, the tracing of influences (see Ch. vii), the textual explications of Lanson and the German school, and the history of ideas after Lovejoy. A vigorous literary criticism and vituperation existed during the Renaissance, mainly among the writers themselves: Scaliger and Rabelais, Ronsard and Saint-Gelays, Marston and Nash, and the other "gladiators," as they have been called.

Around the beginning of the present century, the emphasis in American and European graduate schools was upon literary history and analysis, literary theory, and philology more than criticism. The titles of the new literary journals of that period frequently featured the word "philology," as though equatable with literary history. A major change came in the 1940s with the popularity of the so-called New Criticism, with its emphasis on the poem (or prose) itself, originating in England but sweeping quickly across American college campuses. It deemphasized the author, who in his poetry was referred to merely as the persona. From this period graduate professors and students began to seek enlarged bases for literary judgments in Marxism, Freudianism, Darwinism, structural linguistics, Jungian archetypal criticism, myth and symbolism, phenomenology, existentialism, semiotics, aesthetic reception, and of course social *engagement* or commitment, with poets and other writers, as Corstius puts it, crowding into London's Albert Hall, Greenwich Village, and Moscow squares and crying out against their elders' modes of life and values. With the emphasis now on criticism, many professors coveted the title of critic rather than of scholar. Newspapers and journals now habitually identified their book reviewers as critics. Few had the modesty of the veteran book reviewer Walt Whitman, who questioned the value of his reviews and shrugged, "I'm a hell of a critic." In the words of Professor Mustanoja of Helsinki some academic critics are bent on creating their own "literature about literature."

Obviously this trend is a mixed blessing. No one, of course, wishes our professors to be like the Japanese emperor's art authority, encountered by Yeats in the British Museum, who knew everything about art except what he liked. Despite the polemics of some of their proponents, the widening of the contexts of literary study enumerated in the preceding paragraph has surely been beneficial as well as stimulating. A new development, and probably a fortunate one for graduate students, is the broadening of thesis topics to include writers still living. There is no reason why a doctoral thesis on living poets or novelists is not so worthy of a degree as an annotated edition of the Greek poetry of Theophylactus Simocatta or an annotated bibliography on, let us say, the Querelle des Anciens et des Modernes. Stressing the positive contribution of these twentieth-century critical movements, we must admit that the focus of the New Critics and the explicators on the "poem itself" was a welcome one coming after the nineteenth-century emphasis on biography and milieu. To appreciate the rebellious poems of Dowson to his Cynara, one hardly needs to study the details of this quite banal and inconsequential liaison. There are many exceptions, however, for one cannot dismiss Michelangelo's sonnets and madrigals as mere "poems themselves," for they are the exclusive keys to many of his works of art and to his mind itself (see p. 189).

The twentieth-century critical movements sometimes divide into dissident splinter groups. For the comparatist it is interesting to note their provenience out of individual literatures: the semioticists out of French and Italian, the New Criticism out of English, *Rezeptionstheorie* out of the Germanic area, the formalists out of Russia and East Europe—and so on. As suggested earlier, comparatists should be aware of the entire gamut of them. However, in such newer trends as structuralism and semiotics, with their stimulating statistics and diagrams (see Fig. 18, which summarizes in a mathematical appendix a structural analysis of *Les Liaisons dangereuses* by Choderlos de Laclos, who is of course never mentioned in the article), there is a sustained departure away from the "text itself" (whole or fragmentary), which is indeed a departure from the study of literature itself. Some semioticians, as I have noted elsewhere, tend to view literature as a nonaesthetic "message," as do some structuralists.

FIG. 18. *Structural Diagram on* Les Liaisons dangereuses

MATHEMATICAL APPENDIX

From Christiane and Claude Allais, "A Method of Structural Analysis with an Application to *Les Liaisons dangereuses*," *Review of the International Organization for Ancient Languages by Computer*, 2 (1968), 33.

This section deals with methodological problems and it could be skipped by readers not interested in the mathematical details of the method.

From a mathematical viewpoint, the novel is represented by a $n \times p$ matrix, where n is the number of variables and p is the number of periods. The structure is defined by the $\frac{p(p-1)}{2}$ similarity coefficients between the p periods. In order to facilitate its interpretation, the table of similarity coefficients is submitted to the non metric analysis program SS A1 (Smallest Space Analysis 1). This program, devised by L. Guttman and J. Lingoes, represents the p periods by p points placed into a space of the smallest possible dimension. It requires that the distances between the points be a monotonic function of the value of the corresponding coefficients. A monotonic function means that the order of the magnitudes of the distance is the same as the order of the magnitudes of the coefficients. Therefore it is not quite true to say, as we did before in order to simplify, that distances between points are proportional to the coefficients. Let us illustrate this point by an example: the similarity coefficient between periods 1 and 32 is *.44*, and the coefficient between periods 2 and 3 is *.25*; instead of plotting the points such that the distances 1–2 and 2–3 are exactly in the ratio *.44/.25*, it is just required that distance 1–2 be larger than distance 2–3. The advantage of requiring conservation of order rather than strict proportionality is that it allows the program to put the p points in a space of fewer dimensions. In the example given the space has only two dimensions. This allows a very simple representation of the structure in a plane.

The program puts the points in a space of the smallest possible dimension. If the dimensionality is 1 or 2, the graphical representation is likely to be understood by everybody, but if it is 3 or more, most people without mathematical training are unable to visualize the graph and the main advantage of a graphical representation is lost. Two solutions are possible. Either one sets up the program so as to yield fewer dimensions, in which case the graph will only approximate the table of coefficients, or one does again the same analysis after reducing the number of periods. Since the number of periods is arbitrary, the last method is usually to be preferred. In the example, we have compromised between the two: in order to keep the number of periods equal to 10 we have settled for an approximation of the table of coefficients (Phi = .007, coefficient of alienation = .12).

A few words should be said about the coefficient of similarity. Its mathematical definition is:

$$Sjk = \frac{\displaystyle\sum_{i=1}^{n} |Vij\text{-}Vik|}{\displaystyle\sum_{max}}$$

where

Vij = value of the variable i in period j

i = 1, 2, 3, ... n

j,k = 1, 2, 3, ... p

$\sum max$ = maximum value of $\displaystyle\sum_{i=1}^{n} |Vij\text{-}Vik|$

in the novel. In other words the coefficient of similarity between two periods j,k, is the sum of the absolute differences between the value of the variables. This sum is divided by its maximum value in order to keep the value of s between 0 and 1.

Having observed the new critical experimentation of the present century, one may applaud it only if the underlying disciplines of literary history continue to be provided in our graduate schools: rigorous emphasis on languages, linguistics, bibliographical training, chronology, evidence, and the rest. It is obvious that even as we acquaint our students with the new critics and criticisms moving on and off center stage over the years, our basic obligation to teach the principles of literary history and philology remains constant. It is appropriate to conclude with a conciliatory remark made by the Danish scholar Billeskov-Jansen at the FILLM Congress back in 1963, a congress devoted precisely to the title of this section: "Whenever we read, there is an interplay of historical-philological interpretation, constructive analysis, and aesthetic evaluation. The three attitudes complement one another methodologically." At another panel of this congress Walter Silz of Columbia agreed that the historical and critical methods must be coupled "if the university study of literature is to avoid the extremes of uncritical antiquarianism and uncritical dilettantism." Our dual obligation remains clear, and it is imposed on students of national literatures as well as on comparatists.

Literary Criticism: "Substitute Muse of the Varsity"; Vogues of Criticism

The mechanisms of themes, forms, and movements provide convenient frameworks for the great literary works of all climes and ages. So also does the final "approach" of our discipline, literary theory and criticism. Criticism may be, as Stephen Spender has alleged, "the substitute muse of the varsity," but certainly the great currents of criticism flow long and wide. Just as some great books resist classification within a convenient theme, form, or movement, so also there is a disjunction between some books and given schools of criticism. We have noted elsewhere that there is little to be gained in saddling the *Shakuntala* with Aristotle's generic approach to drama. Some of the most amusing demonstrations of the inappropriate or inapplicable exercise of psychological, bardic, Marxist, Chicago-Aristotelian, sacramental, or archetypal criticism on a resistant work of literature are found in Professor Crews's *Pooh Perplex* (see above, p. 193), with its tongue-in-cheek explanation that the work "for proper elucidation requires the combined efforts of several academicians of varying critical persuasions." This satirical work illustrates three characteristics of academic literary criticism: first, that vogues of criticism come and go; second, that there is an infinite variety of critical approaches, often mutually exclusive and contradictory; and third, that some subjects (e.g., *Winnie the Pooh*) ill befit certain schools of criticism (e.g., the psychoanalytical).

Professor Guyard's pioneer little manual on our discipline notes that the French are especially addicted to evolving vogues in criticism and constantly require an *embarras de choix*. He summarizes the evolution of such emphases through the following phases:

1880–1950	Source studies; history of themes; fortunes of authors outside their native national boundaries; disinterest in comparative study of genres; determinism of Taine
1950–70	Reaction against influence study; diminishing interest in author himself; interpretations of a country through its literature

1970–present *Stoffgeschichte* (Trousson); *la poétique comparée* (Étiemble); sociology of literature (Escarpit); interrelations with music, psychology, fine arts; first- and second-person narrative; cinematic techniques; etc.

Approving the devaluation of the author's life in literary study, Guyard quotes and approves a recent thesis that began: "By a stroke of good fortune easy to appreciate, the life of Pierre Corneille is almost unknown." Should this claim be made equally for Shakespeare?

Another amusing commentary on the mutations of critical approach over the decades is that of Herbert Lindenberger in a recent article from the *Bulletin of the Association of Departments of Foreign Languages*. The ebb and flow of tastes in individual language departments correspond to generational schools of criticism. He writes:

> Knowing the cues within a single discipline also demands sensitivity to the methodological differences between generations. One must know better than to mention structuralism or drop the name of Derrida before a stranger in French who is over forty. Nor should one bring up *Rezeptionstheorie* or the study of popular culture to a stranger in German over forty. If one feels like indulging in the vocabulary of *Geistesgeschichte*, one had best do that with those who are near or past retirement.

In some circles the very word "literature" seems old-fashioned. Unlike such earlier currents as I. A. Richards' "practical criticism," in recent years Lévi-Strauss, Jakobson, Chomsky, Barthes, Benjamin, Goldmann, and Eco undercut the complete texts of literature. At the 1976 New York Comparative Literature Conference a semiotician admitted that his approach worked as well on advertising copy as literary text, and in a revelatory moment he referred to "what we used to call literature." At the 1978 FILLM Congress at Aix literature was being announced by some speakers as a message to be decoded.

One remembers that years ago entire English departments were caught up in the New Criticism, just as entire French, Italian, or German departments are now committed to semiotics. Indeed, such a departmental vogue limits the *embarras de choix* and sweeps even the unconverted into the movement, the unconverted professor and student alike, who must be ready to transform literature into diagram. On this point Lowry Nelson of Yale, in a departmental memorandum, sounded a caution:

> The breadth of the true Comparatist should reach of course to the present. Since he is committed to the whole phenomenon of literature, to exclude the present would be folly. Yet Comparative Literature must guard itself against being captured by preachers of contemporaneity or purveyors of current fashions. To bend literary study to some eccentric, all-explaining version of Freud or to the latest revival of Heidegger (as in the punning philosophizing of Derrida) is simply to parochialize literary study and to cast away its scholarly moorings. In a small graduate department any such ideological capture or preponderance would be stultifying and quickly outdated.

It is surely easier on the student who has a thesis to write to be able to select an adviser from a department with representatives of several critical persuasions. The department most unlikely to be "ideologically captured" by a single viewpoint must surely be Stanford University, where the bulletin lists courses on semiotics, on formalism and structuralism, on phenomenology in drama, on baroque stylistics, on the poem-itself textual criticism, and on *Texthermeneuthik*. It is perhaps the potential lack of unanimity among critical positions of examiners on Ph.D. examinations that leads to an unexpected, almost unbelievable situation recorded in the report of the ACLA Committee on Graduate Programs (1974): "It seems that only rarely does the examination include literary theory and literary criticism specifically."

With comparative literature students doing some course work in one or more national literature departments, however, some tend to expect that current critical vogues like *Rezeptionsästhetik* or semiotics will be found also in their comparative literature courses, even in courses on Renaissance satire or the history of tragedy. Introduced in the sixties by Robert Jauss, *Rezeptions-ästhetik* proposes that a literary text be studied primarily through the original public reaction to it. This approach would be of doubtful value in world literature courses, since the local critics' reactions to Mao Tse-tung's poetry were always enthusiastic, and in primitive times or places the readers' receptions to the *Argonautica* are now beyond assessment.

A student who has not embraced the current critical vogues must be protected from enthusiasts espousing them. One of our candidates with a classical training began to be interrogated by a French scholar at an oral examination on how to decode the message of Ovid's *Metamorphoses* and had to be rescued by the chairman of the jury. As one graduate student complained of this tendency, "Frequently a course supposedly dealing with a literary work turns out to be a course on the criticism about the work." Even vestiges of the New Criticism of the forties are occasionally resurrected by older examiners, and one can breathe more easily when the candidate recognizes an objective correlative. It is obvious that the various ages and specializations of their professors require young candidates in comparative literature to be aware of a greater number of critical approaches and their *mots clefs* than their fellow students majoring in the national literatures. This fact of academic life is amusingly pointed out in a poem that Albert Sonnenfeld of Princeton published in the *MLA Newsletter* of December, 1975. In addition to the compounding of approaches for which comparatists must be responsible, Sonnenfeld parodies the coupling of authors proposed in some of our courses and theses:

COMPARATIVE POEM

Here's to the world of comparative lit.
The students all love it, they call it "lit. crit."
They love Wellek and Warren and Harry Levin,
Horst Frenz, Baldensperger and Claudio Guillén . . .

'Cause Comparative Literature really is fun,
We compare Shakespeare with Shelley,
And Beckett with Donne.
Dante's *Inferno*
With Sartre's *Enfer*,
L'enfer, c'est les autres . . .
Who said that? Voltaire??

We read: Schlegel and Schiller and Sholokhov,
             Hamlet, Don Carlos and Raskolnikov;
             The lower mimetic invented by Frye,
             Wimsatt ever whimsical, Deleuze ever high.

             There's Hegel on Tragedy,
             Bergson on laughs,
             Segal on comedy,
             Chomsky on graphs,
             Abrams on imagery,
             Kenner on rhyme,
             Comparatists really have fun all the time!

Comparing: Chaucer with Hemingway, Blake with Flaubert,
               Frost with von Hofmannsthal, Kleist with Baudelaire:
               Musset with Nabokov, Hugo with Joyce;
               Bely with Herder and Josiah Royce.

Study the influence of: Rousseau on Petrarch, Mencken on Marx,
                            Bert Brecht on Shelley, Skylarks and sharks,
                            Boccaccio on Gorky, Corneille on O'Neill,
                            Influence studies have sex appeal.

Analyze obsessive patterns of imagery in: Dryden, Ariosto, Fontane
                                              and Yeats,
                                              Pushkin and Lermontov,
                                              and, for eye rhyme,
                                              J. Keats.
                                              Strindberg and Ibsen and
                                              Pär Lagerkvist,
                                              Rilke, Novalis, Hebbel
                                              and Liszt . . .

Identify briefly and precisely the following: Tenor and vehicle, *semio-
                                                  texte,*
                                                  Ricorsi, amor fati,
                                                  Goethe's *Urtext,*
                                                  Klassische Dämpfung,
                                                  McKeon's Idea,
                                                  Freudian cathexis,
                                                  Trembling and Fear.

Inscape geography,
And Iconography,
Objective correlative,
Categorical Imperative,
Synchronic,
Mnemonic,
Diachronic
Platonic.

Yes, Comparative Lit. really is here to stay.
Comparing St. Augustine to . . . St. Vincent . . . Millay,
Malory to Mallarmé, Plutarch to Pound,
Like the eternal return,
We drink round after round . . .

The Survey Course on Theory and Criticism

ACLA reports on both graduate and undergraduate curricula in comparative literature make it clear that the survey of literary criticism or aesthetics is a staple requirement. There are several available anthologies of *loci critici* from Aristotle to the present in satisfactory translation. In departments willing to devote two semesters to this survey, the first half normally contains texts from the fourth century B.C. to the eighteenth, or at least to Dryden, who died in 1700. Studying this long period when, in the wake of Aristotle, the principles of criticism derived from a detailed analysis of the texts themselves, it makes sense for one to integrate the reading of theoretical texts with the reading of assigned creative works. Such coupling makes it possible for the student not only to validate literature through theory, but theory through literature as well. The student continues increasing his familiarity with masterpieces of literature even as they are used as demonstrations of theory. In the Renaissance, when every critic's goal was to outdo Aristotle by writing theory, a drama, and an epic as well (Lope, Tasso, and Trissino come first to mind), one has the choice of confronting their poetic arts with either their own or another contemporary's epopeia or tragedy. Thus, Tasso's discourses on the heroic poem can be applied to his own *Gerusalemme liberata* or equally well to the *Lusíadas* of Camoëns. Lope's manual on writing plays can be used to assay one of his own hundreds of *comedias* or, leaving aside its discussion of metrics, to one of Shakespeare's tragicomedies. Thus the sequence of dual reading assignments, including paired texts of criticism and of literature, affords a wide familiarity with the coherence of theory and practice under humanism. Baroque and mannerism, coming at the end of the first semester, are more of a challenge, of course, since the only familiar treatises on baroque deal with the fine arts and mannerism's poetics have to be reconstructed out of its practices themselves.

Whereas the second semester allows for practice and theory of the more familiar movements such as romanticism, realism, and symbolism, criticism itself becomes more varied, more autonomous, and at times almost an end in itself. Some texts of criticism become accepted as creative works. Criticism allies itself with psychology, psychoanalysis, anthropology, logic, rhetoric, politics, and mythology. The first-semester pattern of dual assignments on selections of criticism and of literary texts must be abandoned because of the explosion of contemporary criticism. The comfortable Western Heritage geographical thrust of the first semester is replaced by a tide of new theory and criticism emanating from probing minds in America, Canada, Russia, Poland, Hungary, Germany (both zones), France, not to mention South America. To some extent the course must evolve into a criticism of criticism.

The inevitably differing nature and presentation of criticism in the first and second semesters of the survey is illustrated by the syllabus that follows, in use for several years at New York University. (Professors of the sequence: Clements and Balakian.)

FIG. 19. *Syllabus of Two-Semester Course on Literary Theory and Criticism*

I. First Semester

This two-semester survey will juxtapose literary theory, literary criticism, and creative literature itself from the Greco-Roman period to the present. Theory will not be considered as in a void. It will be accepted as a source for criticism, criticism being often a creative act in itself, and the validity of the theory will be constantly measured by its impact on and its relevancy to the evolving literature.

Pagination of the daily assignments in criticism is keyed to *Literary Criticism: Plato to Dryden*, edited by Allan Gilbert (hard-cover edition, American Book Company; paperback edition, Wayne State University Press).

Students are expected to read the assigned works of literature and the theory itself in the original language if the students' proficiency in that language has been certified.

SEPT. 24   Introduction. Plato on Poetry and Imitation.
            Pages in Gilbert to be read within following week: 1–62.
            Ion, Republic, Laws.

OCT. 1   Aristotle on Drama and Poetry. Longinus.
            Gilbert: 63–124; 144–98. *The Poetics. On the Sublime.*
            READ: Sophocles, *Oedipus Tyrannus.*

OCT. 8   Horace and Roman Theory.
            Gilbert: 125–43. *Poetics* or *Epistle to the Pisos.*
            READ: Vergil, *The Aeneid.*
            CLASS REPORT: Ovid's *Metamorphoses* throughout the
            centuries, a study in evolving literary tastes.

OCT. 15   Mediaeval Theories of Poetry and Allegory. Literature
            as *ancilla theologiae.* Dante, Petrarch, Boccaccio.
            Gilbert: 199–211. *Letter to Can Grande. Life of Dante.*
            READ: Dante, *The Divine Comedy.*
            CLASS REPORT: Malory, "Sir Galahad and the Holy Grail,"
            a meeting of courtly and scholastic traditions.

OCT. 22   Mediaeval Theory and Practice. The Lay Tradition.
            Satire.
            Gilbert: no assignment.
            READ: Lorris and De Meung, *Romance of the Rose.*
            CLASS REPORT: Boccaccio, *The Decameron* and the
            Church.

OCT. 29   Humanistic Theory of Epic. Tasso.
            Gilbert: 466–503. *Discourses on the Heroic Poem.*
            READ: Camoëns, *The Lusiads.*
            CLASS REPORT: Ronsard's theories on epic and his *Franciade.*

NOV. 5   Humanistic Theory of Tragedy. Giraldi Cinzio, Castelvetro.
            Gilbert: 242–62; 304–57. Preface to the *Orbecche,* and
            other texts.

READ: Shakespeare, *Julius Caesar*.
CLASS REPORT: Marlowe's tragedies in the light of humanistic theory.

NOV. 12   Humanistic Theories of Comedy. The Spanish Comedia. Comedy and Renaissance Satire. Ben Jonson, Lope de Vega, Heywood.
Gilbert: 537–39; 540–48; 559–64. *New Art of Making Comedies*, and other texts.
READ: Machiavelli, *The Mandrake* (*Mandragola*).
CLASS REPORT: Ben Jonson's theory and practice as playwright. _____

NOV. 19   Reformational and Counter-Reformational Criticism. The Index. Apologies and Defenses of Poetry. Philip Sidney.
Gilbert: 404–65. *The Defence of Poesie*.
READ: Tasso, *Gerusalemme liberata*.
CLASS REPORT: Tasso's two versions of *Gerusalemme liberata* as illustrative of the poet's dilemma during the Counter-Reformation. _____

DEC. 3   Baroque: a Theory without Treatises.
Gilbert: no assignment.
READ: Rotrou's *Saint-Genest* or Calderón's *La vida es sueño* or Klopstock's *Messias*.
CLASS REPORT: Crashaw's poetry and the influence of Saint Teresa. _____

DEC. 10   Mannerism. The Metaphysicals. Working Back toward Appropriate Theories.
Gilbert: no assignment.
READ: Giambattista Marino, *Adonis* (Cornell University Press).
CLASS REPORT: John Donne's poetry. _____
Góngora's mystical and mundane poetry as linking mannerism and baroque. _____

DEC. 17   Neoclassicism. Malherbe, Boileau, Dryden, Pope.
Gilbert: 565–95. Excerpts from Massinger, Corneille, Scudéry, and Milton.
READ: Racine, *Phèdre*.
CLASS REPORT: Dryden, *All for Love* as a neoclassical work. _____

JAN. 7   Conclusions. Decline of neoclassicism.

Paperback editions of assigned readings. All but one or two of the assigned readings are currently available in paperback editions.

Oral Class Reports. Class reports are not to exceed 20 minutes. Class reports on individual writers will relate their practice to their theories (or to contemporary theory). Reports on theorists will relate their theories to their literary practice (or to contemporary literary practice).

II. Second Semester

FEB. 5   Introduction to Literary Criticism and Theory.
            René Wellek, *Theory of Literature*: "Literary theory, criticism and literature."
            Multiplicity of classifications.

FEB. 12   From Classicism to Scientific Enlightenment.
            Henri Peyre, *What Is Classicism?*
            Paul Hazard, *The European Mind.*
            Arthur Lovejoy, *The Great Chain of Being.*
            Cf. Pope, Boileau, Diderot, Lessing, Kant.

FEB. 19   Romanticism.
            M. H. Abrams, *The Mirror and the Lamp.*
            Jacques Barzun, *Romanticism and the Modern Ego.*
            Albert Beguin, *L'Âme romantique et le rêve.*
            C. M. Bowra, *The Romantic Imagination.*
            Mario Praz, *The Romantic Agony.*
            Cf. Mme de Staël, Poe, Shelley, Hugo.

FEB. 26   Positivism and Determinism. Generic Criticism.
            Irving Babbitt, *Masters of Modern French Criticism:* chapters on Sainte-Beuve.
            Marcel Proust, *Contre Sainte-Beuve.*
            Hippolyte Taine, Introduction to *History of English Literature.*

MAR. 4   Aestheticism, Symbolism, and Decadence.
            C. M. Bowra, *The Heritage of Symbolism.*
            T. S. Eliot, *Essays.*
            Walter Pater, *Appreciations.*
            Ruth Z. Temple, *Critic's Alchemy.*
            Anna Balakian, *The Symbolist Movement: A Critical Appraisal.*
            Cf. Baudelaire, Gautier, Ruskin, Swinburne, Wilde.

MAR. 11   Realism and Naturalism.
Émile Zola, *Le Roman expérimental.*
Gyorgy Lukács, *Realism in Our Time; Studies in European Realism.*
Leon Trotsky, *Literature and Revolution.*
Cf. Harry Levin, *The Gates of Horn.*

MAR. 18   Theories of the Avant-Garde.
Ortega y Gasset, *The Dehumanization of Art.*
Renato Poggioli, *The Theory of the Avant-Garde.*
Edmund Wilson, *Axel's Castle.*
Roger Shattuck, *The Banquet Years.*
André Breton, *The First Surrealist Manifesto.*
Guillermo de la Torre, *Ultraísmo, existencialísmo, y objectivísmo en literatura.*

APR. 1   American New Criticism.
J. C. Ransom, *The New Criticism.*
Cleanth Brooks, *The Well-Wrought Urn.*
William Empson, *Seven Types of Ambiguity.*
Cf. I. A. Richards and Wimsatt.

APR. 8   Philosophical Criticism.
Jean-Paul Sartre, *What Is Literature? Situations* II.
Gaston Bachelard, *La Psychanalyse du feu* (*The Psychology of Fire*).
George Poulet, *La Poétique de l'Espace.*
Cf. Hegel, Kleist, Husserl, Merleau-Ponty.

APR. 15   Sociocriticism and Mythocriticism
Claude Lévi-Strauss, *The Savage Mind.*
Lucien Goldmann, *Pour une sociologie du roman; Le Dieu caché.*
Northrop Frye, *Fables of Identity: Studies in Poetic Mythology;* also *The Anatomy of Criticism.*
Cf. Herbert Marcuse, M. Eliade, R. Girard.

APR. 22   Structuralism and Semiotics.
R. Jakobson, *Selected Writings.*
Richard Macksey, *The Language of Criticism.*
Roland Barthes, *Le Degré Zéro de l'écriture.*
Michel Foucault, *Les Mots et les Choses.*
Cf. U. Eco, J. Derrida.

April 29, May 6, May 13: The last three sessions vary from year to year according to the most recent theoretical writings in Semiotics, Psychocriticism, Hermeneutics, and Reception-Aesthetics. Assignments currently include readings from Robert Scholes, Charles Mauron, T. Todorov, Wolfgang Iser, et al. Collateral references include J. Lacan, Wittgenstein, J. Monod, Merleau-Ponty, et al. Individual student reports also include recent books of substantive scholarship in comparative literature, analyzed from the point of view of their methodologies. (N.B.: Although the theoretical part of this syllabus is in constant flux, Professor Balakian is preparing an anthology representing those critical attitudes and methodologies that have stood the test of time.)

XI

Teaching, Textbooks, Examinations

Ein Lehrer, der das Gefühl an einem einzigen guten Gedicht
erwecken kann, leistet mehr als einer, der uns ganze Reihen unter-
geordneter Naturbildungen der Gestalt und dem Namen nach
überliefert.

GOETHE, *Die Wahlverwandtschaften*

The Comparative Literature Teacher

The qualifications of the comparative literature teacher, whose
training has been touched upon in our third chapter, may be
viewed as relative or absolute. Relatively, as Lowry Nelson
once put it, he must stand somewhere between a Sainte-Beuve
and a Meyer-Lübke, a broad generalist and a concentrating
specialist. Not everyone can be a Lermontov, of whom it was said
in nineteenth-century Russia that although they had no encyclo-
pedia like the *Britannica*, they did have Lermontov. Since the
comparatist must constantly broaden his knowledge and reading
and language skills, it is true, as we tell our new Ph.D.'s, that if
one keeps at it, one may be a comparatist by forty. Indiana is one
of the few universities that offer teaching-training courses (C-
503: Teaching Internship in Comparative Literature). There
must be others, however, for the ACLA Committee Report on
Graduate Programs (1974) lists among the "most frequent course
requirements" for both Ph.D. and M.A. the course Teaching
Literature.

Absolutely, there are some simple qualitative measurements, a
few of which have been noted in our pages on the formation of a
comparatist (see p. 65). The instructor must have an acquaint-

ance with not only the literatures on his course syllabi, but the languages they represent as well. Professors should confirm their commitment to our discipline, and reaffirm their eligibility, by knowing at least one more language than the three that all graduate departments require for the Ph.D. Since the ideal comparative literature graduate course will cover four or five literatures (see course syllabi concluding Chs. vi, vii, and viii), the instructor should have a somewhat broader knowledge of these literatures than required for the immediate course itself.

This is not the place to tarry over personality, didactic effectiveness, judgment, and the other qualities of a good teacher; these staples must be taken for granted while we emphasize the practical demands of one specific discipline. One practical question concerns the relative values of the retooled professor of English, French, or German and the new generation of comparatists whose degree is specifically in our field. With all respect for the pioneers and zealots who have done such a fine job creating comparative literature departments where none existed before, it does seem that the new generations of comparatists should henceforth have the first option of maintaining their major field as a principled, ethical, and clearly defined discipline.

It is not always possible, however, to hire trained comparatists exclusively to teach the departmental courses. When national literature professors contribute so many "manpower units" to the comparative literature department, undertaking the many "housekeeping" tasks for which they are needed (see p. 63), they have every right to assume that they will be allowed to teach an occasional course in the department. Furthermore, during periods of budgetary pressures, deans—who cannot be expected to understand the more complex and subtle problems of staffing comparative literature—may insist that instructors from the cooperative departments be hired as an economy measure—like Professor Nesposobny. In view of the close cooperation that must exist between comparative literature and the national literature departments—a theme emphatically present in both reports of the ACLA Committee on Professional Standards—perhaps a quarter or a third of comparative literature instructors might well be culled from the cooperating departments; but where qualified personnel is lacking, discussions should be undertaken with the cooperating department heads concerning either joint appointments or appointments of new personnel capable of teaching an occasional comparative literature course. Experience shows that the comparative literature department needs at least one "friend in need" or spokesman in each of the cooperating departments to clear up possible misunderstandings (see p. 275).

Another means that many departments have tried is group teaching of comparative literature courses. This has much in its favor, since it apparently guarantees that a course touching six literary bases will have a high degree of expertise throughout. We tried it for years at NYU. Professor Trell taught a course on the history of pastoral with seven guest lecturers. Professor Casson shared his course on tragedy with six specialists, attending each of their lectures and holding a few luncheon briefings with them lest the course represent seven differing viewpoints and cross-purposes. Both the pastoral and tragedy courses drew a large group of satisfied students. Yet eventually Casson, an accomplished linguist in any case, decided that the unity of the course as he conceived it was not coming through and henceforth gave all the lectures himself. If an instructor teaching a class involving six literatures can handle four of these languages himself, then one or two guest lecturers—not enough intrusion to undermine the unity of the course—would seem to be a reasonable concession to specialism. The major difficulty with group teaching is the lack of budgetary provision for it. It thus becomes yet another of those free services that the comparative literature department is required to ask of its next-door colleagues. Another such solution is the in-service briefing session. For undergraduate sections of world literature courses SUNY-New Paltz arranges in-service faculty seminars during which specialists on Russian, Chinese, Indian, and Japanese discuss the backgrounds of assigned texts, provide critical materials, and suggest discussion topics. This is an excellent solution where subject-specialist group teaching is not feasible.

We habitually confine our view of the professor's service to students to what happens in the classroom or during the consultation hour in the office. Yet the teacher's books and articles should be part of the students' education and intellectual formation. The threadbare epithet of "publishing scholar" is not without honor. Comparative literature especially needs publishing scholars to demonstrate the discipline's principles and potentials.

The Classroom

The teaching of comparative literature is a pleasurable and instructive privilege in any case, but increasingly so when the class is large and varied in composition. The first two ACLA reports of the Committee on Professional Standards, as we have noted elsewhere, strongly recommended small classes—reminiscent of the tutorial sessions that the more affluent universities used to feature. There is no need to advance our view once again. The fact remains clear that the limited knowledge of many literatures, and indeed languages, found among students in a small class is less desirable than the many languages and bodies of literature known to a large cosmopolitan class in comparative literature. Many advanced European students in America feel that it is illogical to earn a doctorate in French, German, or Italian in the United States and then return home to France, Germany, or Italy to find a teaching job. Since the United States is now the major exponent of comparatism, these foreign students take their degrees with us and populate our classrooms—adding a considerable dimension of enrichment. They come from all parts of the world. Stated elsewhere (p. 25) is the variety of these nationalities—European, Asian, and African—contributing an international scope that the most cosmopolitan professor cannot contribute alone.

It is thus useful in such classes to allow the students ample opportunity to speak, whether the course be called a seminar or not. The classical mechanism for student participation is the class report, rehearsed to avoid exceeding the time limitation. The disadvantage is that students habitually take twice as long as agreed. Sometimes the quality remains high throughout, but the class timetable is destroyed. Sometimes students need an extra five minutes to distribute sundry pages of Xeroxed materials. Clear instructions to students on a mimeographed sheet to avoid wasting an entire class's time will be called for in some courses. Various expedients can be employed to stem the volubility of class reporters, including the use of a kitchen timer to sound a modest chime after fifteen or twenty minutes. Students who complain of the long papers often proceed to give reports of the same excessive length. Professor John Coleman has students photocopy their reports for classroom distribution and summarize them for five minutes in class. This compromise solution helps instructors to maintain their time schedule and get out of the classroom before the following class starts rattling the door. Another solution, albeit draconian, is to discontinue class reports and try to elicit wider vocal commentary from all the students themselves. Discussion is thus timed and controlled without difficulty.

As has been mentioned, it is not uncommon for outside guest lecturers to participate in a comparative literature course, discussing an author or a work from their special field of competence. In some seminars one may profitably bring in for the appropriate occasion—and to vary the routine—authors, editors, bibliographers, librarians, and so on. My favorite exploitation of this possibility occurred during the final meeting of a course on Don Juan in Literature. The class had argued long and variously about the meaning and value of Max Frisch's *Don Juan, oder die Liebe zur Geometrie*. After over an hour had passed, I called to a small silent man puffing a pipe in the back of the classroom: "Herr Frisch, würden Sie bitte einige Kommentare zu Ihrem Stück geben?"

The author himself walked to the front of the room before the astonished class and lectured for the second hour in his "chosen" English, informing us inter alia that his *Don Juan* was written only a few blocks from the Washington Square classroom.

Students frequently ask two standard questions about the classroom: whether they may record your lecture and whether they may bring a guest. Opinions vary. One may refuse to be recorded for several reasons, not the least of which is the fear that one would be talking for the recorder and not for the students. One reserves the right, which the recorder would deny, of saying anything opinionated, tentative, or frivolous that occurs to one to lighten the class occasionally. If one is talking about the eighteenth-century salons, the recorder would be the censor discouraging the relation of the racy illustrative stories learned in Brandes' *Voltaire* or contemporary memoirs. As for guests, I suppose one always welcomes them. I do remember, however, that after a colleague had uttered some asperities about psychoanalysis in a class, a student introduced her visitor—her husband, a most gracious practicing psychoanalyst.

Teaching Aids: Syllabus, Bibliography, Checklist

Of the materials distributed at the initial class meeting, most of them need little comment here. It is useful to run over the syllabus, showing the direction the course will take, reminding students which books may be purchased and which used in the library, assigning class reports according to the language competence of the individual students, and so on. If the course bibliography is not analytical, the instructor may wish to analyze and evaluate the books listed thereon. It is useful to have the bibliography carry the volumes' library serial numbers.

I should like, however, to stress the value of what I call the Checklist for Study and Analysis, which is also circulated at the first class. Whether a genre, movement, or theme is being studied, the specific elements that transcend national boundaries and together define and limit the subject matter instruct the student from the start what to look for in his reading of the assigned texts. I have found that even the most independent minds in the classroom are grateful for these suggestive listings, even though they might choose to modify them later in the course. I refer not to such other useful memoranda or outlines instructors often hand out, such as lists of the succeeding waves of romanticists (names, dates, works), which are often useful in a romanticism course, but to the checklists of elements and characteristics by which students may seek and judge the traditional commitment of an author or the extent of an author's departure or estrangement from the mainstream course of the genre, movement, or theme.

Such checklists are not drawn up definitively during the first time one gives a new course; they are gradually revised to assume more definitive validity each time the course is offered. Included as figures in this volume are several such checklists from my own courses: on genre (epic poetry and the novella), on movements (baroque and romanticism), and on themes and myths (Don Juan). (See Figs. 4, 5, 8, 9, and 12 on pp. 140, 142, 159, 161, and 174.) You will note that the checklist of elements of epic poetry that were crucial to Aristotle is considerably broadened by a list derived from Ker, Bowra, and other modern critics, as well as from our own class discussions. Because of the breadth of comparative literature courses and the students coming to grips with many authors new to them and in new areas, the checklist becomes an inherent part of the course, useful to students in their reading, their class reports, and their term papers and examinations.

Textbooks

Everyone knows that an exceptional teacher can initiate good students into literature by almost any method—or by no method at all. Yet, as we are now aware, the very name of comparative literature guarantees a method to be followed, to coordinate the efforts of instructor and student before the classroom experience. Successfully educating those Indians on that log outside Dartmouth, Eleazar Wheelock was not initiating them to the subtleties of comparative literature. Nor should we be lulled into supposing that whenever Abel-François Villemain or Joseph Texte opened their mouths to a class, whatever issued forth was inevitably an exercise in your and my favorite academic discipline. The method is fixed in the syllabus, and the syllabus takes its direction from the selected textbooks.

Ideal textbooks for comparative literature classes would of course be annotated bilingual editions of the great books, original readings with English translation. One recalls the great bilingual classics of Greece and Rome that constituted the Loeb Library published by Heinemann in England and Harvard Press here. How magnificently they helped us to get close to the ancient texts. Even when an obscene passage occurred, they kept their bilingualism, not by Englishing it, but by translating purple Greek patches into Latin and Latin obscenities into Italian. Since English is the lingua franca of most American and Canadian classrooms, how convenient it would be if our English renderings of Lope, Pushkin, and Camoëns were accompanied by the original texts. Such readers as the Dent bilingual Dante seem to be disappearing, although an occasional series, like the Edinburgh Bilingual Library, tries to stem the tide.

We have already noted in Chapters vi, vii, and viii representative textbooks in English on specific genres, periods, and themes, which may serve individual comparative literature courses. The ideal textbooks for courses that touch several literary bases do not exist—such as an anthology on European romanticism presenting bilingually crucial passages from Goethe, Manzoni, Chateaubriand, Lamartine, Rivas, Pushkin, along with the already English texts of Byron, Wordsworth, and Irving. As our discipline grows and settles on which courses are most basic in a curriculum —such as European epic, romanticism, symbolism, and a few others—such bilingual texts might become feasible, even if using only Xeroxed pages and, if necessary, established texts out of copyright. Since we have devoted pages to the more specific matter of textbooks servicing specific courses in Chapters vi to viii, let us address ourselves to the greatest textbook need of comparative literature at the undergraduate level, the Western Heritage or Great Books anthology that is to initiate students, including majors or minors in comparative literature, to the comparative study or method of literature.

The Ideal Literary Anthology

Traditionally popular with undergraduate English, French, German, Western Heritage, Great Books, and humanities courses, the carefully edited anthologies were a staple item in the teaching of literature at the college level. The selected-text or *morceau choisi* collection has a long tradition in the French and German secondary schools, where they facilitated teaching of literature through textual explication and criticism. When comparative literature courses were revived at the college level after World War II, instructors from the foreign language departments of course assumed an important role. The professors from France and Germany, as well as Americans trained abroad, were long familiar with the many useful literary anthologies illustrating and pinpointing movements and trends especially. Many of the illustrative texts became familiar. Every French anthology, whether published in France or the United States, took as illustrative of realism the pages from Balzac's *Père Goriot* that describe in oppressive detail the salon of Mme Vauquer's boardinghouse. In French and German courses, at least, the *morceau choisi* (selected fragment) took precedence over the complete text, at least in the prose offerings. It was the suitable and most satisfying medium for the textual-linguistic literary analysis dominant on the

Continent. The shorter excerpt in French or German classes was also dictated by the American student's inability to read his assignment in a foreign language fast and easily. English majors and minors, reading in their native language, were accustomed to longer assignments if not "complete works." Poems, short stories, and one-act plays can of course appear in anthologies as "complete works." The problem was that the Great Books, almost a fetish of comparative literature, resisted being excerpted. One regretted substituting Hawthorne's "The Birthmark," excellent and characteristic as it is, for a scene from the magnificent *Scarlet Letter*. Or the death of Ahab for the entire *Moby Dick*. Or the murder of Roberta for the whole *American Tragedy*. Or the murder of the lady pawnbroker for the long cat-and-mouse thriller *Crime and Punishment*. Yet such excerpts do have a unity and attraction of their own. Provided with a prefatory summary of the work's entire plot, the student could appreciate the selected portion in context and understand it as illustrative of a genre, theme, or movement. The class lectures on these excerpts could thus be exercises in textual explication, placing the individual text in a comparatist setting. Indeed, the organization of anthologies for use in undergraduate comparative literature courses would have to be oriented toward comparison of texts with footnotes and exercises fitting them into the genres, movements, and themes, which are the woof of comparative literature. It is apparent to the reader that we are discussing here an undergraduate comparative literature course that would not be limited to a single theme, movement, or genre alone, but rather serve as an introduction to all unifying approaches to comparative literature. As for anthologies based on an individual form, movement, or theme, these have already been mentioned in Chapters vi, vii, and viii.

The widespread availability of the paperback classic during the sixties and early seventies made it the ideal medium for supplying any and all comparative literature courses, certainly at the graduate level. Instructors and graduate students who were teaching undergraduate literature requested and received "desk copies" of these paperbacks with joyous abandon, and a few of them enjoyed "wall to wall paperbacks," thus indirectly raising the costs for their students and depleting the stock of necessary texts. One could remind one's students how lucky they were to have these paperback classics, recalling that sad day in the Middle Ages when Petrarch and Boccaccio found a manuscript of Homer they wished to purchase in common, but had not between them the money to afford it. Then suddenly in the mid-seventies the cost accountants took over the textbook houses (as the great conglomerates themselves were taking over the cost accounts in these houses) and such useful paperback texts as *Elizabethan Lyrics, The Palace of Pleasure,* and many others were suddenly out of print. At the present writing so many useful paperback editions are off the market that teachers are turning back to the literary anthologies, themselves recently become paperbacks. As stated elsewhere in this volume, the MLA is collecting titles of the valuable paperback texts now suddenly going out of print.

Is the time now ripe for a number of useful anthologies of comparative and world literature for undergraduate classes, to be reinforced with an occasional paperback of complete works in English or the appropriate foreign language? Could such an anthology be so carefully edited for comparatists that it might even provide them with a useful text at the M.A. level? It is perhaps not a vain hope.

Many of the anthologies available—several carrying the misnomer world literature in their title (see Ch. ii)—follow the Homer-to-Joyce pattern, zigzagging through two thousand years of literary texts presented not logically but chronologically. The value of such a course under an inspiring instructor cannot be contested, but its label of comparative literature or world literature is misleading. These anthologies fail to impose a course structure identifiable as comparative. Most of the available anthologies, many of them carefully, imaginatively, and attractively prepared, merely present a bookful of texts in chronological order, without transitions or overall structure.

Now that we are in a period of unavailability of important paperbacks, some anthologies should be so prepared as to endeavor to satisfy the following desiderata imposed at least partially by comparative literature:

1. A course structure to acquaint students with the four most common approaches to the comparative study of literature.
2. An editorial apparatus encouraging the actual comparison of texts as a major activity in the classroom.

3. A content of major and lasting texts, not sacrificing quality for lesser works that might lend themselves to a more obvious exercise in comparison and contrast.

4. A very wide number of avenues to units within these approaches so that instructors unable to assign all the contents could select those approaches and units with which they are most familiar or which they most enjoy teaching.

5. A book that would not be so intent on presenting a method that it might overlook the other objectives of entertaining and edifying students and giving them texts conforming to their current interests and tastes.

6. In this collection, a selection of some texts whose appearance in the most popular current college anthologies attests to their appeal to both teachers and students. If the method is an unfamiliar one, some of the texts at least will remain familiar ones with which the instructor is comfortable.

7. An anthology with simple and clear editing so that instructors from any literature department need not hesitate to teach from it and the less experienced could know in advance what they may profitably do in the classroom. Yet a method flexible and varied enough that inexperienced teachers may depart from it or disregard some of the apparatus in favor of their tried-and-true techniques.

8. An anthology that, even though the texts be short ones, will make concessions to those instructors loyal to the ideal of the "complete text." That is, probably a majority of the selections will be brief forms, and therefore "complete."

9. An anthology that, for the benefit of those same instructors, will allow for substitute or complementary readings in complete text paperbacks within each unit.

This is a formidable list of desiderata to keep in mind as one pioneers in a new type of anthology (Western Heritage or East-West or World) catering to the needs and tastes of young comparatists. After all, it has happened that one fortunate textbook at the right time and place can initiate the methodology of a discipline, just as Professor Sumner's *Folkways* shaped the first course in sociology in our American colleges.

Such an anthology, if maturely presented, might also be usable at the M.A. level, especially if used by newcomers to comparative literature whose B.A. was in a national literature or other humanities department. It could be thus a text illustrative of the principles and methods being taught in the comparative literature seminar.

Examinations at the Graduate Level

Examinations at the graduate level may consist of language proficency examinations, oral or written examinations for the M.A. or Ph.D., and the thesis examination or defense. The foreign language tests have been discussed in Chapter v.

A common type of examination, in either oral or written form, is the Great Books examination. This examination has much in its favor. The listing of great books, from the famous five-foot shelf of President Eliot of Harvard to various commercial series, some even purchasable in chain grocery stores, has been a boon to the culture-starved. Since occasional undergraduate literature surveys are presented as Great Books, this constitutes one justification for the Great Books examination as a requirement for candidates who may be later assigned to teach this same course. The NYU plan was to offer the graduate student ten titles from a national literature, each list compiled by the national literature department itself, from which the students picked two per literature, excluding their own literature of concentration or specialization. Such a test is pyschologically to the advantage of the candidate, for if six examiners represent their own national literature, the candidate will logically know more about any single text than five of the six examiners. A professor of English hearing a candidate discuss learnedly ten masterpieces of Brazil, Spain, Russia, France, and Italy will be chastened and impressed, even if not entirely satisfied with the candidate's performance over his two English texts. Students who have good memories and who improvise easily do well. This examination presents some problems. A professor who has taken the train in from the suburbs specifically to ask questions for a half hour on two Russian books cannot in fairness be silenced after thirty minutes following such an effort. Since various specialists from the cooperating departments are called on only sporadically, there is sometimes uncertainty on their part of what constitutes a uniformly acceptable performance on the part of the candidate. A final drawback is the *coq-à-l'asne* content of the assigned books, which offers candidate and jury alike little chance to draw parallels or integrate such disparate masterworks as *Oedipus*, *Madame Bovary*, and *Werthers Leiden*. The one great advantage of this type of examination with its company of learned interrogators was described by a college dean, who opposed its discontinuance: "It's the only time and place in this entire university where a company of literary scholars from various departments can sit around and hammer out issues of literature." He was not wrong, and it was with some regret that after a student referendum our department replaced it by two written examinations and a special-field oral examination.

There is nothing special to be discussed here about graduate written examinations, since they may have many forms and durations. The one pertinent point to be observed here is that since our Ph.D. examinations consist of one oral thesis-field and two written examinations, we legislate that three of the four approaches to literature be covered in these three examinations. Thus, if a candidate wishes to write a thesis on Mary Stuart in literature (theme), then the written examinations must cover a movement or a genre (although an interrelationship may be substituted for one of the latter). In view of our effort to keep candidates in touch with all four approaches in the courses they choose, this diversity again comes into play in their program of examinations.

Since NYU authorizes a thesis syllabus (also directing the student toward teaching an undergraduate comparative literature course) for the M.A., no other type of examination is necessary under the state Regents directives. The traditional M.A. thesis may be elected as an alternative.

Comprehensives for the B.A. Major

The ACLA Committee on the Undergraduate Curriculum, chaired by Stephen Nichols, has submitted the authoritative report on the B.A. requirements, including examinations. Their crucial paragraph on comprehensive examinations testifies to a general weakening of the line.

For those programs which accept the necessity for some formalized means of providing unity for the major, but for whom the thesis requirement does not seem practical, the comprehensive examination offers a solution. The examinations themselves take place in the final term of study, but the list of readings which the student must prepare before passing the examination serves as a guide for his/her extra-class study for the duration of the program. Of the schools surveyed, it must be admitted that only Princeton, among the existing programs, and SUNY-Binghamton of the new ones, seem to have stuck by the comprehensive examination. Unfortunately, both the thesis and the comprehensive examination must be reviewed rather in the context of prevailing undergraduate usage, than from the viewpoint of disciplinary standards. Whatever the desiderata might be, hurdles such as the comprehensive or the thesis are viewed—at least by students—as institutional requirements, rather than disciplinary ones.

The Committee concludes that it is increasingly difficult for individual disciplines to hold the line in the face of the general retreat from such exercises that marked the sixties.

Pedagogical and Research Tools Needed for Comparative Literature

From 1883 to the present the Modern Language Association has published many types of pedagogical materials to facilitate the teaching of English and foreign language and literature. In the first decade of this century the MLA was abetting the cataloging of early English books in our libraries and making photographic reproductions of them available for research. Later it set up microfilm collections. It inaugurated a series of scholarly books. It initiated the "work in progress" bibliographies. It created an important UNESCO booklet on foreign languages. It sponsored a new course manual of study for beginning Spanish. It cosponsored with the government a committee to study the success of the wartime ASTP and CATP programs. These and the many helpful teaching aids, bibliographical tools, and committee reports were designed to make the teaching in either English or national literature departments more efficient and effective.

By 1976 the Modern Language Association decided that tools it had provided for the English and foreign language departments should be devised for the newer comparative literature departments as well. The Office of Research Programs made it known to then President Haskell Block of ACLA that the Association was now prepared to repair "the serious gaps in the resource materials available to comparative literature teachers and scholars." The letter, signed by Joseph Gibaldi (himself a Ph.D. in comparative literature), made six suggestions of projects that might be undertaken: an updating of the Baldensperger-Friederich bibliography of comparative literature; guides to research on newer areas of study (mannerism, structuralism, semiotics), each volume to contain essays and bibliographies, including one computer-produced; a bibliography of bibliographies; a series of volumes on interdisciplinary topics (literature and society, etc.); guides to the teaching of masterpieces of world literature (readings, bibliography, teaching aids, sample questionnaires, term paper projects); options for the teaching of comparative literature and interdisciplines—pedagogical approaches solicited from scholars and teachers from around the nation. ACLA was invited to list its highest-priority needs, and set up an ad hoc committee chaired by the present writer. Some of the first projects proposed by ACLA members were a bibliographical guide for students of comparative literature (to be undertaken by George A. Thompson, librarian at NYU, who prepared the Selective Bibliography of Bibliographies at the end of this volume); a history of the teaching of comparative literature; a bibliography of comparative literature doctoral dissertations in the United States; a more complete annual bibliography of comparative literature; a volume updating or replacing an earlier book on literary interrelations, with syllabi and bibliographies, prepared by a team of collaborators directed by Jean-Pierre Barricelli and Joseph Gibaldi; guides to teaching masterpieces like the Norton Critical Editions, but with greater emphasis on the works' international sources and influences; reprints of bilingual editions of masterpieces. Ideas are always welcome from comparatists and can be channeled through MLA in care of Professor Gibaldi.

XII

The Thesis

A man will turn over half a library to make one book.
SAMUEL JOHNSON

The Ph.D. Thesis

Certain optimum procedures safeguard the student during the
thesis phase. The department chairman or graduate student adviser should be informed of the thesis topic as soon as the
candidate and the thesis adviser have agreed upon it. The chairman must be satisfied that the topic fits the definition of a
comparative literature thesis, verify that proposed readers have
graduate status, are not scheduled for imminent sabbaticals, etc.
The preliminary thesis outline, specifying the nature, content,
purpose, and chapter division or structure of the thesis with a
summary bibliography, should be submitted to the thesis adviser
and appropriate readers, with a copy for the student's file in the
department. At a later point the student files a thesis abstract and
a diploma application card in the Graduate Recording Office.
    The thesis may be doubly "comparative" in the sense that it
embraces literatures and an interrelated discipline or disciplines.
Two or more literatures representing separate language areas
must be drawn into the interdiscipline. "The European Romanticists and Music Theory" is thus legitimate, whereas "André Gide
on the Leitmotivs of Wagner's *Ring*" would not qualify. Nor
would of course "André Gide's Preference for Verdi over Wag-

ner." Appropriate would be such interdisciplinary topics as "Freudian Psychology and the Theater of the Absurd" or "The Concept of Law in Dostoevsky, Kafka, and Camus."

Since some theses require a trial run to see whether the topic is feasible, whether competent readers can be found, and whether library facilities are adequate, it is advisable that departments offer for this purpose a credit-bearing course, Guided Individual Research, to be reserved normally for the final semester of the candidate's course work.

The selection of readers for a comparative literature thesis is not so simple as it is for a national literature candidate, who requests as readers three professors within his department. In some national literature departments chairmen wish to have requests for readers channeled through their office, disapproving of direct solicitation of a departmental colleague by comparative literature students. This is natural, for the chairman of that department knows best the expertise of his staff. He also knows who is carrying an overload of theses and must not be given new dissertations to evaluate. Since there is usually no recompense for such "outside" readers who read comparative literature theses, it is best for students to avoid asking this "free service" of a potential reader on their own, even—curiously enough—if they have taken a course or two with that particular instructor and felt a compatibility. In such cases it is best for the comparative literature department to petition in writing for thesis readers, submitting the thesis abstract and other data. Let the candidates check out the correct protocol from their chairman or graduate adviser. In some schools the formalities may be fewer.

Universities will vary on the number of thesis readers as well. This writer recently sent a questionnaire to twelve comparative literature chairmen on the East Coast asking the number of professors attending the defense. Four schools replied five, four replied four, and four replied three. Where a jury of five professors is required, three principals will have probably sealed the candidate's fate and the final two (called *Sitzfleisch* jurors in some schools) are usually present to ratify that decision. If a thesis includes five literatures, a complement of five jurors is obviously in order.

The student usually channels the chapters of his thesis through the comparative literature department unless readers permit delivery of chapters to them in person. To prevent the thesis writer's receiving three contradictory reports, the thesis adviser should be responsible for ironing out suggestions from the readers before the chapters are returned to the student. Since professors are often overburdened, the candidates are usually permitted to submit further chapters while still awaiting return of earlier ones. Once the chapters have been approved and returned with only minor suggestions by all three readers, the candidate can proceed, after appropriate wassailing, to put the thesis into final form. Since so many corrections involve styling, the candidates should keep on their table the *MLA Handbook for Writers of Research Papers, Theses, and Dissertations*, an adaptation for students of the *MLA Style Sheet*, a manual that has stood well the test of time (see p. 251).

One rule an adviser may forget to inculcate is that footnotes of Ph.D. theses are to appear at the foot of each page rather than be collected at the end of each chapter. The reason for this rule is that most theses are microfilmed and will thus be used with a microfilm reader, making visible footnotes desirable.

One final safeguard must be mentioned concerning possible duplication of thesis topics. Many candidates naïvely feel that the responsibility for duplication lies with their advisers. In such a vast field as comparative literature this assumption cannot be accepted. As for theses and books already in print the bibliographers in the university library will be helpful to the student with their retrieval techniques and resources. The thesis adviser can of course acquaint the candidate with names of authorities in the field or fields of the thesis for investigative correspondence. As for theses and books in preparation the candidate should write to the Director of Microfilms Incorporated (300 North Zeeb Road, Ann Arbor, Michigan 48106) requesting a search of the proposed topic. (For telephone inquiries, dial 313-761-4700.) This bibliographical center has extended its thesis research area into Europe as well as America. A modest service fee is charged for this crucial service. It is apparent that the more literatures involved in a thesis, the less duplication of topic will result.

Still speaking of safeguards, students who are satisfied that they have made a real contribution in their theses, or are so informed by their jury, would be wise to arrange through the Recording Office to copyright the material for a year or more.

Theses Written in Foreign Languages

In what language should a thesis be composed? English would seem the simplest solution, since many universities require a jury of three (M.A.) to five (Ph.D.) readers and thus English would be the same lingua franca for the thesis that it is for the classroom and, usually, examinations. There are many reasons favoring English. It may be that American universities are wary of a person not in a foreign literature department who does not write his thesis in English. Fred Nichols writes from CUNY, "My own experience at the Graduate Center is that every single student who has asked us to waive this rule was in fact someone whose English was shaky. But we've always made them do it in English, and so they finally learn the language." Some of these candidates are required to take courses in English composition. Nichols might also have pointed out that the rigid styling and practices in the *MLA Handbook* can be enforced in English, but have less application in the Western European or other languages.

At times NYU candidates have been allowed to write theses in their native languages. Some of our foreign candidates plan to pursue their careers in their homeland, and the demands of English styling need not be imposed on them. Furthermore, upon returning home—or even when remaining—a young scholar will have an easier time publishing there a thesis in his native German, French, or other. When the European language is a familiar one, many thesis readers would prefer to read it than a weak English that leaves them copy-editing. (To protect such readers from inadequate English, the thesis adviser must insist that the candidate enlist a competent copy editor to undertake a thorough check on the thesis script.)

The Difficult Choice of a Thesis Topic; Breadth of the Topic

There is little doubt that the choosing of a thesis subject is as important as the writing of it. The choice of the topic should ideally originate with the candidate. In many departments this subject will fall within a special field on which the candidate has passed a preliminary oral or written examination, in which case the initial choice may have been made under time pressure. If the candidate has forgotten the Horatian caution about a prudent choice ("sumite materiam vestris aequam viribus"), then he must be reminded of it before, and not after, that special-field examination. This same sentiment, at a lower level, is expressed in the 1976 ACLA Report on Professional Standards, as follows: "If the requirement is held to firm standards of scope, substance, and originality—then the weak student is likely to discover too late that the degree is beyond him. The risk, all too often, once the mediocre student has reached this stage, is to tailor the project to his abilities."

It is hoped the candidate will have been influenced by course work taken from a regular professor of the department, which could solve the question of topic and advisement at the same time. The student should be cautioned against hasty choices inspired by ephemeral subject matter or vogues of criticism. Although many theses of value were written in the seventies on feminist topics, others were of less consequence. It was difficult in that period for a male adviser to question the lasting value of a dissertation on minor women poets published only in the little magazines. One way to take a hard look at a potential thesis topic is to ask oneself whether the university press would ever consider it seriously for publication. The editors of the press will ask themselves: Does it make a substantive contribution to knowledge or is it merely a new personal viewpoint and interpretation?

We are all familiar with amusing thesis topics such as one remembered with dismay by Professor Guyard, "Les accouchements dans la littérature." Another classical stereotype mocked by Pichois and Rousseau concerned Béranger's influence in Persia, which must indeed have been a slim dissertation. Such research products become more mechanical than analytic as they are compiled from a box of file cards bearing sentences or passages taken out of context. Despite the familiar comment of students that there are no more thesis topics left, the breadth of comparative or world literature allows for many unexploited, meaningful topics to be pursued with patience through several bodies of literature, with much play left to creativity and imagination. A thesis on the plague in literature, a topic we have mentioned earlier, would consider the various social, moral, psychological, and other values attached to pestilence in the works of a variety of authors.

The broad spectrum of courses that the candidate will have taken by the time for a thesis, buttressed by the reading knowledge of four languages (including English), should allow for the handling of a broad theme, bridging three or four literatures, or more. There are two cogent reasons to recommend, other things being equal, the embracing of three or four literatures. As stated above, such a thesis reduces the risk of duplicating other books or dissertations that have appeared or are about to appear. Almost as important, since some theses become more definitively demonstrated in a broad international context, their eventual chance of publication is enhanced.[1] It is obvious that a book on some aspect of romanticism will be reduced in value if only two or three national literatures are to be explored. Then, too, the old-fashioned thesis that encompasses only two authors or countries (which some recent European scholars call with slight deprecation the "binary" thesis) is one that can be handled in a national literature department and does not need the large apparatus of a comparative literature department to accommodate it. English departments, with a long history of administering literature-in-translation courses and with their own demanding foreign language requirements, would see no justification for having a thesis on Gosse and Gide sponsored by others than the professors of English with the aid of the French department colleagues. This feeling is obvious from the complaint of John Fisher (himself an English mediaevalist), quoted elsewhere, that the new MLA Comparative Literature Sections were sponsoring topics on a single literature coupled merely with another discipline or another literature.

---

[1] The number of distinct language areas represented in our first dozen published departmental Ph.D. theses at New York University (with England and America counting as one, as do all Spanish-speaking areas) is tabulated as follows: *Writers in Arms: Literary Impact of the Spanish Civil War* (4), *Space, Time, and Structure in the Modern Novel* (6), *The Real and the Ideal in the Novella of Italy, France, and England* (5), *Poetry of the Spanish Civil War* (6), *Giudizi Critici nei Poetices di Scaligero* (4), *Ancient Greek Myths and Modern Drama* (4), *La Liebestod dans le roman au 18e siècle* (3), *The Theater of the Marvelous* (3), *Dada and Buddhist Thought* (3). Only three published theses concern two language areas: *The Narrow Act: Borges' Art of Allusion*; *Hamlet: A Window on Russia*; and *Translations of French Sentimental Prose Fiction in Eighteenth-Century England.*

The Single-Author Thesis or Course

The topic of a thesis on a single author has been touched upon very briefly in Chapter ii above, where it was involved in a definition of the minimal dimensions of comparative literature. At issue was a thesis on Virginia Woolf and her literary opinions. The thesis was probably brilliantly done, but one suspects that it was a thesis more appropriate to an English than a comparative literature department. A rigorous application of logic would exclude a thesis not only on one British author, but on two or three.

Haskell Block on several occasions has upheld the more emancipated view.

> I see no reason why a single author or a single work may not serve as a valid subject for a study in Comparative Literature, provided only that the author or work be approached from a broad perspective. The student of Comparative Literature with his command of several languages and his interest in a variety of literatures should be able to illuminate the individual work of art in ways not possible for the more narrowly trained specialist. Literary studies have gained enormously in recent years from the development of increasingly sensitive and refined techniques of analysis and criticism. The claims of the concrete individuality and uniqueness of works of art should be recognized by the comparatist, who should seek out strategies that will encourage and support the simultaneous use of analytic and interrelational methods. If the breadth of perspective is sufficient, the comparative aspect of the study will be reflected in the results, even if the title may seem to be limited to a single author or work.

Professor Block has further written:

> As today's dissertation is often tomorrow's article or book (or if you will, today's book may be yesterday's dissertation), we ought to take a closer look at what constitutes an acceptable dissertation in Comparative Literature. . . . To my mind, a thesis on Gogol and the art of comedy or on Gogol's art of comedy can be just as comparative as a study of Gogol and Molière, and it might be a good deal more interesting.

Now it is quite true that over the years candidates have developed great and proprietary enthusiasms over a single author and wonder just how they might fit him or her into the requirement of a comparative topic. Such enthusiasm should not be stifled, and there are ways to legitimize the thesis. The first time it came up at NYU was when Michael Anthonakes, whose adaptation of Kazantzakis' *Greek Passion* was accepted as the Yale Drama School's annual production, wished to do a thesis on the Greek novelist and epic poet. At our suggestion he did a thesis on the critical reception of Kazantzakis in Greece and Western Europe. It turned out to be a rich contribution to the study of not only the Greek author but contemporary criticism. This first solution also was paralleled by theses on the universal critical reactions to Carson McCullers and Scott Fitzgerald, dissertations advised by English professors. Again, each proved to be a rich contribution to European critical modes and indeed their evolution in successive decades. These thesis writers of course had important cooperation from the publishers of McCullers and Fitzgerald in several Western countries.

Another solution often satisfactory to candidates enamored of a given author is the familiar old solution of influence study. Thus we have had a thesis, eventually published, constructed on the influence of American and English writers on Borges (an influence Borges repeatedly acknowledged) even though a less pedestrian title was found for it. A similar thesis by Professor Carol Slade, most of whose chapters have now appeared in print, centered on Dante—specifically on the unexpected reappearance of his ideas and scenes in such twentieth-century novelists as Unamuno, Malcolm Lowry, Solzhenitsyn, Joyce, and Camus.

There are other solutions, making the thesis on Gogol's art of comedy less appropriate and less necessary. The principal reason a topic such as Gogol's art of comedy seems inappropriate for a comparative literature department concerns the reactions of the cooperating (in this case, the Slavic) department. I have consulted chairmen of my cooperating departments of national literatures, and I find among them grave reservations if not hostility about hopping across those good fences that make good neighbors. They can understand how a two-literature or three-literature thesis can be legitimate as a comparative thesis topic. They cannot agree that a thesis solely dedicated to Cervantes,

Voltaire, or Gogol would not be an intrusion, an implication that their own authors are not being written about or even taught with sufficient depth and breadth. A truly offended chairman or specialist might well carry the case to the curriculum committee, which determines policy in such matters. The latest ACLA Report of the Committee on Professional Standards claims that a cordial, cooperative relationship with its neighboring literature departments is "indeed crucial" to comparative literature.

Nor am I sure that the chairman or professor of comparative literature would be happy if the roles were reversed and the national literature departments all began to assign three-literature theses to their candidates. Those fences Mr. Frost wrote about can be crossed in both directions. Once the principle of nonintrusion is abrogated in the case of theses, it can be broken in the case of course topics as well. Happily, I have not had any professor from another department ask to teach a comparative literature course on Cervantes, or Voltaire, or Gogol. Or a course on European romanticism in his own department. À Dieu ne plaise!

One must conclude herewith as we examine these less welcome, narrower dimensions of comparatism that the two-author or two-literature courses could be compounded only with difficulty to constitute a satisfactory curriculum in comparative literature. A compounding of courses on Hemingway and Baroja, Opitz and Boileau, or Theocritus and Sannazaro cannot add up to an ethical curriculum. Furthermore, the limitation of resulting methodological values has been well voiced by Wellek in his *Theory of Literature.* Furthermore, as we have already pointed out in Chapter ii, the premium on geographical extension is explicit in the requirement of three foreign languages that most of us impose on our Ph.D.'s. One of the practical attractions of the plural-literature thesis is that there is always something new to probe and the candidate will hardly discover to his chagrin that someone had already written it years before.

Discussion of the breadth of a thesis leads, illogically enough, to the question of its length. While most departments maintain a laissez-faire policy concerning the length of both the M.A. and Ph.D. thesis, City University of New York rules that the Ph.D. dissertation must observe a minimum length of 200 and a maximum of 250 typed pages. Professor Fred Nichols writes:

Looking back over the dozens of dissertations I have read in line of duty at three institutions over the years, I do think that the monster of 300 pages and upward never says anything that cannot be said more effectively in 250. Weaker students in particular want to put in every single thing they've dug up. They should learn to select from the fruits of their research.

Taking the page lengths of our first dozen departmental theses to appear in book form, varying from 138 to 343 printed pages (and recalling that a printed page holds a third again as many words as a typed page), Nichols' maximum length is exceeded by six of the printed theses and his minimum length underreached by three of the twelve theses. It is obviously difficult to legislate, or even generalize. It should be kept in mind, however, that many publishers are now disinclined to undertake all the stages required to produce a scholarly book of merely 40 to 150 pages, which must risk being overpriced.

Before leaving the question of the thesis and its nature, we must consider a question sometimes asked by advanced doctoral candidates: Could the edition of a text replace the conventional thesis? This type of research project has an honorable antecedence and has been especially attractive to classicists and mediaevalists. The ACLA committees approve the alternative, but with one minor reservation: "Editions of texts are acceptable as dissertations, in our view, only when accompanied by introductions of substantial length and substance: a minimum might be seventy-five pages."

A few scattered universities will let a translation project replace the conventional thesis. Here very considerable caution must be exercised, if indeed the project should even be considered. If the translation is of some difficult and arcane manuscript out of antiquity or the early Middle Ages and presents difficulties of obtention and verification, such as the Dead Sea Scrolls, then a translation with variant texts, footnotes, and a lengthy introduction would seem legitimate. One thinks of the difficult "translations" of Professor Kristeller's Committee on the Repertorium of Mediaeval and Renaissance Translations and Commentaries on Greek and Roman Authors. Or some projects like the *Codices* of Arator published by the Mediaeval Academy. Being a veteran member of the Kristeller Committee, I could hardly fail to applaud such philological projects. However, once the privilege of substituting translations for theses is authorized, all sorts of regrettable excesses and simple projects may ensue. A young scholar on the West Coast who had received a Ph.D. with the "dissertation" of a translation into English of a fairly familiar Spanish Renaissance play explained apologetically to me that he undertook the project because his thesis adviser did not read Spanish and needed a translation of the work for a project that that worthy professor was working on.

CUNY permits its young comparatists to submit a translation in lieu of a thesis on two conditions. The accessory matter (introduction, notes, etc.) should be about half the length of the whole, and the introduction must discuss the work in a broader context than that of the single literature involved. Furthermore, the work must have the status of international importance. If it is a question of a modern work, the student must be sure that there will be no copyright problems: since dissertations are published, technically even when microfilmed, the student translator must hold permission from whoever administers the translation rights.

One incidental thought about theses might be added here. Students should be calm if they find that their thesis timetable has gone awry, that it cannot be defended on time for the usual June or October degree. Typing and restyling always take more time than expected. The student should remain calm and submit the thesis only when it is ready and right, not letting the deadline become an end in itself. Missing a deadline by a week or a month is disappointing but not a tragedy, since the chairmen in most universities (and even deans in others) will certify in a written letter or document available to the candidate that all requirements for the Ph.D. were satisfied within a day after the successful thesis defense.

The Master's Thesis; the Syllabus-Thesis

The master's thesis, although increasingly considered in America a minor affair, is still required by most state education boards like the New York Regents. Some universities have managed to have the thesis requirement replaced by the presentation of three term papers already accepted as part of the candidate's class-work. This compromise solution was approved in a more accept-able form by the 1976 Report on Standards of the ACLA, specifying "two or three essays, *written independently of courses.*" At the University of Indiana, for example, one may substitute for the M.A. thesis an expanded term paper for two to six hours of credit or merely submit a term paper to show evidence of schol-arly potential, for no credit. Since the master's candidate in comparative literature must usually have a reading proficiency in two foreign languages, the thesis might well promise some inter-esting and broad research. Nevertheless, since the best jobs are open only to possessors of the A.B.D. ("all but dissertation") or Ph.D. category, the master's thesis continues to be of less voca-tional utility.

One alternative adopted for all M.A. candidates at NYU is the syllabus-thesis. In an earlier, simpler version it is the term paper for the required comparative literature seminar, which consists of a detailed syllabus for a one-semester course at the undergradu-ate level. It is a plan of some 18 to 20 pages outlining an under-graduate course selected by the candidate from a standard list of movements, genres, themes, or interrelations. The syllabus must contain the basic six items:

1. Topics and general lecture themes of class meetings
2. A reading assignment of appropriate literary text or texts for each of these class meetings
3. Subjects of two oral class reports by students for each of the class meetings on authors, works, or topics illustrative of the topic of each class
4. Bibliography-per-lesson
5. General course bibliography
6. Six essay questions of twenty minutes constituting the final ex-amination of the course

The total number of these familiar syllabus (or course) topics is restricted to about thirty, since the instructor of the seminar has only a small nuclear group of colleagues to help him grade the syllabi. These course syllabi must be checked thoroughly, since they constitute the first phase of an eventual M.A. syllabus-thesis, a carefully expanded and enriched document of some thirty-five to forty pages. The later syllabus-thesis includes a long introductory essay on the value of the course's approach, with a conversion of the bibliography-per-lesson and the general bibliography to analytical status, with sample examination questions and the desired answers, and so on. A memorandum explaining the conversion of the seminar-assigned syllabus to an M.A. "thesis" is provided to all M.A. candidates.

The advantages of the M.A. syllabus over the conventional thesis are several. The motivating reason advanced by several faculty members is its practicality. A young M.A. being considered for a teaching post already has a "teaching specialty" (another reason for keeping the students from choosing esoteric and impractical topics). Then, too, the several types of discipline (organizational, ratiocinative, bibliographical, etc.) required by the syllabus are just as valuable as those usually demanded for the M.A. thesis. Furthermore, the candidate now has a special field for further doctoral examinations or thesis writing usually broader than the specialism gained by a narrower M.A. thesis topic.

The privilege of presenting such a syllabus fully developed is not extended to a candidate for the Ph.D.

For the benefit of departments interested in the syllabus-thesis as a required or optional substitute for the M.A. thesis, there follows part of a memorandum that includes the four areas of expansion that will convert the shorter syllabus into a legitimate M.A. syllabus-thesis. Such expansion would raise the initial pagination *grosso modo* from twenty to forty typed pages.

1. The Introductory Explanation of special viewpoints or premises of the *topic* should be enlarged to include a historical conspectus of the *topic* itself, including critics and theorists who have dealt with it in a major way.
2. The syllabus-thesis should be augmented considerably by an essay of several pages on the value of the particular *approach* to literature (movement, theme, form, or interrelationship) within which the *topic* lies. Read and quote from specialists who have defended or espoused your chosen *approach* (not forgetting the useful prefaces in textbooks and readers, as demonstrated in class), evaluating or extending these borrowed ideas.
3. After the listing of the subject of any given class, devote a page

to an outline summary of your introductory lecture on this subject. This useful addition may in itself add a dozen pages to your original course syllabus.

4. The General Bibliography for the course should be a descriptive listing of the most relevant background works, affording the accurate bibliographical data. The Bibliography-per-Lesson should be expanded by making the bibliographical entries analytical (not necessarily critical), with the addition of a few sentences clarifying content and scope of each entry.

The general reaction to this type of project has been almost universally favorable, and almost never do we receive a request from someone to undertake the more traditional M.A. thesis. Since the topics are "mainstream," it eliminates the possibility of the student choosing a trivial or dubious topic or one where it will be difficult to find two readers. Appraised by two professors, it also eliminates the more personnel-consuming M.A. oral thesis defense. It eliminates as well the potential duplication of subject always lurking behind many theses. Recalling a distinguished but suspicious professor at Harvard years ago, who used to spend hours in the stacks near his Widener Library study checking on plagiarizing in theses, it occurs to me that the syllabus-thesis eliminates the temptation to copy or to pad from more remote sources. The only problem that occasionally comes up is the student who seeks permission to undertake a topic legitimately comparative literature in nature, but way out of the mainstream of his future teaching or the competence of the available thesis readers in the department.

The Undergraduate Thesis

For many years undergraduate concentrators in an English or a foreign literature department have enjoyed the privilege of intensifying their work as honors candidates by undertaking special examinations or a thesis. Such is often the case in the comparative literature department. The Nichols inquiry discovered that about half the institutions polled accept the B.A. thesis as an "indispensable instrument of focus" for an honors group, requiring a senior thesis varying from fifteen to a hundred pages in length. At

Princeton two "junior papers" are required, one of which "might serve as the beginnings of a senior thesis," the latter composition averaging about 20,000 words. The language announcing the honors thesis usually seems to reserve this paper for an elect group.

> For superior students, the departmental honors program offers an opportunity for independent study and research under the guidance of a faculty member during the senior year. [Indiana University]

> An exceptional student may be invited by any member of the staff to work on a special project, the honors program, during his senior year: senior thesis, a course supervised by two members of the instructional staff. [University of California at Riverside]

The Nichols Committee regretted that the thesis was so often made an instrument differentiating regular majors from honors majors. "All students can benefit from the defining process of researching and writing a thesis, no matter how modest an undertaking it may be. To turn it into some kind of an academic equivalent of the Grail would seem to remove from them an exercise which could only serve to strengthen and encourage the regular concentrators." An inquiry into this thesis requirement at Dartmouth affirmed that students involved in the composition of such a paper "were unanimous in describing the project as perhaps the most meaningful academic exercise they have undertaken."

The Graduate Term Paper: Sixteen Counsels

Over the years I have drawn up a list of suggestions that answer most of the queries students raise concerning comparative literature course term papers. Rather than write at length on this smallest unit of composition required of the graduate student, I shall set down these sixteen counsels herewith. Obviously several of them apply to graduate theses as well, and may echo ideas developed more lengthily on other pages of this work.

1. Be as accurate and thorough as though you were writing for publication. Indeed, term papers written by graduate students have occasionally seen their way to eventual publication.

2. There is no excuse for incorrect or inconsistent typescript styling. The *MLA Handbook for Writers of Research Papers,
Theses, and Dissertations* is available in the university bookstore, and must be your inseparable guide and chapbook.
Other and more costly manuals such as that of the University
of Chicago are useful, but the MLA practices have been accepted by a majority of the learned journals in this country.

3. In selecting a topic, remember Horace's counsel about choosing a limited subject. By choosing a limited subject and
mastering it, you will achieve a more personal contribution,
and you will be less likely to duplicate work with secondary
sources. Obviously, "Melancholy in Romantic Literature" is
too vast a topic for a term paper. More suitable would be a
narrower field such as "Ethical Justifications of Suicide in the
Romantic Novel." "Petrarch's Theory of Poetry" would be
difficult to embrace, whereas "Petrarch's Evaluations on
Greek Poets" would be more suitable.

4. Once you have settled on your theme, do not pad your paper
or waste time on known introductory facts. Former investigations on or around the subject must be presented with the
greatest economy. Get down to the problem without delay
and proceed to your solution, interpretation, or conclusion.

5. Append a minimum bibliography or reading list. If you lean
heavily on two or three secondary sources, state the fact out-
right and acknowledge by footnote every borrowed thought.
This is better than having your professor discover your un-
acknowledged cribbing, which becomes an ethical issue. Do
not overload your paper with lengthy quotations from secondary sources!

6. Everything about your source must be included in your footnotes: author, title, series (if one is involved), publication
place and date, and pages. Omitting any of these data on first
citation is a minor offense.

7. Do not write an essay or impressionistic criticism. A research
paper is called for; that is, a logical study more cautious in
reaching conclusions, and bearing the burden of proof of those
conclusions.

8. There is no proper length. If papers usually run between fifteen and thirty pages, this does not mean that an important
contribution could not be made in a half dozen pages. Einstein

worked out his theory of relativity on an envelope. In any case, there is not a Parkinson's law decreeing that the longer the paper is, the better its chances of an honor grade.

9. An *explication de texte* is acceptable as a term paper if it is of such merit and acuity that one could seriously submit it to the few journals publishing explications.

10. A really thorough book review (as opposed to a "notice") of an important new literary study, done at the professional level and with thorough research behind it, would be acceptable with prior approval and indeed might be submitted to a learned journal.

11. Keep footnotes at a minimum by using them for sources and not for additional information. Footnotes may be grouped on your last page.

12. Some subjects will require constant quoting from the primary literary source. To prevent your pages from appearing like pages of an anthology, resort to judicious paraphrase. Indeed, poetry can also be absorbed directly into the body of your text if integrated into sentences. In such cases use slashes to separate lines of verse, of course.

13. Always quote foreign sources in the original language (including classical languages). Quotations from the Bible, however, are traditionally given in the Latin; otherwise, if you are dealing with English language authors, these generally refer to the King James Version. You can buy in major bookstores the Vulgate Edition of Jerome, the official text recognized by the Roman Church. Do not modernize the spelling of excerpts from mediaeval and Renaissance sources, for the original spelling may tell us much (regional provenience, historical period, pedantry of the author, etc.) that modernization wipes out.

14. If scholarship lacks relevancy sometimes, it is frequently the fault of the scholar himself. After you have gathered your materials, interpreted them, and reached your conclusions, summarize briefly just why your paper is significant.

15. I have not touched upon the subject of who chooses the term paper topic. A student doing sufficient reading for a course does not usually have to admit midway through the semester that he has found no topic to work on. Start early to make a list of potential topics as you read, including those suggested

in class. When the course is seven or eight weeks along, bring the list for discussion with your professor. The topics which you propose then will reveal something of your interests, language abilities, and training, and they will supply areas within which your instructor may make further suggestions.

16. Although some comparative literature departments or individual instructors do not demand that a term paper must include two or more literatures, others do. Be sure to make your instructor clarify his wishes on this. If you are writing a paper on an interrelationship, you must remember that comparing one literature with one or more disciplines does not equal a comparative literature paper. Furthermore, where principles of comparatism are being maintained, you cannot devote a term paper to an author or work whose language you cannot read. As suggested elsewhere in this volume, you would be unable to read not only the works with professional accuracy, but the critical studies about the author in the language in question.

The MLA HANDBOOK

The need of a style manual for writers of theses led the University of Chicago as early as 1906 to the preparation and publication of a handbook that guided young scholars until the forties. Late in that decade William Riley Parker, Executive Secretary of the MLA, decided to edit a new style manual, less detailed and less expensive, for the broadest possible distribution. He solicited the major learned societies in the country and convinced them to accept common norms of styling. Even the Mediaeval Academy gave up its beloved British stylistics (Mr for Mr., -ise for -ize, etc.). A million copies were printed between 1951 and 1970, when it was replaced by a revision prepared by John H. Fisher and others. For almost three decades the *MLA Style Sheet* guided the conventions of scholarly publishing by most journals and university presses.

Although the popular *Style Sheet* served scholars and students alike, some complained that the work, originally compiled for scholars, was inadequate for students. Thus, to serve as a classroom text and a supplementary reference guide, the present *MLA Handbook for Writers of Research Papers, Theses, and Dissertations* was prepared.

Compiled by Joseph Gibaldi and Walter S. Achtert of the Association, themselves publishing scholars, the *Handbook* was prepared in cooperation with college and university language and literature departments throughout the United States and Canada. It contains an introduction to the writing of research papers (selecting a topic, using the library, compiling a working bibliography, taking notes, avoiding plagiarism, outlining, writing drafts); a compendium of the mechanics of writing (punctuation, numerals, spelling, titles in the text, quotations, capitalization, names of persons, transliteration); recommendations for preparing the manuscript (typing, paper, spacing, margins, the title, divisions of the text, tables and illustrations, pagination, corrections and insertions, binding); a survey of the purposes and practices of documenting the research paper; a discussion of the content, form, arrangement, and placement of the bibliography; a list of abbreviations for common reference words, for the Bible and the works of Shakespeare, and for proofreading and correction; an appendix on the preparation of theses and dissertations; and sample pages of a research paper.

Such a book must obviously stand within the scholar's and student's reach. With the gradual disappearance of the methods and bibliography seminars in our graduate schools, the *MLA Handbook* becomes increasingly necessary.

XIII

Evaluation and Standards

> Truly at the day of judgment we shall not be evaluated on what we have read, but as to what we have done.
>
> THOMAS À KEMPIS

Standards and Criteria

Probably every chairman in the United States and Canada who has a flourishing comparative literature department would respond to the suggestion that his department be evaluated with Professor Kittredge's bewildered reply: "But who would examine me?" Indeed, it was only when the American universities, public and private, had proliferated to such a point as to regard budgets getting out of hand, that the matter of outside evaluation and self-evaluation came up in all departments. In the mid-seventies the Regents Board in New York State sent out its first teams of evaluators into departments of history, philosophy, English, French, Spanish, and German. Administrators fearing the arrival of the Regents' out-of-state examiners immediately called in teams of their own choosing to make a preliminary assessment of these departments. Since no general criteria by which to evaluate a department were given out, a certain confusion and fatalism resulted, as though evaluation were an act of God.

The Greene Report of the ACLA was at this moment thinking about professional standards and evaluation:

All of the changes we face raise questions about standards in the broadest sense: about the value of what we are doing and should

253

be doing, about our function in the academic community and the larger intellectual community, about our responsibilities to our students, our colleagues, and ourselves. Standards are admittedly difficult to define; they permit finally no quantification; they depend ultimately on the judgment of each scholar. The scholar, in turn, sets the level of his standards primarily during his graduate training. By definition, any crisis of undergraduate training could be a crisis of graduate training.

This committee, whose very title made them custodians of standards, saw their mission as modestly alerting their colleagues to dangers, recommending norms and goals for the present that perpetuate the best of the past, and suggesting means by which the Association might affect the direction of standards in the future.

Since only five universities in New York State were authorized to grant the Ph.D. in comparative literature, they were not high on the priority list of the Regents' curiosity. Yet when one major English department was evaluated, the Regents' evaluators suggested that the department release the discipline of comparative literature from its grasp and let it be truly autonomous. When the Regents this same year authorized a new M.A. in Comparative Literature at New York University, they economically validated the existing doctoral program at the same time. Other disciplines over the Empire State did badly—traditional departments like history, chemistry, philosophy, and others being instructed to fold up, phase out, or make visible improvements within a year or two.

It was in this atmosphere that the second Report of the ACLA Committee on Professional Standards wondered whether it might not be helpful to the profession to intervene—that is, to organize evaluating groups under the aegis of the ACLA. The fourth article of the Report read as follows:

> In view of the growth and diversity of so many programs in Comparative Literature as well as conflicting conceptions of its scope and role, we recommend the creation of a permanent Committee for Information and Evaluation. Many institutions that plan to initiate or expand programs would in our belief welcome suggestions and advice from representatives of the ACLA. Many would welcome a visit from such representatives to

evaluate ongoing programs, if it were offered in a courteous spirit of collegial cooperation.

Perhaps remembering that some schools, like Harvard, had their own Visiting Committees (of whom an occasional member, taking his title too seriously, would drop into a busy classroom and slip into a rear seat to the consternation of the instructor), the Committee continued:

A good number of institutions seek out periodic evaluations of their programs as a matter of course. Some are required to do so by law. It would be in the interest of our discipline if all those invited to visit could speak with authority concerning the various approaches to Comparative Literature pursued elsewhere, if they could suggest activities, arrangements, and curricula already proven useful, and if they could indicate to their hosts those points on which their professional society has determined no compromise to be acceptable.

Thus the ACLA found itself being invited by its distinguished committee to enter the evaluation business even before it had formulated any collective standards subscribed to by a clear majority of its members.

The Report proceeded to the constitution of such a committee. It should be chaired by a senior member of outstanding reputation. It should include as many as fifteen scholars, chosen for their distinction, their judgment, their fairness, and their geographical distribution about the country. Each member might be asked to serve for a renewable term of three years. The Report suggested that the existence of this committee be publicized by the *ACLA Newsletter*, by the *MLA Newsletter*, and along with other appropriate means, by letters from the ACLA secretariat to chairmen and deans. A small number of the committee members —perhaps only two—could be delegated to visit a given department or program when and only when the committee was invited by the institution in question. It was proposed that the delegation spend two days at the host institution, offering suggestions and counsel. It was further specified, of course, that the visitors would submit a report to the appropriate chairman or dean. A second copy would be filed at the secretariat of the ACLA.

It is our hope that the creation of such a committee would help to dispel confusion about the nature of our discipline. It would also provide a clearing house for ideas and news. It would ensure the solid professional calibre of each evaluating team, and it would supply the ACLA secretariat itself with fresh information. Finally it would demonstrate our continuing pursuit of excellence to the academic community and—not least of all—to ourselves.

This proposal has not yet been converted to reality. Probably it would have been more useful if it had been proposed in the first ACLA Committee Report. As Dean Herbert Weisinger said in a dissent: "The [second] Report in two or three ways ignores the fact that there is a new generation of young Comparatists rigidly trained in the principles and practices of comparative literature now teaching and endeavoring to put their learned practices into action all over the country."

It is true that whereas during the sixties chairmen of large departments received many inquiries and requests for descriptive materials from smaller institutions all over the country, these inquiries are fewer now, partly because of the reason assigned by Weisinger, but they have by no means disappeared. A more obvious reason why departments would be slow to invite in an evaluating commission results from rumors, true or false, of subjective and unfavorable evaluations submitted to Albany and other state capitals by outside investigators. "Visitors" is an anodyne, reassuring word, as used in the ACLA Report, but many of the "visitors'" reports to Albany were contested—in a few cases successfully—and the right to confer the Ph.D. was narrowly regained. Obviously chairmen would prefer to invite their own evaluators or have them invited through intermediaries who bear them good will. From my own experience as an evaluator, it is clear that at least three days of careful inquiry in many sectors are needed if one is to carry out the commission with accuracy. The ACLA Report, hovering at a somewhat philosophical level, does not clarify the financial details that would be involved. One would assume that no honorarium—only travel costs and sojourns —would be involved, since the goal is defined as "assisting institutions and departments and individual scholars toward an excellence whose vision is shared almost everywhere if seldom achieved anywhere."

Objections to Outside Evaluation

The academic community, comparative literature included, was for reasons explained above scarcely in a mood in the mid-seventies to have outsiders intruding. Herbert Weisinger, who rated the first two reports on professional standards as elitist and remote from actuality, finds such an approach at the moment anachronistic. He fears that the ACLA evaluators will insist on "evoking the rule of exclusivity and exceptionality." Does the Committee really intend to eliminate comparative literature where it does not come up to its particular standards? He continues at great length and I quote him without interruption:

For the report defines the role and scope of comparative litera-ture to fit the measure of its own view of it so that one can read the section on the evaluation process only with the greatest ap-prehension. My own experience with evaluations on my own campus (the Graduate School conducts an evaluation by outside consultants of each graduate program every five years), with SUNY-wide procedures, with the N.Y. Regents Doctoral Council, and with the Steering Committee for the research project on the dimensions of quality of graduate education leads me to be ex-tremely suspicious of the guild approach to the evaluation of graduate education. If the evaluation committees were to go forth with the criteria of the report immovably fixed in their minds, the end results would be so predictable it would be unnecessary to send them out to begin with. And I venture to predict that not many departments would extend invitations for evaluation under such circumstances. If I have learned anything from my experi-ence of evaluation techniques, it is that graduate education is far more complex than we have assumed, that the criteria are many and varied, and that the perception of faculty performance can-not be limited to peer observation alone. Most important, unless the results of evaluation are made available, not only to depart-ments and administration within institutions, but to prospective students, employers, and those who fund universities outside them, there is no real hope of improvement. Self-perpetuating and self-regulating professions, such as medicine and law, have not established an impressive record of self-criticism, and I see no evidence that academia does or will do better. Nor am I clear as to the role the Secretariat is to play in the process; surely it is not

to be cast in the part of the enforcer of academic respectability,
your committee definition? There is no greater incentive to work
well and truly done than public disclosure; *caveat emptor*, to be
sure, but in the light, not of ignorance, but of knowledge.

Under the New York State evaluation project it was possible to
lose authorization to award the Ph.D. or the M.A. Another consequence, dismaying to many, began to spread in 1977. After the
graduate departments of German had been evaluated at Columbia, New York University, and the City University, the daily
Times announced, perhaps somewhat prematurely, that the three
departments would henceforth become a consortium. The an-
nouncement read: "The impetus for the joint venture in German
came from a state-appointed academic review team that examined the German departments and found that, collectively, they
would provide a very strong doctoral program. The review was
part of a statewide evaluation of doctoral programs initiated by
the State Board of Regents."

Since comparative literature departments show only the tip of
their instructional iceberg, with a nuclear two or three teachers
reinforced by instructors from the cooperating departments, an
educational efficiency expert might easily conclude that all
comparative literature departments in metropolitan areas should
be coalesced, especially since so many geographical and subject
matter specialists would seem to be needed. With the comparative literature department, however, the "consortium" already
exists with its own cooperating national literature departments—
the best consortium anyone could conceive of. Is there any
wonder then that Dean Weisinger's assessment of departmental
reluctance or truculence is often a justified one?

The power of such evaluating committees should be circum-
scribed by their title. At best any outside team should not be
called an evaluating committee, a committee on standards, or
even an examining committee (an Albany term), but something
more modest like a "committee on normative procedures." For
what is wrong in so many new departments is not the weak quality of instruction—far more difficult to assess in any case—but
rather departures from normative principles and practices that
could be spelled out and used as a measuring stick, something
more comprehensive than the minimal decalogue of only ten

guiding rules (see p. 264). Indeed, if the principles and procedures were worked out in a manual or booklet and prepared by ACLA and circulated on request to any chairman, modifications and improvements could be undertaken intramurally without the specter of a visitor or visiting committee too elitist, too powerful, or too rigorous, like the famous *inspecteur* who terrorized French schoolteachers. The ACLA could endorse the principles and practices that indirectly determine "standards" without even mentioning this almost subjective term.

Indeed, the present volume was inspired by the obvious need of normative principles, requirements, and procedures that may keep the comparative literature department on *la bonne voie* over long periods and changes of personnel. When new chairmen, eager to build a qualitative department or program, write to those of us long in the profession, it is to ask for memoranda, sample examinations, course syllabi, thesis regulations, curriculum structures, language requirements, bibliographies, and the like. Over a quarter century, I cannot remember any such request mentioning "quality" or "minimum standards," so much a part of ACLA Report I. Nor have they sought advice about whether, as phrased in Report I, comparative literature "should not be introduced without a great deal of institutional heart-searching." Nor have they asked to what extent to limit enrollments to be assured of quality. But they do write, and this was wisely mentioned in Report I, to "make a careful scrutiny of the facilities and requirements elsewhere."

The uncertainties of our discipline at the present involve the dimensions of our subject matter, latitude of theses, the ancient language requirement, and the rest. New or small departments welcome answers on these basic matters; they are not asking for qualitative evaluation, involving outsiders and deans. Being a successful comparative literature chairman demands an ability to provide constant decisions and solutions. It is these that our newer colleagues want us to share with them.

Intra- and Extra-University Evaluation

The University of California at Riverside has adopted an evaluation questionnaire drawn up by the local Graduate Council and applicable to all local graduate programs. It would seem to include useful criteria. A rating sheet is sent to "faculty at se-lected institutions" requesting ratings ranging from 1 (among the top few in the country) to 6 (poor), allowing for a rating of 7 for "no opinion, insufficient information." Evaluated in turn are (1) overall quality of the faculty, (2) overall quality of the program, (3) quality of faculty in the evaluator's subdiscipline or area of specialization, and (4) quality of graduate program in the evalu-ator's subdiscipline or area of specialization. Further comments are optional. The recipient of this evaluation sheet is furnished with a photostat of the catalog entry for comparative literature with all courses, course descriptions, and instructors' names and degrees. "The Council hopes that you will be able to complete the questionnaire on the basis of your knowledge of our faculty and program through disciplinary contact. The enclosed description is intended to serve primarily as a reminder." Since many faculty members in comparative literature programs are borrowed part time from other departments, it is very difficult to recognize and evaluate more than a few of the eighteen teachers listed. As Owen Aldridge responded to the Council, brief vitae of all the teachers would have completed the materials needed for an ac-curate evaluation. However, an evaluation is quite possible on the comparative literature curriculum, for most of the needed details other than staffing are present: course content, dimension and level, number of credits, number of approaches, etc. It is thus possible to certify that this curriculum chaired by Jean-Pierre Barricelli has been carefully thought out, adhering to principle on spread (Western cultural tradition), variety of approaches, in-terdisciplinary thrusts, language requirements, and the other elements that concern us in the present volume.

A totally different and less effective approach was recently taken by the University of Michigan (Ann Arbor) to "review and evaluate its Comparative Literature program." Professors of na-tional and classical languages, anthropology, art history, and psychology were the evaluators. Respondents around the country were asked some twenty-one questions about their own depart-ments (size, staff, degree requirements, curricular structure, etc.). Several questions seem to call into question the value of comparative literature itself and its training. ("Would you accept applications from Comparative Literature graduates?") Finally, one is asked to evaluate any Michigan Ph.D. in this field whom one might happen to know. One is assured that replies will be held in "strict confidence" as though one might be embarrassed to speak out about one's own department. Rightly or wrongly one senses that the comparatists in Michigan's "program" are "on the carpet," that one need not risk taking the pains to answer at this late date of our development a questionnaire asking for general information about comparative literature already available to the committee through ACLA publications, UNESCO, reports, and elsewhere. Indeed, these could have been supplied with little effort to the committee by their local colleagues in comparative literature. The Riverside evaluative approach is obviously more professional and meaningful.

Examining committees, intramural or extramural, might well be provided with an adequate minimum list of criteria for evaluation, although potential registrants in a department might like a longer list of items to investigate. Let us draw up, then, a two-level evaluation sheet: *A* for professional evaluation; *A* plus *B* for students.

FIG. 20. *Checklist of Elements for Departmental Evaluation*

A. Professional Evaluation

1. TEACHING STAFF: Names of full-time, part-time, and visiting professors, with vita of each one (education, degrees, publications, awards and honors, lectures, foreign residence, languages read or spoken). Membership and offices in learned societies or listings in national or international registries. Academic rank, tenure status.

2. COURSES: Photostated catalog pages showing all courses taught in department each biennium or triennium, with instructors and brief descriptive paragraphs. Double-listed courses. Cross-listed courses. Basic methods seminar on the profession; on literary criticism; research and thesis courses. Summer courses. Changes and withdrawals. Numbers of hours and credits. Auditing policy. Four approaches of representation of comparative literature: Themes, Forms, Movements, Interrelations.

3. DEGREE REQUIREMENTS: Ph.D., A.B.D., M.A., B.A. Number of credits; transfer of credits; course distribution, comparative literature and noncomparative literature. Number and types of examinations: oral and written; number, duration, and content; time limit; number of examiners; how many tries? Change of major; diploma application.

4. ADMISSION REQUIREMENTS AND CLASSIFICATIONS: Graduate Record Examination scores, cumulative average grades, grades in major; nonmatriculants; transfer credits (major and nonmajor) allowable for Ph.D., M.A., B.A. Letters of recommendation. Other credentials. Requirements for full- and part-time status. Admission procedures; permit to register. Ratio of teachers to active students. Ratio of full-time to part-time students.

5. LANGUAGE REQUIREMENTS: Ph.D., A.B.D., M.A., B.A. Timing of ETS or departmental language examinations. Standards and scores for certification. Number of tries. Language class auditing privileges. Languages spoken; languages read. Token use of foreign language in classroom and assignments. Other means of assessing language proficiency: graduate and undergraduate courses in foreign language and literature; language department exam; foreign schooling in residence.

6. ACCREDITATION OF COLLEGE AND UNIVERSITY: American Association of Universities, regional accrediting association, or other. Academic standing. Recognition and subsidies: NEH, Foundations, etc.

B. Additional Criteria of Particular Use to Potential Candidates

7. STUDENT ADVISEMENT AND REGISTRATION: Registration periods and hours in comparative literature and cooperating departments; guidelines; prepared materials on degree requirements, thesis writing, examination structures. General course requirements: paper, examination, etc. Preregistration. Mail registration. Deadlines. Policy on late grades. Changes and withdrawals. When courses are taught: A.M., P.M., evening. Full- or part-time requirements. Counseling services. Ombudsman. Foreign students. Transfer of credits. Student visas. Remedial reading courses. International student advisement. Number of Ph.D. and M.A. candidates.

8. FINANCES: Fees; scholarships; fellowships. Teaching assistants. Exemption for employees and faculty kin. Work-study assistants. Prizes, loans, thesis grants.

9. THESIS: Breadth; outline; approval of topic. The Ph.D., M.A., B.A. breakdown. Major, minor readers. Defense. Options of Language of Composition.

10. EXTRACURRICULAR ACTIVITIES: Departmental seminars, colloquia, student association, receptions, newsletter, annual conference, student room, alumni solidarity, literary journal, attendance at functions and lectures of national literature departments.

Undergraduate Program Evaluation

The Nichols Committee Report would reassure us that often the maintenance of standards at the college level is more securely upheld by the students than by the faculty, the latter perhaps motivated by registration statistics. In any case, the student sentiment seems to be such as to invoke the disputed word "elitist":

> If this report has tended to stress standards which make the undergraduate discipline more, rather than less rigorous, the inspiration for that thrust has come from the students themselves at institutions as diverse in orientation as large State Universities, such as Wisconsin and Kentucky, and small liberal arts colleges, such as Beloit and Dartmouth.

While recognizing that model programs proposed in the appendix of the Committee Report do incorporate a minimal set of standards in recognition of the fact that comparative literature has a role to play in institutions where the humanities resources are limited, the Report nevertheless cautions that:

> . . . it would be a grave disservice to the discipline and to the students themselves to move generally in the direction of minimal standards or to make a marked distinction between the honors major intended for those who know in advance that they want to continue in the profession, and a so-called "terminal B.A."
>
> On occasions when students majoring in Comparative Literature have been asked to evaluate their programs, the responses combine a refreshing blend of idealism and practicality. Often students can sense, behind faculty questions concerning the stringency of requirements, a nostalgia for greater numbers of majors. The students sometimes respond to such questions with frustration. Why do we spend time worrying about the hypothetical students we do not have, rather than concerning ourselves with the needs of those we do have? This intelligent response sounds a useful note of warning.

The Report concludes that our students, presumably like ourselves, have chosen the discipline for its challenge, and the faculty members must neither disappoint them nor compromise themselves by courting expediency.

A Decalogue of Principles for Evaluation

1. Entrust comparative literature courses only to bona fide comparatists with the outlook and training that your students will recognize as professional. Give more serious consideration to the new generations of trained comparatists than to national literature professors who will require retooling.
2. Offer only courses that "touch all geographical bases," that is, involve four, five, or more of the literatures of concentration represented by your students, with further literatures being covered in possible class reports.
3. Set the most essential or required courses on a two-year rotation and others on a three-year cycle, thus giving students the broadest possible choice of courses.
4. Schedule courses at hours convenient and possible to the students, including those who work and teach, and not merely at the convenience of the instructor.
5. Offer each academic year two or more courses on each of the four major approaches of genre, movement, theme, and interrelation.
6. Do not entrust the administration of comparative literature to a scholar who is not a full-time comparative literature professor capable of dedicating to the department or program full time, energy, and undivided interest.
7. Do not double-list courses as a matter of convenience or compromise, even while encouraging reciprocal cross-listing.
8. Do not assign comparative literature graduate courses to instructors who cannot read at least the three foreign languages (preferably more) required of their advanced students.
9. Do not through ambition, generosity, or expediency annex departments of national literature to the department of comparative literature.
10. Do not echo the misuse of the phrase "world literature," except to refer to a dimension of comparative literature that includes texts from Asia and Africa.

XIV

Academic Diplomacy and Politics

I have been a looker on in the Cockpit of Learning these many years.

ROGER ASCHAM, *The Scholemaster*

Academic Diplomacy: Good Fences, Good Neighbors

A French scholar who wrote on Renaissance literary rivalries and contentions entitled his book *Les Gladiateurs de la république des lettres.* The basic premise of a successful department of comparative literature is that gladiators are to be kept away from the arena. The university republic of letters was relatively peaceful during the early years of this century, before the return in force of comparative literature departments and programs. As our New England poet reminded us in a lighthearted context, good fences make good neighbors. The literature departments knew their traditional area of responsibility and had few territorial aspirations to unsettle the academic climate. True, the Department of Hebrew, where one existed, complained in vain that the old required course on the Bible as literature was really its property. English departments rarely conceded this, pointing out that only when the Hebrew texts (like the Greek) were ennobled in Jacobean English did they really become literature. The English department held in custody the broad courses of literature in translation. Under this hegemony a young English scholar whose thesis treated the satire of Marston, Nash, and Donne was considered ready to teach not only the Bible as Literature, but also texts of the Great Books, Western Heritage, and humanities courses. It was also true that Romance language departments, unaware that Romanistik was a rich, rewarding area pioneered and given a method by German and French scholars, set up their fences in curious ways. They often split into departments of French and Italian, Spanish and Portuguese, Italian and Spanish, French and Portuguese, and so on, for local reasons other than academic or philological. Overlooking such vagaries as these, one concedes that the fences were good and they made good neighbors.

Into this world of well-defined precincts and responsibilities comparative literature tried for several decades to inch its way. As we have shown (p. 16), the earliest attempts at Harvard and Columbia, each in its separate way, came to naught. At the close of the Second World War, however, owing to the positivistic forces mentioned in Chapter i, the national literature departments were obliged to make room for departments and programs of comparative literature.

The accommodation was eased by the fact that in the absence of trained comparatists in the 1940s, the first generation of comparatists kept one foot, and indeed a part of their loyalty, in their department of origin. Seldom did a program ask for more than one or two full-time appointments in comparative literature. The roster of comparative courses was kept at a minimum, usually four or five at the outset. Students coming to most universities were informed that they must take a large complement of courses in a single literature. Thus, the national literature departments, which of necessity contributed three types of direct service to the comparative literature department—examination jurors, thesis readers, and occasional lecturers in multiple-staffed courses— were rewarded by the presence of young comparatists taking at least a third of their courses in French, English, Slavic, etc. This cautious start, probably wise, corresponded to the spirit of the first Report of the Committee on Professional Standards:

We can scarcely overemphasize that our relationship with the sister departments should be one of close collaboration, rather than rivalry; that we should not be living up to our standards unless we are also fulfilling theirs; and that, if we succeed, we shall be realizing together the richest potential of the humanities.

The same Report of 1965 sought and found a silver lining in the fact that a few universities

> still require the M.A. in a single field as a prerequisite to the Ph.D. in Comparative Literature. This implies an even dimmer view of the undergraduate major, and makes it rather difficult for the candidate to progress from the one-or-two languages stage to the three-or-four. At the other extreme, it is noteworthy that a number of institutions have thus far been concentrating their efforts on a meaningful master's degree in the field of Comparative Literature itself.

The grafting of comparatism on the body academic was obviously successful. Haskell Block has explained that inevitable growth as a rejection of entrenched patterns of literary study:

> The rise of Comparative Literature can be explained in large part by the narrowness of literary study in more traditional disciplines, the sacrifice of breadth for the sake of minute specialization, and the effort to define and systematize the study of individual national literatures as wholly autonomous fields.

It is certainly true that the comparatists shied away from narrowness, and they played well their modest role of caution and cooperation. They did not complain of the lack of two-way traffic while comparative literature students took many courses in English, French, and other departments whose registrants were kept right at home. However, the gladiatorial rivalry occasionally burst forth, as in Herbert Weisinger's preface to Étiemble's *Crisis in Comparative Literature*. On a slight and indirect pretext, this preface points a finger of suspicion and competitiveness at the "chauvinistic" departments of national literature. Discussing the nature of comparative literature, he suddenly writes, "For there is no agreement as to what it is, except that it is a good thing, and of course even this harmless proposition is hotly denied by the chauvinists of the traditional departments of literature." (See fuller quotation on p. 2 above.)

By 1960 many young Ph.D.'s in comparative literature were infiltrating faculties, confident of the *droit de séjour* of their now entrenched discipline and impatient for its growth. As their numbers grew, the comparatist's task of sailing safely through shoals increased. The situation is amusingly summarized by Herbert Lindenberger of Stanford:

> One of our most lively and respected comparatists once described his role as that of a diplomat who must constantly mediate among the various nationalities that comprise the language and literature family at every university. I, too, as one forced by his job to mediate ever since graduate-school days between literary scholars unable to communicate with one another, can testify that one must learn certain cues to maintain one's credentials with people in the individual national disciplines. If I happen to mention my admiration for Nietzsche to a classical scholar, I am quick to add that I know Nietzsche was dead wrong about Greek tragedy. If I speak of the importance of Ezra Pound to either a classical scholar or a Sinologist, I make clear my awareness that Pound's linguistic boo-boos must have made him an unacceptable graduate student of Comparative Literature during his brief period in that role. If I discuss a French literary work before an American in the field of French, I assure him that I have read the work in the original, only hoping that my quite imperfect pronunciation of the title will not discredit any literary insights I have to offer.

The problem of interdepartmental harmony looms importantly in the second ACLA Report of the Committee on Standards:

> The first requisite of a healthy department or program in Comparative Literature is an adequate staff, and the second following close upon it is the department's relationship to the other literature departments. Every department or program ought to have at least one and preferably two trained comparatists on its staff, normally in positions of responsibility. Normally the staff is enlarged by recourse to the strength of neighboring departments. One useful means of promoting collegiality between departments is the joint appointment, an arrangement which commonly promotes communications and properly supplies a structural basis for a spirit of cooperation.[1]
>
> Such a spirit is indeed crucial. Any Comparative Literature program must depend heavily on its neighboring departments of national literatures, indeed on all the Humanities departments. Without a strong English department and strong foreign language teaching, Comparative Literature cannot itself be strong.

[1] A recent Ph.D. from NYU commented on this sentence: "For new assistant professors, the road to tenure is difficult enough to tread in a single department."

The dependence of comparative literature on its good neighbors became accentuated during the early seventies when severe financial restraints were imposed on both public and corresponding private universities. At the same time the undergraduate foreign language requirement was widely abandoned and graduate requirements were lowered. The crisis was echoed in the 1976 ACLA Report:

> The present deterioration of support encountered by many graduate programs in the languages threatens our discipline with grave consequences. It is by no means certain that the enlargement of comparative literature programs can offset the decline of departments of foreign languages and literatures even when serious efforts are made to assume their specific functions. Our relations with our colleagues in those programs must in fact be symbiotic. Cooperation should occur at almost every level of departmental activity . . . and it should occur in two directions.

The report urges every sort of cooperation: cross-departmental freedom of enrollment, cross-listing of course offerings, exchanges of instructors, borrowing of staff for oral examinations; their use as codirectors of theses, their assistance in administering language examinations, their participation in colloquia, panel discussions, conferences, and similar activities. "Collegiality is implicit in the very term *university* as well as *college*. Without this spirit of fraternal participation in a common humane endeavor, Comparative Literature cannot thrive; indeed it cannot exist as a dynamic enterprise." The report wisely draws the line at double-listing—as opposed to cross-listing—of a single course.

Thus, whereas the first ACLA Report appealed for a more and more central role for comparative literature within the university, shrinking budgets of cooperating departments were making that role more inevitable. Yet such budgets, granting cooperation and collegiality, cannot help but make the competition for students (although fortunately not always the same students) a more obvious fact of life.

Competition for Students, Majors, and the Budget

The welfare of the comparative literature department, as we have seen (p. 61), is often determined by the budget officer rather than the academic dean. It is the bottom line that matters. Like the director of the university press or the football coach, the chairman of comparative literature must break even financially, and his balanced budget must be even more apparent than those of the established departments. At financial discussions you are reminded by Dean Midas: "Every tub on its own bottom." The statistics on majors, minors, and other students (full- or part-time) and course registrations are somehow memorized in advance by budget officers.

"You are down 72 points this semester," says Dean Midas. "Spanish is up 28 points."

"May I point out," you suggest, "that 20 points of that surplus indicates comp lit students studying with them this semester. The same holds for the other lit departments. We are not down. They are down."

Dean Midas, famous locally as a statistical genius, can never grasp this simple point. The temptation to attract students, possibly even set your admissions score at 3.1 instead of 3.4, sweeps momentarily over you. Certainly at the undergraduate level, where the language requirement has often been dropped, the scramble for students is great. Since Stephen Nichols' Committee Report on the Undergraduate Curriculum draws conclusions both realistic and idealistic about "body counts," we defer at length to that report:

> It is unfortunate that the leitmotif of "number of majors" should recur with such regularity in discussing such aspects of the undergraduate program as the language requirement and the senior thesis. The quantitative emphasis on majors threatens to beguile us, at times, into pretending that the Comparative Literature major has popular appeal, or, worse still, into reducing our standards to the point where—as literature-in-translation—it can attract a large number of student concentrators. While individual courses may attract undergraduates, the nature of our discipline predestines it to a limited clientele. Most undergraduates are not sure enough of their direction to justify investing the extra effort

necessary to meet the requirements of most Comparative Literature programs. It is a fact that our undergraduate major is more rigorous in its demands than most undergraduate majors in the humanities today. Rather than apologize for this rigor, or attempt to disguise it, we should not flinch from making a virtue of necessity.

The relatively small number of majors we can honestly hope to attract should serve to allay the fears of neighboring departments which would certainly become alarmed if we started attracting large numbers of majors. The strongest argument against worrying about the major "head count," however, lies in the domain of administrative statistics. Most deans simply do not figure instructional hours per student in terms of numbers of majors. Rather, they figure FTE's and supporting budgets in terms of enrollments. The case of the program at Dartmouth may be instructive in this respect.

In 1969–70, Comparative Literature had enrollments of 409 students with approximately six majors. There was no secretarial help budgeted to the program and only 3.7 FTE's which translated into seventeen instructors teaching part-time in the program (only two of whom were regular appointments budgeted for more than fifty percent of their time). In the academic year 1974–75, with a two-year history of more than 800 enrollments—*but still only an average of six majors*—there were 4.7 FTE's or twenty-one instructors teaching part-time (four of whom were regular appointments). In addition, a half-time secretary was assigned to the program. All these gains came about not as the result of an increased number of majors, but of an increase in the number of enrollments. It is important to note, for those who believe it necessary to reduce requirements in order to attract greater numbers of students, that there were no changes in requirements during the period in which increased enrollments were achieved and maintained.

Why Not Combine Comparative Literature with Portuguese?, or the Departmental Bouillabaisse

Concerning the bouillabaisse principle, which many administrators fondly dream of if they note a decrease of registrants in Slavic, Portuguese, or other language departments, several facts of life must be faced squarely. It is easily comprehensible why a state evaluation committee admonished a major department of English to release its tight, exclusive grip on comparative literature. The answer is simply that their departmental goals, dimensions, and interests are quite distinct. If an Italian or Portuguese department is foundering, then the logical—even welcome— merger should be within the Romance area. There can be no objection to the merging or coalescing of the Romance or Slavic or Near Eastern (including Hebrew and Arabic) linguistic families, for respected and logical unifying forces should encourage it.

When this writer had some years ago organized the Ph.D. in Italian at NYU—within the Romance languages department—he was invited to organize the doctoral program in comparative literature, a task he had participated in elsewhere. No one suggested that he renounce the administration of Italian studies. Nothing was more painful therefore than the writing of a formal letter of withdrawal from Italian, which he felt obligated to submit. One cannot have it two ways.

Since deans often hope nowadays to effect economies in attaching national literatures to a successful comparative literature department, it does not bother them when they are making de jure comparatists out of teachers who are not. Perhaps occasionally chairmen of comparative literature may be flattered to see their authority extended and their manpower pool increased. Yet mergers too often move manpower about like so many pieces on a chessboard, uncritically and to no advantage. If the transfer of personnel is done critically, after consultation and study of departmental needs, a valid solution to the bouillabaisse problem might be found. If national literature departments are overstaffed and in deficit, let the major comparatists study the qualifications of the most convertible individuals, if any, who might be transferred. These qualifications are by now familiar: knowledge of three or more foreign languages, a broad literary perspective, recognized broad competence in a given period or genre, and a willingness to retool and offer a meaningful rotated course or two in comparative literature. This last resort would alleviate the budget of his department of origin, add new viewpoints and thrusts to the comparative literature department, and make him or her available for the many units of manpower (see p. 63) required by theses, examinations, and other duties. This measure should be adopted only when the budget will not absorb a full-time Ph.D. in comparative literature.

In a number of schools where the bouillabaisse syndrome became especially evident, deans and budget officers dreamed of combining not only profitable with unprofitable departments, but unprofitable ones with themselves. Thus, if English, Spanish, and comparative literature were holding their own financially, the bouillabaisse might be a meager one of Slavic, classics, Portuguese, and Italian. To put it in a cynical way, those departments that not only were traditionally popular but had been carefully administered to weather the storm might—there was no certainty of it—or might not be thus rewarded by union with those that had not been so administered. In most schools the prosperous English department was less vulnerable to merger. Yet one could never be sure. A young Ph.D. in our field is quoted in the Chambers Report: "It seems the chairman thinks my being in the English department will forestall a dean's plan to merge the English and Foreign Language departments into a single unit."

A few deans have even considered a final accretion of all language and literature departments. The general was not to absorb the particular. The chairman of the amalgam might be, let us say, an Italianist or classicist who had clout with the administration. Comparative literature truly stood to lose its particular identity under any of these projected umbrellas, losing its identity and philosophy by having to absorb untrained and uncommitted—perhaps even unconvinced—colleagues. The individual department chairmen also were not happy at the prospect of general anschluss. This concern of theirs was somewhat allayed in a speech of Herbert Lindenberger to a gathering of foreign language department chairmen when mergers were the topic of the day:

> Perhaps I should assure you at this point that I do not advocate the extinction of language departments. Nor do I advocate their amalgamating to form a large department of literature. However attractive the latter possibility may sound in theory, forcing the national literatures into a single administrative entity is like forcing nation-states to become part of some world republic: since each national literature would enter such a department with its own local ways of thinking and acting, the best one could hope for would be a loose federation of language areas which, even

though housed in a single department, would not differ signifi-
cantly from the departmental groupings we now know at present.
Given the long fragmentations of literary study into these areas,
we cannot expect the ease of communication between specialists
in national areas that one finds in fields such as history, art history, and musicology.

During the mid-seventies this threat of total merger of all
language departments under the semantically attractive title of
comparative literature was so widespread that the Regents accreditation office was "keeping an eye on this tendency," and I
was informed there that Albany would find it very difficult to
"legitimize" such a patchwork arrangement. The ACLA Report II
would have done well to take a strong stand against this real, not
theoretical, threat. Such a threat should be occupying us much
more than the lesser divisive issues of an ancient language requirement or the "happy few" theory of student admissions. The
major problem, now and in the future, is to arrest charlatanism,
opportunism, and abandonment of principle as long as language
departments remain on the defensive in our colleges and universities. If the Levin Report of 1965 was right in stressing that
autonomy brings budgetary advantages, indeed independence,
we must reject mergers. Even if such mergers left us at the top of
the heap, we should have sold out our principles and, what is
worse, our colleagues, not to mention our students. At New York
University when a merger of this kind was contemplated, the
students sent formal protests to the chancellor pointing out the
illegality of such a move (see p. 278).

Perhaps unworthy of discussion are those departments willing
to absorb another alien department for other than financial reasons. Yet cannibalism exists. I think of one department of our own
discipline that suddenly annexed Italian and Portuguese. When I
asked the chairman how this ever happened, he replied, "Well,
the Portuguese couldn't get along with the Hispanists, nor the
Italians with the French. So we took them in." A brief glance at
college catalogs suggests that one could make a census of these
mésalliances in a number of colleges and universities. The ACLA
should take a stand on this issue, it seems. If it ever creates an
evaluation mechanism or dispatches visiting committees, let them
do their best to discourage these *mésalliances* and hasty mergers.

The Interdepartmental Advisory Committee

During the infancy of a comparative literature program, some administrators have set up an interdepartmental advisory body not only to involve and allay concerns of the other literature departments, but to gain a broader base of strength. Each neighboring department of literature will have one or two *sympathisants*, perhaps even one who occasionally teaches for comparative literature. Such committee action is most useful during the period of expansion when pressures are needed to obtain more secretarial time, more space, more personnel, more courses. Such amici curiae help counter the two-edged criticism of comparative literature: that it poaches on the teaching preserves of national literature departments and that it competes for students with them. With an interdepartmental committee, restricted to an advisory function, serving as a watchdog over the program, the first objection is more easily countered. As for the second, the committee members can convince their own home departments that well over three quarters of the graduate students come from earlier schooling elsewhere (the situation apparently differs with respect to the B.A. majors), and that in any case since graduate students must take a generous quota of their course work in noncomparative literature departments, our department actually swells the roster of students in the national literatures. Such committee colleagues serve as welcome missionaries or ambassadors to the other department chairmen. When something is placed on the agendum of possible concern to these chairmen, the latter may, if strategically desirable, be invited to attend meetings ex officio.

Most useful at such meetings is a small student representation, so that student members, whose interests are vitally concerned, will be present armed with their vote. Sometimes student action can accomplish what the administrators of a small department cannot. As stated above, in our own university, student representations to the president and chancellor nipped in the bud a contemplated departmental merger involving comparative literature. After all, the student committee insisted, they had paid considerable tuition for a diploma in a specific department, validated by the Board of Regents, and the university was legally bound to confer such a diploma.

Once the program has been solidly entrenched, achieved equality, and been successfully accredited as a department, the value of the interdepartmental committee is somewhat reduced, since faculty protocol will provide many occasions for the comparative literature chairman and teachers to be in direct contact with other departmental peers. Indeed, at that point there will be times when the comparative literature chairman may be in a position to reciprocate past favors. Nevertheless, some chairmen may prefer to retain the interdepartmental advisory mechanism for future emergencies. Consequences of their favorable intervention may be of a lasting nature, such as their arranging free auditing in elementary and intermediate language classes for students of comparative literature, who must learn two or three foreign languages.

Diplomacy and the Jacquerie: Student Power

The present volume rejects the premise that a principle of elitism derives from the number of students admitted to our discipline or with the amount of scholarship monies they are awarded. Neither bigness nor smallness is inherently preferable, but I have stated above that teaching classes in which the students represent over a dozen nationalities and languages makes me opt for largeness. The multinational texture of our student body is especially appropriate to comparative literature. Their availability to untraveled American students makes their presence desirable. Since we have discussed elsewhere this happy affinity, let us conclude this chapter by discussing rather the role of a large body of students in the diplomacy and governance of academe.

There are three assumptions concerning administration which we shall briefly elaborate. First, one must find ways to stay in touch with the students. Second, one must find ways to let them share in the departmental decision making. Lastly, one must acknowledge and use their collective power and influence in the res publica of comparative literature.

One of course stays in touch with individual students through classes, consultation hours, receptions, frequent colloquia where faculty and students mingle, the annual regional conference, and even, for that matter, oral examinations. Our departmental student association, with funds from the Graduate Student Association, sponsors two parties a year. They have created an informal atmosphere in a small office, space formerly used for storage. There is each fall a chairman's cocktail and buffet, where the new students meet the old. About once a year there is mailed from the office a state-of-the-department letter to present and former students. (Alumni are often included in the invitations to events and, sometimes, the mailings listed above.) In the spring the students themselves compile a newsletter about the department, mainly about their own activities and accomplishments, which is sent to students, alumni, faculty, and even administrators (you see, we are still in the area of diplomacy). The colophon on the title page of this volume is borrowed from the front page of the student newsletter. The students themselves, who attend classes in several different departments, make an effort to stay in touch with one another. (An occasional marriage attests student solidarity.)

The students are eager to have a hand in the discussion and making of decisions. For this reason they have been represented at meetings of the Interdepartmental Advisory Committee, as suggested earlier. A basic revision of the structure of our Ph.D. oral and written examinations was made during preliminary discussions in the Advisory Committee, a student delegation present. This was followed by questionnaires to all students and then balloting by mail. The intervals between oral and written examinations were set by a student vote. Not all decisions concern intradepartmental matters. Our departmental delegation to the student governing body of the graduate school sometimes consults departmental professors before casting votes. The students of the graduate school occasionally publish a booklet rating chairmen and professors, somewhat more dependable than the *Harvard Crimson Guide* to undergraduate courses. Thus, they hold a legitimate influence over our performance.

With the mention of public, printed ratings of faculty we are in the presence of our third assumption, that of student power. Our students exercise power in their own graduate school councils and in our department. We are probably conscious of this power in everything we do, with the result that we are seldom petitioned or requested to innovate or change policies and practices.

That this power seems more potential than actual lulls us into forgetting its existence. When the department needs it, or when the students see that their interests are at stake, it is a great power indeed and must not be forgotten. We have already mentioned how our students reacted with vigor and unanimity against a plan to merge our department—the more difficult because the plan was never really brought into the open. The student meetings, vocal and written protests, and finally veiled threats of legal action totally thwarted the plan. One factor—and one neglected area of student power—that has not been mentioned in connection with this example of blunt diplomacy is that our departmental alumni over the country banded together through correspondence for a second wave of attack, which, fortunately, was never required. The prospect of bringing together the currently enrolled graduate students in comparative literature of an entire geographical region is surely an attractive one, and Yale's comparative literature department has organized the first such meeting in New Haven.

XV

The Future of a Discipline

Voltaire said that a man has as many personalities as the languages he speaks. He could have said as well the literatures he reads.

WELLINGTON BRUNDAGE

Comparatism and International Understanding; Images; Mirages

As these pages are written, we are roughly a score of years from the twenty-first century. Considering such achievements of science and technology as landings on the moon, radar, color television from Mars, probings of the sun's unreliability and its effect on our life, research potential of computers—useful also to our own studies—one would expect that sociopolitical strides forward would keep pace. We have too many evidences that such is not the case. As my friend Édouard Roditi bluntly stated it, "Our sewage systems are a great advance over the Roman cloaca, but their burden has not improved." There were very few years during the twentieth century when America was not at war or in a state of bellicose confrontation. The need for understanding among peoples is greater than ever. Despite the creditable job being done by educational television to bring the peoples and places from all corners of the world into the home and the classroom—especially when a "bowl" football game or a crime drama does not divert ninety percent of the viewers—the increase of international understanding is not keeping up with the increased tensions and dangers. More and more nations are now equipped with nuclear overkill, and more liberated nations are feeling the excitement of militaristic nationalism.

279

Courses in comparative literature—Western Heritage, East-West, or World in dimension—are one of the few ongoing media for international understanding, a potential for "cultural exchange." As Professor Guyard wrote in his useful little manual:

> Everyone knows that cultural exchanges are one of the fragile hopes for humanity. Comparatism, as it writes the history of international literary relations, shows that no literature has ever been able to isolate itself without becoming atrophied and that the finest national masterpieces have always leaned on foreign contributions, that these masterpieces assimilate them or affirm their own identity more clearly either in juxtaposition to them or thanks to them. At the same time, comparatism helps every people to trace within itself the birth of those mirages that it may too often take for faithful images—a lesson of lucidity and humility as valid as the lessons of history: little known, but certain.

Several others have written on the role of cultural images in our discipline. In his *Comparative Literature: Matter and Method*, Owen Aldridge defines mirage as

> the impression which one national culture makes upon another through literature. Like the mirage in the desert, this impression may or may not resemble reality. Going beyond the portrayal of national types, such as the stolid Englishman, the volatile Frenchman, or the materialistic American, which are mainly caricatures, the mirage comprises the total effect which one nation makes on individuals of another.

The method was brought to perfection by the French comparatist Jean-Marie Carré. It may be seen in several of his works, including *Les Écrivains français et le mirage allemand*. In this work Carré showed how inevitably an excessive Germanophilia was replaced after 1870 by an excessive Germanophobia. In the Aldridge anthology Harry Levin's essay, "France-Amérique: the Transatlantic Refraction," probes the reciprocal imagism of the United States and France. "The mutual attraction of the two cultures is that of opposites: ours has had a centrifugal movement, as well as an outward perspective, while theirs has had a centripetal tendency, along with an inside viewpoint." Also suggestive on *images* and *mirages* is the chapter "Images et psychologie des peuples" in the manual of Pichois and Rousseau.

Paul Van Tieghem has seen comparative literature as a resurgence of Renaissance humanism, "broader and more fecund than the former, better able to bring nations together. Comparatism imposes on those who practice it an attitude of sympathy and understanding toward our fellow human beings (*frères humains*: the phrase of Villon)—an intellectual liberalism without which no work to be commonly shared by all peoples can be attempted." All the humanitarian and social values that Gorki read into the concept of world literature had already been implanted in comparative literature by the generation of Van Tieghem.[1]

Cultural Exchange

It is easy to exaggerate the effect of cultural exchanges. They do not always operate as one hopes. Even the international Olympiad now breeds political assassinations. The Institute of International Education, which has labored so admirably in this field, found that sometimes immersion in a foreign culture would backfire. A francophobiac student, writing his end-of-the-year report to the Institute on his sojourn in France, which he cut short, criticized everything about the French, even that source of national pride, French cuisine. One gem from his annual report read: "And as for the *choux de Bruxelles*, they were so tough that they should have been rolled back to Brussels with a billiard cue." Yet for one such exception there were a thousand successful transplants. Similarly, it is unusual for a student immersed in comparative literature to drop out for any reason other than health or penury.

All comparatists who have taught a course—especially a widespread course penetrating six or seven cultures such as European romanticism—have witnessed the students' sense of excitement on "connecting" with a masterpiece from an unfamiliar literature. Students who wondered at the outset why a course on epic should require a reading of Camoëns' *Lusiads* end up with the realization that it was the Portuguese who first had the global vision and

1 By sheer coincidence, a fuller version of Van Tieghem's praise of comparative literature is included in the GSFLT French examination above, page 113.

did something heroic about it. Much of the writing until now on the cultural exchanges of our discipline has of course centered on the familiar literatures of England, Germany, and France. In the twenty-first century students will probably be learning of equally great feats of epic heroes from *Gilgamesh*, the *Mahabharata*, and the *Shah Nameh*. The mirages to be offered by world literature will be no less exciting than those offered by Aztec culture to the astonished Cortés.

In his apologia for the contribution of comparatism to cultural exchange, Guyard assigned an important role to influence study. As comparatism spreads across its world stage, influence and source studies may become more difficult to establish and less important—even as comparisons and contrasts may become more exciting.

In any discussion of cultural exchange we are assuming that our Ph.D. candidates will read their three required languages with facility, and not barely slip by with a low passing score. One shares the hope of Pichois and Rousseau that they will travel. Just as French concentrators became imbued with sympathy, if not enthusiasm, for French culture, and German students similarly sensed *Heimweh* for things German, the multiple intrusions of young comparatists into several cultures should produce the healthy cosmopolitanism that we almost unthinkingly assume on their part. All the more reason to incite them to probe further into an Asian or African literature.

We always encourage our students to learn even more languages after they finish their schooling. Yet if the decline of foreign languages continues in America, we may have to become more indulgent about literature in translation at the undergraduate level. Against our most deep-rooted principles, we may have to accept the fact that some cultural exchange must be effected through translation. One evening just before the peace in Vietnam our department sponsored with the Asia Society an evening of public readings of contemporary Vietnamese social and political poetry translated by Unguyen Ngoc Bich and others. Texts were read in the original by Asians and in translation by young Americans. Carpet-bombing and napalming were reaching their intensity in Southeast Asia. A large crowd of American and Asian students sat mute in Loeb Student Center for two hours, traumatized by these gentle, disturbing poems. If you have read "What

Were They Like," by Denise Levertov, identical in spirit with the Vietnamese poems read, you can understand their katharsis. The students left—one could almost say slinked away—without a word. The Vietnamese texts played for the Americans a minor, if useful, role of lending authenticity. It was the words in English that effected the purgation. Here is one of the poems read that night, Te Hanh's "The River Back Home,":

> At home we had a blue river,
> limpid waters reflecting bamboo.
> My mind was a summer afternoon
> as sunlight glittered over the surface.
> I wonder if waters keep track of time,
> if memories remain in your flowing streams,
> o river that has bathed my whole life!
> For you my love is still fresh,
> for you, river of my land, river of youth,
> river of our beloved South!
>
> Birds chattered in the bamboo hedge,
> fish leaped through the air
> as we, in bands of seven or five,
> young birds, swam in the stream.
> I spread my arms to embrace the water,
> the river opened and gathered me in.
> We grew up, each went his own way:
> Some were fishing all the day,
> others plowing in sun and rain.
> I took up a gun to fight far from home,
> but still my mind, like a squall, a storm,
> rushed back to the river it loved,
> the image of a girl with ruddy cheeks.
>
> Now the North has made me its son,
> but in my heart I still hear the whisper,
> the two sacred words, "South Vietnam."
> Who can console me for the loss
> of that yellow sun, that emerald sky?
> I miss even people I never knew . . .
> Sometimes, under trees in the afternoon,
> I am suddenly overwhelmed
> by the image of a cool, fresh river
> that flows on, bathing me as a spray.
> Native land! My mind is also a river:

Love between North and South runs in one stream,
a stream no rapids or falls can stop.
I will go back to the land of my dream,
I will go back to the river of my land,
I will go back to the river of my love.[2]

Since we are in this final chapter speculating on the future course of comparative literature, one cannot help hoping that wherever comparative literature is not part of a college curriculum, the inevitably present literature-in-translation will penetrate the vaster dimensions of East-West or World Literature. Since we are hoping, however, let us envision that these broad courses in translation will be taught by trained comparatists and linguists.

The ethics of prophecy does not permit wishful thinking. One gathers from the Nichols Report that the spread of literature-in-translation may continue to exceed that of comparative literature at the undergraduate level. The continuing programs of translation in the English-speaking world recorded in UNESCO's *Index Translationum* and elsewhere make it clear that if the present rate continues, major works of East-West or World origins will be more easily available in translation as textbooks or assigned readings than in their original form. Indeed, where the professor of a graduate course touching six or seven linguistic bases knows only three or four foreign languages himself, the specter of literature-in-translation already haunts the classroom (see p. 303). *Au royaume des aveugles les borgnes sont rois.* To thwart the specter, either guest-lecturing or a much higher standard of polyglottism must be called for in the future. As more "new" literatures will demand a modest *droit de séjour* in classes, the problem will become accentuated.

One solution to this problem would be to increase the number of comparative literature courses taught each semester, even at the cost of a smaller enrollment per class. (We do not refer here to double-listed courses.) A department now offering six courses a semester might offer eight. Thus, if each course concerns four to six bodies of literature, room could be found for more of the "new" literatures. Furthermore, linguists familiar with the less common national languages and literatures would have their "day

2 Te Hanh, "The River Back Home," trans. Ngoc Bich, with Burton Raffel and W. S. Merwin, in *A Thousand Years of Vietnamese Poetry*, ed. Bich (New York: Knopf, 1975), pp. 182–83.

in court." Such an expansion may occur in the future at the graduate level.

The Job Market Present and Future

The first major survey to ascertain how Ph.D.'s in our field were
faring on the employment market, what they were teaching, what
their departmental affiliations were, and what their vocational
expectations, was conducted by Leland Chambers for the ACLA
poll A. It was a difficult task carefully undertaken, for which we
are all grateful. Some 145 questionnaires (63 percent of those
polled) were returned, approximately two thirds of the respondents being male. Chambers found after studying their answers
that the variety of institutional arrangements and modes of existence made legitimate conclusions largely very general. Since the
year 1974 was a year of recession in college language and literature departments, the tightness of the job market was reflected in
the replies. Turning to the two-year colleges, Chambers sent 151
questionnaires also to chairmen of English, humanities, language
arts, and communications departments (poll B). Finally, to ascertain the total picture of the job market for Ph.D.'s in comparative literature, he sent 140 questionnaires to chairmen of English
and related departments of four-year colleges and universities
across the country (poll C). To simplify this summary, we have
called these three investigations A, B, and C respectively.

Fifty-eight percent of the Ph.D.'s in poll A reported that their
comparative literature degrees gave them an edge over those
candidates with narrower specializations; 11 percent thought this
possibly true, and 31 percent reported that their teaching was at a
level that precluded their using their comparatist's training.
Many of the unemployed reported that the comparative literature
degree hindered their chances in some areas, particularly in foreign language departments. Of the recent comparative literature
graduates 41 percent taught in English departments, 12 percent
in comparative literature departments or programs, 11 percent in
foreign language departments, and the rest in various departments or combinations of literature or the humanities. Many
institutions expected from comparative literature graduates the
versatility of the generalist and a professional expertise in two or

more languages. The report showed that many of the graduates had already occupied their teaching posts before completing their degree, with 41 of 128 graduates having assumed their current posts upon obtaining the Ph.D. within the previous twelvemonth.

As they sought positions in comparative literature, a sample group of young Ph.D.'s was asked by Professor Chambers what advice they would give to a job-seeker just starting out. A few of their answers were especially pertinent:

> Inquire about positions in all language and literature departments, not just comparative literature and English.
>
> Try two-year institutions. Their enrollment is not declining.
>
> Be specialized enough in one or more languages to qualify for joint appointment.
>
> Follow the current fashions in specializations and be forewarned.
>
> Publish. No one will look at you until you do.

Since most of the present generation of full and associate professors had to wait impatiently through their apprenticeship teaching elementary or intermediate foreign languages or English composition, it is no surprise that the new generation of Ph.D.'s polled on being obliged to teach at this rookie level find it "uncomfortable" and embittering. New Ph.D.'s have felt this way since time immemorial. Those respondents who had a legitimate grievance were the 17 out of 145 (approximately 11 percent) who had not yet found employment. Professor Chambers was disappointed that the entire group surveyed "demonstrated relatively little esprit de corps," few belonging to the MLA and not more than ten to the ACLA. He concludes:

> If we ourselves believe that such organizations have a place as a forum for discussing what we are most interested in, as a place for expressing our views, as a means of gathering together for common causes, we should really make a better effort to enroll our students somewhere along the line into our organizational activities.

Although Chambers states that "less than half of them" belong to the MLA, this is probably comparable to the percentage of the

American language teaching profession as a whole. Perhaps this is the place to agree with Chambers about solidarity, with not only the ACLA, but the MLA as well, for the many interviews arranged between employers and candidates at the MLA convention have proved to be extremely valuable. The recent decision of Executive Director William D. Schaefer to list comparative literature jobs in both the English and the Foreign Language Job Information Lists makes these available at small cost to the comparative literature departments, for which we are all grateful.

Poll B was addressed to community and junior college chairmen of English, humanities, language arts, and communications departments. Their courses included Great Books, humanities, genre or archetype, Western Heritage, and literature-in-translation. Chambers' conclusions are as follows:

> In general, both 2- and 4-year colleges seem relatively receptive to hiring teachers in Comparative Literature, when "Comparative" is taken to mean interdisciplinary. But they do not favor hiring Ph.D.'s. Several insisted that they wanted "generalists," that the Ph.D.'s were "too narrowly specialised." Since Freshman Composition is a large part of the teaching load at such institutions, qualifications for teaching such courses are the most sought-after quality, I should suppose. Several respondents mentioned that they would be interested in CL or interdisciplinary majors only if they were able to teach Freshman Composition and if they understood the philosophy of a junior college. One respondent took the trouble to volunteer his opinion that interdisciplinary studies of some sort seemed the coming thing at the junior college level.

The Report, moreover, further noted that a dozen schools would hire English Ph.D.'s as better qualified to teach freshman composition, although thirty-one indicated a preference for specialists in "Interdisciplinary literatures." Twenty-eight of the chairmen indicated a willingness to make dual appointments. A majority of the schools indicated that readings in "world literature" (see Ch. ii) were offered in the contexts required by freshman and sophomore courses. None of the community or junior colleges at the date of poll B offered a minor in comparative literature, but three of the larger community colleges were planning majors in comparative literature leading to the B.A. degree.

Poll C taken by Professor Chambers concerns the employment potential of Ph.D.'s in comparative literature in the four-year colleges and universities throughout the nation. These schools, he specifies, varied in character: private and public, denominational and secular, metropolitan, suburban, and relatively rural; liberal arts colleges and specialized schools. His conclusions are encouraging and coincide in passing with the results of the polling undertaken by Professor Stephen Nichols:

> In the schools returning questionnaires (79), the chairmen of English departments demonstrate a great deal of openmindedness toward CL majors. Ph.D.'s are wanted, at least with regard to the limitations suggested in the questionnaire, yet very little hiring is contemplated. A most interesting phenomenon emerged from the answers to these questionnaires: the number of new CL departments or programs either under way or definitely planned is increasing greatly, particularly at the undergraduate level.

Among the summary of data concluding this report are several interesting facts: to teach the undergraduate Great Books and congeneric courses, 86 percent would hire Ph.D.'s, while 13 percent would hire M.A.'s or A.B.D.'s. Thus, it would seem that limitations of budget are not an imperative consideration. Of the 68 percent, thirty-one wanted comparative literature graduates, twenty-one preferred English graduates, and sixteen would take either:

> The possibilities for dual appointments are not likely to help CL majors very much. Less than half—35 institutions—indicated the possibility of dual appointments, but not many seemed enthusiastic about them. Furthermore, the partner departments most often mentioned as sharing dual appointments were departments such as Black Studies, American Studies, Education, Humanities, none of which, when paired with English, seems made to order for CL majors. Furthermore, half (39) of the institutions indicated no possibility (or at most, only a remote possibility) of dual appointments.

Of the seventy-nine institutions that returned questionnaires to Professor Chambers, forty-one offered "world literature" in undergraduate courses (see p. 42 above), though "not as a required course in most institutions." Only six of the seventy-nine institutions offered an undergraduate minor in comparative literature; three offered a minor in comparative literature at the graduate level. As proved to be the case in poll B, Chambers found that twenty institutions that did not already offer B.A.'s or M.A.'s in comparative literature were definitely planning comparative literature majors or giving the prospect serious consideration.

Whereas the statistics on the growth of comparative literature as an academic discipline gathered in these three significant polls are already undergoing modifications in favor of a growing discipline, the factors determining the employment possibilities will be conditioned by the general health of the body academic. The trend toward the spread or growth of comparative literature clearly indicated in the Nichols Report is corroborated in that of Professor Chambers. Vocational opportunities will inevitably reflect the trend. As the male and female rabbit, held at bay in a cave by a pursuing hound, agreed hopefully, "The future is on our side. We'll outnumber him."

In the peripheral applications of comparative study, there are some optimistic reports. SUNY's translation curriculum at Binghamton (see p. 303) reports that its majors are finding jobs without difficulty. So also is the report on M.A.'s completing Iowa's Program of Asian Studies: "Career opportunities in East-Asian studies are plentiful at the present and there is every indication that they will increase markedly in the next decade as cultural exchanges with Asia develop further."

During decreasing prosperity chairmen and graduate advisers are interrogated constantly about the job market, from prospective registrants to students writing their final theses. The chairman must volunteer to examine and edit the graduate's vita to be filed with the employment bureau. The department must order annually the Modern Language Association's job information lists (comparative literature being included with both the English and foreign language lists) and call these to the student's attention. Letters of recommendation from the department must be prudently, if honestly worded, since one single negative statement during hard times and severe competition may disqualify a candidate. Sometimes one can transmit enthusiasm for a candidate or lack of it by the letter's length instead of its wording. This is particularly true where the freedom-of-information policy

(Public Law 93-380) allows a student the option of reading what his professors have written. A student should be advised to waive that right, for a strong statement bearing the information that a student has access to its content may impress a potential employer less than a confidential statement of support more moderately worded.

One of the ironies and disappointments in a large department during the late spring is that senior professors are more often asked to recommend a candidate for an associate or full professorship than for an instructorship or assistant professorship. A job candidate should not fail to try the college employment agencies, which must continue to place teachers or close their doors. An advantage of graduating from a department with large enrollment is that departmental alumni already placed in colleges—occasionally even as administrators—sometimes manage to hire the department's later qualified Ph.D.'s.

When Dean Weisinger was contesting what he called the elitism of the first and second ACLA Reports on Professional Standards, which called for small departmental enrollments, he attacked their argument that it would be hard to place graduates in this field, charging professors with disregarding this function of theirs.

> Nor need these students be unemployed if we seriously and directly address ourselves to the various requirements and even more numerous possibilities of the market. We tend to forget that, in this country at least, the purpose of graduate education is the preparation and placement of students, and that double obligation cannot be offloaded onto the students themselves, as may easily be the case where the research interests of faculty take precedence over other responsibilities.

Not only does the Modern Language Association assist in arranging interviews for candidates at the annual conventions, as well as distributing the job lists mentioned above; the American Comparative Literature Association has started to publish a list of new Ph.D.'s in our field, with descriptive materials on them, including languages and field of specialization.

The understandable concern of students over the specter of unemployment is one we all share. One can sometimes allay their fears by pointing out that many graduates of the past, during the years of the Depression, did not know in early June where they would be teaching the following September. Those who were fortunate found jobs teaching eighteen hours a week. With budgets now being approved later and later in the year, jobs are also being offered later.

It is good to remind students that jobs *are* being filled, even if theirs have not come through. Our department issues every spring a previously mentioned newsletter of about eighteen pages, recording achievements, travels, publications, vital statistics, acts of God, and the employment status of both degree candidates and alumni out in the arena of learning. This newsletter, mailed out widely to students, alumni, and interested faculty and staff, inevitably presents a picture of high employment among both candidates and alumni. This statistical evangel appears in April, a period when jobless candidates need to be reminded that our students have obtained and are obtaining teaching positions, that all hope is not lost.

Publish or Perish?

Finding employment is not the only obstacle facing the young scholar today. A very common problem for those who do find teaching positions is survival in the academic world. The current job market has produced the increasing expectation that the fund of knowledge that a student acquires in graduate school may be applied in even other ways than teaching his students and guiding their theses. Unless he is a Diogenes, who learned merely for the sake of learning, he is expected to get his ideas into print. This expectation leads to a variety of comments among those who do not get into print. These comments have crystallized into the cutting phrase "Publish or perish."[3]

---

[3] This phrase has evoked satirical comment now part of academic lore. Rumor has it that it was coined by a quinquegenarian assistant professor who had never broken into print, but piously explained to his publishing colleagues that he had no time for writing, devoting himself totally to teaching his students. An equally widespread sarcasm owed to this individual was that to maintain tenure at the University of Chicago, one must publish three and a third articles each year. But his best was his constantly repeated maxim, "When you copy from one book it's plagiarism, but when you copy from two books it's research." Unfortunately it is told that he was always ranked poor on the student faculty ratings, while his publishing colleagues fared better.

It is sometimes alleged, as in the footnote, that time taken out for writing means less time to devote to teaching. Another charge often heard is that the more a professor publishes, the more diluted or repetitious his or her production becomes. This may or may not be true, but it is true that not all scholarly published books or articles are serious contributions to knowledge. The satirical poem on the papers at the MLA Convention, composed by Morris Bishop some years before he served the Association as president in 1964, reminds us how remote and overspecialized research may become.[4] Yet, in view of the competition for publication in the major learned journals at this time, only papers of substance are now usually accepted. For every article published

[4] *A Salute to the Modern Language Association*
Convening in the Hotel Pennsylvania, December 28th–30th

The Modern Language Association
    Meets in the Hotel Pennsylvania,
And the suave Greeters in consternation
    Hark to the guests indulging in their mania

For papers on "Adalbert Stifter as the Spokesman of
    Middle-Class Conservatism,"
    And "The American Revolution in the *Gazette de Leyde*
    and the *Affaires de l'Angleterre et de l'Amérique*,"
And "Emerson and the Conflict between Platonic and
    Kantian Idealism,"
    And "Dialektgeographie und Textkritik,"

And "Vestris and Macready: Nineteenth Century
    Management at the Parting of the Ways,"
    And "Pharyngeal Changes in Vowel and Consonant
    Articulation,"
And "More Light on Molière's Theater in 1672–73
    from Le Registre d'Hubert, Archives of the Comédie Française,"
    And "Diderot's Theory of Imitation."

May culture's glossolalia, clinging
    In Exhibit Rooms and Parlor A,
Sober a while the tempestuous singing
    Of fraternal conventions, untimely gay;

May your influence quell, like a panacea,
    A business assembly's financial fevers,
With the faint, sweet memory of "Observaciones sobre
    la aspiración de H en andalucía,"
    And the "Stimmsprung (Voice Leap) of Sievers."

From *New Yorker*, 31 December 1938, p. 18. The reader can be assured that these lectures were indeed taken literally from the program of the 1938 MLA Convention in New York City.

by a learned journal nowadays nine are rejected, and of the book
scripts submitted to a university press, only one out of twelve is
accepted. Thus, the blanket charges against the quality of scholarly publishing cannot really stand.

As the century has advanced, the areas for publication by professors of literature have multiplied. Many areas of creativity are
now recognized. Not only is scholarship accepted and encouraged, but poetry, novels, narrative, dramas, polemics, translations, and other literary activity enhance one's academic standing
and are recognized as potentially making one a broader teacher.
It is no longer necessary for professor-novelists, like Morris
Bishop, to write a mystery novel behind a pseudonym. It is interesting to recall that after Professor Thornton Wilder finished such
memorable works as *The Bridge of San Luis Rey* and *Our Town*,
he returned to complete a definitive bibliography and chronology
of the plays of Lope de Vega. A further evidence of this new
definition of scholarly publication is the fact that many university
presses now publish faculty poetry and plays, and would probably take a chance on novels (a few of which have indeed
appeared) if the trade publishers would not lower the boom on
them (protesting their tax exemptions). In any case, many comparatists are beginning to publish even during their graduate
years, as our annual departmental *Newsletter* abundantly
proves.

Breaking into Print: Book Reviewing
and Textual Explication

The pressure on all young scholars, comparatist or other, to
publish in the area of literary history or literary criticism is a
recognized fact of life. The Chambers Report indicated that one
must publish even before one's first teaching job (see above, p.
286). Almost every college and university dean will expect to find
evidence of printed articles or books before he will recommend
promotion or academic tenure. The publishing of articles, while
difficult of achievement, presents no special problem of technique
or procedure. The alternative of what eighteenth-century England called reviewage, however, must be considered. Several
practical steps that may facilitate publication of book reviews

will be set down shortly. First of all, we must look into the matter of book reviewing and its respectability and desirability. Under what circumstances may the reviewer qualify as a genuine literary critic and his review qualify as a publication fit for a curriculum vitae?

The present remarks have grown out of the realization that I have devoted a substantial period of my life to what Chesterton called "the easiest profession in the world." I evaluated my first scholarly book in *Modern Philology* as a graduate student years ago and my first trade book in the *New York Times* six years later. I encountered the familiar attitude among my colleagues that if you reviewed for *Speculum* it was a feather in your cap, but if you reviewed for commercial media it was "journalism." Later in life a dean at my university who determined my salary observed that I must be making a wad out of my "journalism" in *Saturday Review*. He shared the opinion that reviewing required less thought and research and demanded a style less chastened. Some academicians, notably F. R. Leavis, erected a Chinese wall between literary speculation and book reviewing. In other words, the reviewers, even top ones like V. S. Pritchett or Edmund Wilson, who evaluate a novel on its appearance are thus less respectable at that stage than when some years later they dedicate a learned essay to that novel and reach much the same conclusions.

Perhaps on the premise that literary criticism courses stand firmly behind the formation of book reviewers, no university to my knowledge offers a course on book reviewing. I do not say that such a course is necessary. Indeed, the opposite may be true. There may be wisdom in teaching the theory and then letting it filter down into varied applications. Joshua Reynolds rightly advised sculptors to learn anatomy and then forget it. However, at NYU part of a class in the comparative literature seminar is devoted to this important subject.

In book reviewing the ethical issue is immediate and sometimes dramatic, since we are no longer speculating about Homers or even Gides, but of living authors whose fortunes are dependent upon, if not at the mercy of, the ethics of the reviewer. If the ultimate issues arising in the discussion of book reviewers' ethics remain the traditional ones of insincerity, mendacity, the intention to deceive or distort, there are more immediate issues depending on who should review books and how they should undertake the task. Among the ethical issues arising from the choice of a reviewer there are, to begin with, the reviewer's commitment to read every word of the book assigned, the restraining of one's killer instinct, and the suppression of egotism and hubris. Then there are the questions of ignoramuses and unqualified reviewers, the clique critics indulgent with friends and colleagues (or wives, if one remembers Shelley's rave notice of *Frankenstein*) and harsh to those outside the circle, merchants of prejudice and fixed ideas, and the question whether authors themselves make the best reviewers. Finally, there is the sticky ethical question whether nonlinguists should review translations. These specific issues I have elaborated in a talk at Cambridge University, summarized in the Acts of the 1972 Congress of FILLM in England.[5]

One takes risks if one becomes stigmatized as a "book reviewer." The ethics of a reviewer have been attacked since the eighteenth century or earlier by both authors and more academic critics. Any attempt to juxtapose the parallel activities of literary criticism and reviewing collides with a time-honored prejudice. This is the complaint of men of letters (articulated by Cervantes, Pope, Addison, and many others) that "reviewers are people who would have been writers if they could." True, this charge is laid sometimes at the feet of academic critics, but reviewers are more frequently victims of it, perhaps even justifiably so in some cases.

Leavis' views are extremely interesting, for he set up not two but three categories of literary arbiters: real critics (excessive modesty or "particularity" does not lead him to exclude himself from this group), Higher Reviewers (with capital letters), and routine reviewers, whom we might with a bow to Gissing call Grub Street reviewers. Higher Reviewers Leavis sees as a fraternity of *manqués* or *ratés*, "who in the process of making a living have inevitably left behind what critical qualifications they may have had." They have made their pact with publishers and authors "at those little dinners at the Berkeley, those cocktail parties, and so on." The lower, Grub Street reviewer has not sold out to the Establishment. He is simply a myrmidon scurrying about the world of literary journalism.

[5] This subject is developed at length in *Directions of Literary Criticism in the Seventies* (Cincinnati: Univ. of Cincinnati Press, 1972), pp. 53–86.

The *New York Times Encyclopedic Almanac* of 1970 attempts, in a page devoted to critics and other commentators, to draw a line between critics and reviewers and in doing so awards academics the palm. Critics (twenty-nine familiar names are mentioned) satisfy one or more of three criteria: members of a university faculty, representative of a specific social or aesthetic canon of criticism, authors of books or extended studies of theory or criticism. *Tout le reste n'est pas littérature.* Forty-six more reviewers are mentioned. One wonders whether Malcolm Muggeridge was satisfied with his identification as "book reviewer, Esquire."

The comparison of critic and reviewer actually allows for overlap, of course. Nevertheless, the following distinctions may be made. The literary critic analyzes and measures a work from a critical—even dogmatic—premise or philosophy and, if possible, under the aspect of eternity. The reviewer may possess a critical stance, less elaborately displayed or sustained, but his chief task is to elucidate and evaluate the work under scrutiny while summarizing its contents. Critics usually deal with books already established as literature, sometimes contradicting previous assessments. Thus, in *Scrutiny*, F. R. Leavis will turn to Matthew Arnold, D. W. Harding to Coleridge, or F. O. Matthiessen to James. Meanwhile reviewers cope with the incoming volumes piling up in the mail room of the review medium. The critic may parade himself to his heart's content in his essay, whereas the reviewer must maintain a more modest presence or profile. The critic is usually given more time and more space than the reviewer. The clinging opprobrium attached to book reviewing is expressed in T. S. Eliot's belief that poets are the real critics and that reviewers are merely useful "second order familiars" of literature.

From these prefatory pages one may draw certain conclusions useful to our younger comparatists. The first lesson to emerge is that one must not be exclusively a book reviewer, that book reviews must constitute only a part of one's publication record. To have done some reviewing is obviously desirable. For the younger scholar who needs to appear in print, reviews offer several advantages. First is that they appear very quickly after being submitted, whereas a learned article may be delayed a year or two before publication. Second, reviews in newspapers and

periodicals are paid for. Third, reviews of textbooks are not difficult to place in academic journals. Fourth, one may order off-
prints of reviews just as easily as one orders reprints of articles.
Fifth, it is possible to take the initiative in getting a review published, as I have often demonstrated to students.

One may, of course, request from a learned journal the assignment of reviewing a forthcoming volume, but this is less likely to
be granted to a graduate student. On the other hand many students at my suggestion have published book reviews by checking
future publications in Bowker's latest *Forthcoming Books*, and
successfully requesting from the publisher a copy for review. (In
a few cases they were obliged to buy the book.) With this book in
hand they have submitted unsolicited reviews to journals that
had not received review copies from the publisher. If they were
not yet instructors, we lent them a departmental letterhead for
this correspondence. This stratagem works especially well with
books published in England, France, Germany, Italy, or other
foreign countries that do not usually send review copies to the
American learned journals. After having verified in the university
library order department or an import bookstore that a forthcoming scholarly book is to appear abroad and after ordering it for
purchase, the student informs an American journal editor that he
has received an important foreign book and offers a brief review
of it. Since the learned journals of America seldom receive review
copies from European presses, the editors are usually glad to accept a brief notice without cost, thus broadening their coverage.
One student whom I convinced to try this method found it so
successful that within three years after graduation he had published or placed seventeen reviews. I began to feel concern for his
future, lest he be identified with what Eliot defined as "a mind of
the second order." My fears were in vain. Within two years he
was appointed associate professor in a Western state university.

Textual explication is a second possible way to break into print.
During a boom period of textual explication some twenty years
ago it was possible to publish brief examples either in *Explicator*
or *Modern Language Notes* published in America, or in *Notes
and Queries* published in England. Some exponents of structuralism and semiotics have revived the explicative method, and it is
prominent in their published works. As first elaborated by the
German and French "text critics," structure was always one of the

method's three major elements. Rather than elaborate on text-kritik and its long history, I shall present the outline of an explication (see Fig. 21), re-created from a course on French Renaissance poetry that I took at the University of Bordeaux under the distinguished Paul Laumonier. The professor's own explicative method was less disciplined than would appear here, and during a week spent on one Pindaric ode of Ronsard, twenty minutes could be devoted to proving that the frogs in Greece, unlike those in France, did indeed croak as Aristophanes reproduced their *Brek-ek-ek-ex, coax, coax.*

FIG. 21. *Checklist for Textual Explication of a*
French Renaissance Poem

1. STRUCTURE, FORM
    Identify poetic form (ode, sonnet, eclogue, dizain, etc.); on Du Bellay's approved list? ancient or modern form?
    Metrics, versification, vers baïfins, etc.
    Rhyme scheme (usual, unusual)
    Syllable count: mute *e*'s, caesuras, etc. (donq/doncques, etc.)
    Length and visions of thought blocks; relation of structure and length to thought or general content; prolixity; brevity
2. LANGUAGE
    Langue de la cour, de la ville, des portefaix. Regionalisms, gasconismes, etc.
    Scholarly language. Gallocrec, Latinisms
    Clarity and obscurity: intentional or unintentional
    Contemporary grammar; orthography
    Contemporary idioms and words (nymphette, seulet, etc.)
    Proper names (real, fictitious, pastoral, etymological meanings, etc.)
    Audience intended
3. CONTENT
    Main ideas (social, religious, psychological)
    Progression of ideas or emotion
    Typicality of idea to poet, to school, to period
    Originality and sources; plagiarism, imitation, or *innutrition*; quality of translation if borrowing from foreign source
    School or movement, if any (marotique, mannerist, baroque, etc.); passing reflections of these movements; taste, standards
    Date and circumstances of composition; history of composition, if known
    Variant readings and manuscripts: Did author see definitive form? A *pièce retranchée*? Disputed wordings?

Relation to author's other poetry of same period; of earlier period; of later period; of total production (cf. Ronsard's Pindaric vs. Anacreontic period)

Erudite references; mythology; allegory

Personality, impersonality, le moi haïssable; sincerity

New revelation of authors supplied; conscious or unconscious?

4. CRITICAL COMMENTS

Criticism and mentions by French or other literary historians

Your own summary: strengths and weaknesses: *utilis* or *dulcis*

How does it illustrate principles of Pléiade, if a Pléiade poet? If not?

Renaissance versus contemporary evaluation of the poem

Other comments

Publishing Scholarly Books, Textbooks, and Trade Books

Let us begin this section with some generalities involving all three areas. One's first scholarly or trade book can be accepted more easily if accompanied by a subsidy or grant-in-aid from a university, foundation, society, or other source. However, vanity presses—often used by poets—carry little or no prestige. European publishers often manufacture scholarly unbound volumes more economically than American presses and with a smaller press run. Contract and royalty arrangements should be checked by your own university press editor, by an author's agent, or against an ideal contract, which may be obtained from the Authors Guild. Check financial advance, hard-cover and paperback royalty arrangements, life-of-book provision, plans for advertising, translation royalties, and copyright charges beforehand. Submit to your publisher a style sheet appropriate to your work to assist the copy editor if your work is at all specialized. If you publish further books or become well known in your field, you may be invited to serve a trade or textbook house as an advisory editor, a series editor, or a frequently used consultant reader. These are inevitably rewarding assignments professionally and financially. They will consume time but allow you to influence trends in your field. They also offer various fringe benefits. However, since every textbook you accept means that eleven will be rejected, one risks losing friends among one's colleagues.

Scholarly books bring more prestige than financial reward, of course. Indeed, as suggested above, they must usually be accompanied nowadays with a modest grant-in-aid of publication. This is in no way to be confused with vanity publishing, which is done without regard to the content of a book provided all bills are paid by the author. Sometimes even a scholarly book will attract a large public, such as Professor Schlesinger's *Age of Jackson* or Hasek's *The Road to Serfdom,* which was such an unexpected best seller that the University of Chicago Press turned the marketing over to a major trade house. The choice of a thesis topic, as was mentioned in Chapter xii, is as crucial as the writing of the thesis itself, precisely because of the necessity of its eligibility as a printed book.

It is obvious that trade books sell more easily through the office of a literary agent, whose approval is equated with that of a first reader in the trade house. Yet, an unpublished author now has a hard time acquiring an agent. The publisher Henry Robbins advised our seminar students to make use instead of an intermediary friend, especially a professor of literature who can write a letter to the publisher even if he has not seen the manuscript. A grant-in-aid is not needed for trade books, and indeed the offer of one might create an unfavorable impression.

Scholars are most involved with publishing houses in the area of textbooks, which can sometimes be more profitable than trade books or, certainly, scholarly tomes. Textbook publishers are usually the most agreeable to work with, for even as you are trying to sell them an idea for a text, you never lose your identity as an important customer of theirs. The editors and travelers must keep abreast of trends in every area of the humanities, sciences, and social sciences. They maintain a broader knowledge of current educational problems than most deans. They are thus aware of the inevitable growth of comparative literature, the very field in which you might have an idea for a book project.

Even before young scholars have completed their thesis and start knocking on the door of a publisher, they are well advised to appear modestly in print. Remember one final time that job applicant polled by Professor Chambers who replied bluntly "Publish. No one will look at you until you do." Thus, if you are a student and are able to get a chapter of your future thesis into a journal as an article, you will have a valuable entry for your curriculum vitae or résumé, as it is called in the world outside academia. Yet the easiest first publication for the enterprising student is usually the academic book review, as elaborately demonstrated above.

Vocational Options Other than Teaching

Of the seventy Ph.D. alumni of the NYU department at this date, the vast majority are of course engaged in teaching. We would not, however, be revealing the complete picture if we did not note that there are other positions open to graduates in this diversified discipline. Of the NYU group taken as example, two have become novelists even while teaching, taking advantage of grants and sabbaticals to pursue this difficult calling. In an age of women administrators, two of the women Ph.D.'s are deans in different parts of the country (Sarah Lawrence and the University of Illinois at Chicago). One of the Ph.D.'s is a research administrator of the Modern Language Association. One is about to become a priest and teacher. One is a director of a school in the Indian state of Kerala. One has organized our discipline at the University of Oporto, Portugal. Two are librarians in the New York area. One recently turned down a major comparative literature chairmanship in Australia to enter the fascinating commerce of aboriginal African art. One is a writer living in Italy. One teaches but occupies as well the directorship of a major Latin-American institute. One organized and chaired a world organization of junior industrial executives. In any case the interdisciplinary drive that is incorporated into our studies constitutes in some cases a centrifugal force that propels into other areas. More often it merely shows up as activity enriching our teaching: writing, acting, painting, traveling, collecting, photography, playing the market, and all the rest.

Research seminars are now being initiated to determine the diversified types of employment in major businesses and industries for which Ph.D.'s in literature might be eligible. The NYU Graduate School of Business Administration and the New York State Regents Office have offered summer grants to fifty doctoral candidates to determine in such a seminar their alternative vocational opportunities.

Much of the discussion in this chapter concerns the vocational opportunities of M.A.'s and Ph.D.'s in comparative literature. Less predictable are the opportunities available to the undergraduate who majors in our field. This concern constitutes the last paragraphs of the Nichols' Report on the undergraduate major, which states in part:

> "What can you do with comparative literature?" The question might just as well be asked of any major, since undergraduate training in North America tends to be theoretical, rather than practical in orientation. Nevertheless, whereas economics seems to suggest business, or physics a scientific career, comparative literature does not have any inherent image of career orientation. The most useful response to the question is probably the most honest one. Comparative Literature is a humanities discipline and, as such, prepares the student for almost any career in which analytical thought and verbal communication are important. A course or major in comparative literature can be part of the preparation for a wide variety of careers. Graduate and professional schools look favorably on applicants who have been adventurous enough to depart from the usual majors.

The findings of the Nichols investigation uncover undergraduate majors and minors subsequently working in fields ranging from business to medicine, from law to the performing arts. The Report also lists the more obvious vocation of secondary or college teaching of literature and its related discipline of foreign languages. One logical full- or part-time occupation is not stressed in the Report, so we shall devote a few pages to it.

Translating

Comparative literature is an excellent training for a translator. Some of America's leading translators today, such as Gregory Rabassa and Michael Benedikt, are professors in our discipline. Whereas single-language departments sometimes offer courses in translation, Professor Rabassa teaches such a course in CUNY's comparative literature department, as Erich Segal did at Yale. Thus we may consider translating as a full-time vocation or as a source of additional income. The ACLA Report of the Committee on Graduate Programs (1974) makes the surprising assertion that one of the courses most frequently required for the Ph.D. in our universities is the Art of Translation.

The affinity between comparative literature and translation is nowhere better established than at CUNY-Binghamton, where the department houses a Center for Translation and Intercultural Communication. The M.A. student who has taken three semester courses (Translation Workshop/Advanced Topics in Translation) receives a degree combining academic study with high-level vocational preparation. Students from the social sciences also enroll in these courses.

Translation, being a great and difficult art, is obviously an honored one. Kings themselves, like Alfonso the Wise and Alfred of Britain, engaged in translation. There were days when the translator—Amyot working over Plutarch's texts or Florio Englishing Montaigne—enjoyed great prestige. Some Renaissance theorists like Jacques Peletier held translation to be the truest type of creation. Robert Hillyer hails this Renaissance endeavor in his lines:

> The great Elizabethans' education
> Thrived less on lore than on superb translation.

Who can dismiss as less than masterpieces in their own right Jowett's Plato, Gilbert Murray's Greek tragedians, Hoby's *Book of the Courtier*, Schlegel's Shakespeare, Lermontov's Goethe, Baudelaire's Poe, or Nabokov's *Igor*? Three of this group were also professors.

That a translation can never capture the total meaning of the original is amusingly attested by many (we have already quoted Cervantes earlier), including the Hebrew poet who regretted that reading a translation is like kissing one's sweetheart through a veil, or Paul Valéry with his oft quoted quip that translations are like women, the more beautiful the less faithful, and vice versa. The difficulty of translating poetry discouraged Nabokov from rendering *Onegin* in verse. When his prose version came out, Anna Akhmatova observed with sarcasm that if Pushkin had wished to write *Onegin* in prose, he was perfectly capable of doing so.

Translations are obviously needed, in the field of literature as well as elsewhere, especially for comparatists venturing into the remoter areas of study. The thousands of translations from almost all languages into the more current ones that one finds in UNESCO's *Index Translationum* assures us that this vocation is universally required and practiced. Many American graduate students of literature have already undertaken commercial translating. In America and Europe it is a successful vocation and so acknowledged by the National Book Awards and PEN Club, both of which have awarded financial prizes for outstanding translations. As we shall see below, the PEN Club constantly campaigns for better payment and recognition for translators. The same effort is more vigorously sustained by the American Translators Association, which holds annual conventions and workshops.

To assess the ground that has been gained recently by professional translators, the Translation Committee of the American Center of PEN has issued reports and guidelines. These stress the problems of the translator, who must achieve the same masterful style of the author he translates. Translators must capture the rhythms, assonances, structure, and style of the original. Working from some languages like Japanese, one must patiently examine each sentence, break it into its separate parts, and then refashion it before it can be turned into English. The translator must have a total command of both languages. It is thus unlikely that translation is an art that can be taught. At our university press we have found that even graduates of the famous Translation Institute in Geneva, Switzerland, had to be double-checked for occasional mistranslation of words and especially idioms. In 1976 the Division of Research Grants of the National Endowment for the Humanities reminded us that there is money for translation by announcing an experimental program to support translations into English of major works of cultural value in foreign languages, including Chinese and Islamic (Arabic, Persian, Turkish). Applicants might request support for the duration of three years, starting in 1977.

It is stated in Chapter xii that under very special considerations a translation can be substituted for a thesis (see p. 243). If you are considering translation as a vocation or as an activity to supplement your scholarly work—translations do constitute legitimate items on your curriculum vitae—or your income, you will be pleased to learn that the American Translators Association, the PEN Club, and several New York publishers have agreed recently not only on a fixed minimal fee ($30 per 1,000 words) for routine translations, but also on what is called the Translator's Bill of Rights. It is inspired by the list of rights drawn up by the British Society of Authors. In 1967 the British group stated allegiance to four principles:

1. A translator is the creator of a literary work, within the meaning of the British Copyright Act of 1956, and is therefore the owner of the copyright of his text unless and until he has assigned it.
2. The copyright embraces publication rights in all languages, in volume and in serial publication, public performance, film and other mechanical reproduction rights.
3. Translators, particularly established translators, should make every effort to secure "license" rather than "assignment" agreements.
4. Assignment of copyright and lump-sum payment do not necessarily go together.... The translator should bargain for the best financial terms he can get—not only the rate for 1000 words, "but further payments for subsequent uses of his work."

The eleven principles enunciated by the American PEN Translation Committee have been accepted in principle by the major trade houses in this country:

1. The professional translator should receive a regular contract, similar to an author's contract, stipulating the terms of the agreement between him/her and the publisher.
2. The translator's name should appear on the title page of the work, on the jacket, and in all publicity releases and advertisements.
3. Copyright in the translation, whenever legally possible, should be in the translator's name. In any case, the translator's name should appear on the copyright page.
4. The translator of literary prose (fiction, criticism, biography, etc.) should receive a rate of *not less than* $30.00 per thousand English words. As the general price level and book prices in particular advance, this minimum should be raised proportionately. Translations of difficult languages and of difficult manuscripts should command a higher fee.
5. In addition, the translator should have a continuing share in all income derived from his/her translation of the work. To

begin with, that share should be expressed in a royalty on sales of the work. The suggested royalty should be a minimum of 2% of the list price of the original published edition. For a translation of a work in the public domain, the translator should receive a royalty of not less than 5% of the list price.

6. The translator should have a continuing share in all subsidiary earnings deriving from the use of the translation—including first and second serial rights, book-club sales, sales of the translated version to foreign publishers, paperback and cloth-bound reprints, anthologies, dramatizations and recordings in all media, etc., as are stipulated in the publisher's contract with the author of the book. The translator should also enjoy a continuing share of revenue deriving from the sales of trans-lations made from his/her translation.

7. The translator should receive 10 free copies of the work he/she has translated, and shall have the right to buy additional copies at the standard author's discount of 40%.

8. If a translated work goes out of print, the right of full owner-ship in the translation should revert to the translator, who may then attempt to place it elsewhere with another publisher, subject to agreement with the author or other holder of the copyright to the original.

9. The translator's contract should specify a time limit within which the work must be published. A suggested limit is 18 months to 2 years after delivery to the publisher and accep-tance by the publisher of the completed translation. If the work is not published within a reasonable period, the transla-tor should request that the rights revert to him/her, and all moneys already paid to the translator by the publisher should be non-returnable.

10. It is assumed that the publisher will furnish the translator with the copy-edited manuscript and/or galleys for the translator's approval.

11. Since the translator is the author of his/her text, its integrity should be respected and no changes in it should be made without the translator's consent.

Such resolutions are included in the splendid volume *The World of Translation* (New York: PEN Club, 1971), an anthology of the papers presented at the Conference on Literary Translation.

An element in the future growth of translation is of course the computer, which has developed much sophistication in the case of several languages, especially Russian-English and French-English. Illustrating this point, there will follow below the brief exchange between Pierre and Prince Andrey in Tolstoy's *War and Peace*, first as translated by Constance Garnett and then as Englished by the IBM Mark I computer. I arranged for this comparison in preparation for an article on electronic translation published in *Saturday Review*, remaining astonished by the results. The electronic translation was slightly post-edited, a rapid mechanical process. The time required by the entire process (input, output, post-editing) was probably four minutes.

Lest the reader feel from this example that the advent of sophisticated electronic translation will do away with the need for translators, let him be reassured. Computer translation can be a time-saving process by preparing a first draft for the translator, who can undertake not only the mechanical corrections required of a post-editor, but the further styling that the Mark I or the PDP 10 cannot embody in a sophisticated literary text. Furthermore, electronic translation is so expensive that it cannot soon meet the bargain cost of $30 per 1,000 words for human translation, but it will be used by wealthy employers such as the military or industrial or diplomatic agencies.

"War and Peace": Two Translations

HUMAN TRANSLATOR	ELECTRONIC TRANSLATOR
PIERRE LOOKED AT him in surprise. "But you know they say," he said, "that war is like a game of chess." "Yes," said Prince Andrey, "only with this little difference, that in chess you may think over each move as long as you please, that you are not limited as to time, and with this further difference that a knight is always stronger than a pawn and two pawns are always stronger than one, while in war a battalion is sometimes stronger than a division, and sometimes weaker than a company. No one can ever be certain of the relative strength	PIERRE WITH SURPRISE looked at him: —However, — said he, — after all, they say, that war is similar to a chess game. —Yes,— said, prince Andrey, —with that only difference, that in chess at every step you can think, sufficiently, that you are there outside of conditions of time, and yet with that difference, that the knight always is stronger than a pawn and two pawns always are stronger than one, but in war one battalion sometimes is stronger than a division, but sometimes weaker than a company. The relative

HUMAN TRANSLATOR

of armies. Believe me," he said, "if anything did depend on the arrangements made by the staff, I would be there, and helping to make them, but instead of that I have the honor of serving here in the regiment with these gentlemen here, and I consider that the day really depends upon us tomorrow and not on them . . . Success never has depended and never will depend on position, on arms, nor even on numbers; and, least of all, on position."

"On what then?"

"On the feeling that is in me and him," he indicated Timohin, "and every soldier."

Prince Andrey glanced at Timohin, who was staring in alarm and bewilderment at his colonel. In contrast to his usual reserved taciturnity, Prince Andrey seemed excited now. Apparently he could not refrain from expressing the ideas that suddenly rose to his mind.

—CONSTANCE GARNETT

ELECTRONIC TRANSLATOR

strength of troops not can be known. Believe me, — said he, — that if any thing depended on the orders of headquarters, then I would have been there and would have made orders, but instead of that I have the honor to serve here, in the regiment, here with these gentlemen, and consider that on us actually will depend tomorrow, but not on them . . . Success never depended, and will not depend, not on position, not on arming, not even on the number; but already least of all on the position.

—But on what then?

—On that feeling, that is in me, in him, — he pointed to Timokhin, — in every soldier.

Prince Andrey glanced at Timokhin, who frightened and puzzled looked at his commander. Contrary to his former restrained silence, Prince Andrey appeared now agitated. He, apparently, not could hold from the expression of those thoughts, that unexpectedly came to him.

—MARK I (slightly post-edited)

Still, despite the virtuosity exhibited here, translations will remain in the domain of scholars for a long while in the foreseeable future. For during the past few years computer research in both America and Europe has turned away from foreign language translation to other more urgent interests.

Staffing Comparative Literature in the Distant Future

A question still unanswered concerning the future expansion of comparative literature regards the thrust of staffing. The first chairmen of our discipline during the forties were identified in two ways. They were usually the product and practitioners of a national language or language-family department; they were usually considered specialists in a specific literary period. Their breadth of interest and publication may have weakened their identity with only one language or one literary period, which was often enough in those days to certify them as candidates for the chairmanship of the then program in comparative literature. To meet the challenge of teaching broader movements, themes, and genres, they undertook to retool, either by heightening or by deepening their knowledge of the movements, and so on, within their major literature or by widening geographically the knowledge of the movement or genre of their specialization. The chairman would then expand his staff by adding two or more colleagues, half or full time, from a neighboring language department. A chairman risen from the ranks in Romance languages might choose as graduate adviser an English scholar and two part-time teachers from Slavic, classics, or German. Thus, comparative theses and examinations were manned, if not courses as well.

Since that time several generations of Ph.D.'s in comparative literature have been trained. They are broader in their linguistic abilities and in their literary acquaintanceships.

For this reason, it is likely that by the end of the century staffing will be undertaken by a criterion different from that described above. Since the next generation of trained comparatists will know three or more foreign languages beyond English, the dearth of polyglots *as such* will be repaired, whereas the need of period, genre, and theme specialists will remain pressing. Of these three specializations the most appropriate for the future will surely be the period. The tradition of the well-rounded English department, with its specialists manning the Old English Chaucerian, Elizabethan, Jacobean, and other neatly packaged periods listed on page 147 will probably adumbrate the broader period specializations suitable for comparatism: Scholastic, humanist, baroque, neoclassical, romantic, and the like. For the logical candidates for employment in the future will be trained comparatists whose languages will overlap (especially if they know more than three), but their periods of specialization will not. Yet, considering the 120 unbudgeted units of manpower about which you complained to Dean Midas on page 62 (and who will by the year 2000, it is hoped, have found some slush fund for the purpose), there will always be, to borrow the slang of the moment, a piece of the action for any colleague truly interested in comparative literature, no matter what his or her language or specialization.

In Conclusion

So now we must part. Boileau would have disapproved of the *moi haïssable* inevitably crowding into the preceding pages, but I count on the *vous aimable* to understand why it had to be. For I have doubtless spanned more of the twentieth century than you, this century that has witnessed the greatest transformation in the study of literature since the invention of printing incited a desire to read vernacular texts, and to own them, in the rising burgher classes of Europe. In a search for normative principles and practices, and recalling my own trials and errors, I have taken throughout these pages many a stand. Let me lean on the example of Luther, who advanced strong positions and theses mainly to provoke free discussion among his fellow professors at Wittenberg. However, free discussion of these stands has indeed taken place with the many colleagues who have read the book script whole or in part and whose names appear in the introduction. Their suggestions, criticisms, and objections have infiltrated these pages. Even a few graduate students and alumni have generously accepted to read the text and make comments. A study of the comparative literature pages of dozens of university bulletins here and abroad clarified current collective departmental practices and came up with many a surprise.

Having concluded and stated which principles and practices seem most consistent, productive, and ethical, I am only too aware that the breakthrough of comparative literature even now is conditioned by economic factors in our colleges and universities, and that in the governance of our departments many will have to make occasional compromises with principle as well as practice. These same economic factors will occasionally oblige you readers who are students to make similar compromises of your own, such as taking a language examination when you think you can pass it rather than when you really know the language. Whether professor or student, *cher semblable*, tighten your belt and your resolve, adhere to principle whenever you can, and know that the goal will justify your effort and perseverance.

Appendix: Organizational Structure of the Discipline

If all the structural elements of the world's academic body are eventually fitted within the pyramid of the Union Académique Internationale, we comparatists cannot deny that we fit within this structure under the International Federation for Modern Languages and Literature, centered at Cambridge University, England. If UNESCO sets IFMLL (known in the Romance countries as FILLM) on a parallel with the International Comparative Literature Association (or AILC at its secretariat presently in Utrecht), its altimeter is not functioning well, for, as we explain below, AILC was a spin-off organization of FILLM, on a level with the Modern Language Association, the Associazione Internazionale per gli Studi di Lingua e Letteratura Italiana, and comparable groups. Indeed, at the triennial meetings of the FILLM, all associations of the level of AILC send a delegate to the governing bureau of the FILLM. Furthermore, as I learned while representing AISLLI at the FILLM Bureau session in Sydney, Australia, FILLM has usually solicited and received UNESCO funds on behalf of the triennial congresses at the AILC level.

International Federation of Modern Languages and Literatures

The parent organization of all academic literary associations is, as stated above, the FILLM, the French acronym of the International Federation of Modern Languages and Literatures, situated at the top of the pyramid housing the ILCA, the MLA, the ACLA, and the entire aggregation of sixteen language/literature

311

associations of the world, with members in eighty-seven countries. Founded in 1928 as the International Committee on Modern Literary History, it changed to its present structure in 1951. Its objective is to establish permanent contact between historians of literature, to develop or perfect facilities for their work, and to promote the study of the history of modern literature. Obviously, a look at any recent program of the Federation's triennial congresses will easily convince one that the Federation is as much interested in literary criticism as history. The Federation has been from the beginning under the direction of an English directorate (see below). It has held congresses in such off-the-main-road centers as Pakistan and (Sydney) Australia. FILLM is the official unit of UNESCO that negotiates subsidies for projects and publications in modern literatures and (as stated) has indeed obtained monies for the ICLA.

Like PEN Club, it has sometimes been an activist in problems of academic freedom. Once traditionalist and philological in its approach to literature, it has become willing to "flow with the tides," as demonstrated during the planning of the 1978 Congress at Aix, stressing structuralism and semiotics. It is committed to a policy of opening its meetings to more Asians and Africans. Yet it is more programmatically advanced toward study of individual literatures of the world than the ICLA. Its publications are the *Répertoire Chronologique des littératures modernes* and the *Acts* of the triennial congresses.

Presidents are elected for a three-year term; the two most recent have been from Japan and Australia. The secretariat is presently located at Ste. Catherine's College, Cambridge CB2 1RL, England. Its pioneer secretary-general under its present structure has been Professor S. C. Aston.

International Comparative Literature Association

When the International Federation of Modern Languages and Literatures met in Oxford in 1954, its sixth triennial gathering, a group of comparatists broke away and founded the International Comparative Literature Association (also AILC). Both associations continued their triennial meetings, avoided a conflict of dates, and the parent FILLM continued to encourage and help obtain subvention for the ICLA, especially from UNESCO in subsequent years. The first ICLA meeting was held in Venice the following year with a unifying theme of Venice in modern literatures. Its first copresidents were Jean-Marie Carré of the Sorbonne and Carlo Pellegrini of Florence. The second congress met in Chapel Hill and chose as its theme methodology in comparative literature. Elected copresidents were Marcel Bataillon of the Collège de France and Werner P. Friederich of North Carolina. Successive congresses were held in Utrecht (1961), Freiburg (1964), Belgrade (1967), Bordeaux (1970), Montreal (1973), Budapest (1976), and Brussels (1979).

In view of the discouragement of the study of foreign literatures under Premiers Stalin and Brezhnev, it was welcome to find an increasing number of delegates from the Socialist Republics in attendance after Belgrade. However, the Marxist or sociopolitical emphasis of so many of the delegates from Western Europe has tended to polarize the papers and discussions. It is hoped that two major bibliographical projects will transcend this polarization: an international dictionary of literary terms and a European history of literatures. The inclusion of Asian and African literatures in the program of the meeting at Bordeaux indicated a centrifugal trend in interest and parallels a similar trend in the parent organization, the FILLM.

A general office is located at the Institut de Littérature générale et comparée, 17 Rue de la Sorbonne, 75005 Paris, France. The secretariat for the Americas is located at the Comparative Literature Department, State University of New York at Binghamton, Binghamton, New York 13901. The secretariat for other parts of the world is located at the Institute of Comparative Literature, University of Utrecht, Utrecht, the Netherlands.

PEN Club International

The PEN Club was organized in London in October, 1921, right after the hostilities of World War I, with John Galsworthy as president. The name was an acronym for poets, playrights, editors, essayists, and novelists. Publishers, professors, critics, book reviewers, and literary agents are also active in this agreeable confraternity. Within six months Anatole France presided over the Paris Center, and by April, 1922, the American affiliate held its first dinner meeting in midtown Manhattan. It was to be a habitat for activists and comparatists, following the first tenet of its charter, phrased by Galsworthy:

> Literature, national though it be in origin, knows no frontiers, and should remain common currency between nations in spite of political or international upheavals.

Like FILLM and ICLA, PEN Club sponsors international literary congresses, but on an annual basis. These have been truly cosmopolitan, having occurred in such faraway places as Buenos Aires, Stockholm, Tokyo, Rio de Janeiro, Oslo, Abidjan, and Seoul, as well as in more predictable Western Heritage countries. Its eighty-two centers spread over the globe, many of them publishing news bulletins. (This writer has lectured to PEN Club chapters in such out-of-the-way centers as Teheran and Manila.) It is the one literary association that serves as watchdog for freedom of the writer and the press the world over. Persecution of authors triggers collective action under the vigorous leadership of such recent internationalist presidents as Arthur Miller and Heinrich Böll. It seeks continual improvement in the lot and freedom of writers and translators and serves as a conciliating force between writers and publishers.

Many academics belong to PEN Club. Although membership is by nomination and members have to qualify with two or more previously published books, many panels, speeches, discussions, and conventions of PEN are open to all interested literary scholars, translators, and editors. Since the dues are nominal, and the round tables and receptions so stimulating, this association whose international perspectives coincide with those of comparatists provides a natural climate for us, and an informal opportunity to exchange ideas with active writers and publishers. The American Center is located at 156 Fifth Avenue, New York City 10010.

American Comparative Literature Association

The American comparatists founded their own association in 1960, seven years after the first triennial meeting of the ICLA so that their gatherings would always trail by one year the congress of the parent organization. The founders and first presidents were Werner Friederich of North Carolina, René Wellek of Yale, Harry Levin of Harvard, Chandler Beall of Oregon, Horst Frenz of Indiana, Haskell Block of SUNY-Binghamton, and Anna Balakian of New York University. It has held triennial meetings in all parts of the country, as well as special events, such as a bicentennial colloquium in Philadelphia and a binational meeting with our Canadian colleagues. It maintains its close affiliation with ICLA and plays a role in the planning of the international congresses. It is estimated that almost one third of the membership of ICLA is made up of its American component. ACLA supports a valuable *Newsletter*, containing essays, reports, announcements, and statistics. A spin-off publication, independently edited, is the annual *Yearbook of Comparative and General Literature* published at the University of Indiana. Special reports and bulletins supported by ACLA treat of professional standards, undergraduate studies, vocational opportunities, and the interrelating of the arts with literature (the *Heliconian*). The ACLA takes a special interest in two periodicals, *Comparative Literature* and *Comparative Literature Studies*.

The various activities and thrusts of ACLA are revealed in the names of the active committees, renewable every three years: publications, research tools, bibliography, literature and the other arts, undergraduate programs, doctoral programs, professional opportunities, honors and awards, the constitution, and a recently created finance committee. Much of the researches of these committees and their reports has been utilized in the writing of the present book.

Provision is made for closer relationships with regional associations such as the Southern and the South Central Comparative Literature Associations or the Eastern Comparative Literature Conference, held annually since 1964 on Washington Square, in New York City. Meetings of the Advisory Board are held at the conventions and in connection with the MLA annual meetings. Comparative literature panels, as well as the evening comparative literature meeting at the MLA congresses attest to a close relationship with MLA, both of these associations being parallel constituent members of the American Council of Learned Societies. Students are especially welcome as members.

The secretariat is currently located at the Department of Comparative Literature, State University of New York, Binghamton, New York 13901. The secretary-treasurer is Frederick Garber.

Modern Language Association of America

The MLA, like commencement speakers, "needs no introduction." The Philological Society of England (1842), which compiled the *New English Dictionary*, and the Early English Text Society (1864) inspired the founding of two comparable organizations in America, the American Philological Society (1868) and the Modern Language Association, which first met at Columbia University in December, 1883. It was partially inspired by an appeal of Charles Francis Adams, in a Phi Beta Kappa address at Harvard, for a lesser stress on classical languages and a greater one on the modern ones. However, since a philological journal was proposed at the end of the first meeting and since some of the major pioneers were literary scholars of prominence, it was fated that the MLA should divide its attentions between language and literature. From its first secretary-editor, A. Marshall Elliott of Johns Hopkins, to his present successor, William D. Schaefer, a distinguished roster of scholars has raised it to its eminence and influence, buttressed by constituent or satellite language organizations all over the country. Indeed, Canadian scholars as well are active in it. In addition to its quarterly florilegium of scholarly essays, the quarterly *Publications* (*PMLA*) since 1929 has published the unique International Bibliography of Books and Articles on Modern Languages and Literatures. The first MLA Section on Comparative Literature met during the Washington, D.C., session in 1946, although Werner Friederich has written in *YCGL* that the MLA Congress of 1948 (in New York) heralded acceptance of our discipline. MLA has published many texts and teaching aids for departments of English and foreign languages, and is now planning to do the same for comparative literature (see p. 232). As stated in Chapter xv, it plays a role in finding jobs for young scholars of literature, including comparative literature.

It was the MLA that rallied linguists, philologists, and anthropologists with grants secured from the government and

Rockefeller Foundation to set up the multilingual ASTP and CATP army language programs. These programs dispelled the linguistic isolationism of America and made possible the resurgence of comparative literature immediately after the war. Slowly the MLA, whose executive secretaries have traditionally been professors of English, has become a strong supporter of comparative literature. That the long-hoped-for close cooperation between MLA and ACLA has come about at last is especially appropriate now that both are equally constituent members of the American Council of Learned Societies.

The MLA roster of honorary members includes some of the most distinguished foreign scholars, while its honorary fellows number many of the world's greatest writers and thinkers.

The annual MLA convention, always occurring in the dead of winter, between Christmas and New Year's Day—as in 1883—is one of the established fixities of American academic life. Characterized by competing lectures and sessions, publishers' cocktail parties, job interviews, trade and university press book exhibits, planning and policy sessions in smoke-filled parlors, these congresses are calculated to last up to the point preceding complete exhaustion. The variety and sometimes overspecialized nature of the papers read have been commemorated in the satirical poem composed by Morris Bishop (see p. 292).

The secretariat of the Modern Language Association is located at 62 Fifth Avenue, New York City 10011. The executive director is William D. Schaefer.

A Multiplicity of Choices

It becomes clear from the preceding pages that professors and students of comparative literature may rub (and lift) elbows at a considerable number of conventions during a given triennium. For example, in that period of time a conscientious comparatist could attend three MLA conventions, one ACLA convention, one ICLA congress, one FILLM congress, three PEN meetings, and at least six annual regional conferences of comparative literature. Thus, in a triennium our conscientious colleagues could find themselves attending at least fifteen such literary events. Colleagues interested in world literature would also be attracted to the triennial

Asian Writers' Conferences or the East-West meetings at Tamkang College in Taipei, Taiwan. Medievalists would surely attend the conventions of the Mediaeval Academy. Other societies that attract comparatists to meetings are the Renaissance Society, the Society for Eighteenth Century Studies, the Center for Inter-American Relations, the Conference on Christianity and Litera-ture, the International Arthurian Society, to mention only a few. We are surely provided with a movable feast.

In order that we may attend congresses of the parent organiza-tion, the FILLM, and its derivatives, ICLA and ACLA, these meetings are staggered to avoid overlapping. Thus, when FILLM meets, for example, in 1978 and 1981, ICLA meets in 1979 and 1982, and ACLA meets accordingly in 1980 and 1983. Such congresses, each one dedicated to a few chosen themes, comple-ment the crowded and diversified annual conventions of the MLA, which in 1968 drew the till now maximum total of 14,000 faculty and students.

National Associations and Research Institutes of Comparative Literature[1]

A variety of national comparative literature associations has proliferated and still proliferates on all continents, parallel with the ACLA on the pyramid crowned by the FILLM. Below the peak are a number of well-known institutes.[1]

CANADA (since 1969)
Association Canadienne de Littérature Comparée
Department of Comparative Literature, University of Alberta
Edmonton, Alberta T6G 2E6

Institut de Littérature Comparée
(address as above)
FEDERAL REPUBLIC OF GERMANY
Deutsche Gesellschaft für allgemeine und vergleichende
    Literaturwissenschaft

---

[1] A South Korean association has existed since 1959, an Algerian association since 1964, a Philippine association since 1969, and a Hungarian association since 1971.

University of Bonn
Bonn

Institut für Komparatistik
Technische Hochschule, Aachen
Templergraben 55, 55 Aachen
FRANCE (from 1954)
Société française de littérature comparée
Institut de Littérature Comparée, Université de Caen,
Caen

Institut de Littérature générale et comparée
Université de Paris
17 Rue de la Sorbonne, 75005 Paris
JAPAN (since 1954)
Nihon Hikaku Bungakai
Aovania Gakum University
Shibuya-ku, Tokyo
NETHERLANDS
Nederlandse vereniging voor algemene literatuurwetenschap
c/o Institute of Comparative Literature
University of Utrecht, Utrecht

Instituut voor algemene literatuurwetenschap
Rijksuniversiteit Utrecht
Ramstraat 31, Utrecht
REPUBLIC OF CHINA
Comparative Literature Association of the Republic of China
National Taiwan University, Taipei, Taiwan

Western Literature Research Institute
Tamkang College, Tamsui, Taiwan
ROMANIA
Comitetul national pentru literatura comparata
Str. Onesti 11, Bucharest
RUSSIA
A. M. Gorki Institute of World Literature
Vorovskogo Street, 25a, Moscow

Bibliography

I. Books on Comparative Literature

Aldridge, A. O., ed. *Comparative Literature: Matter and Method.* Urbana: Univ. of Illinois Press, 1969.

————. *Comparative Literature: East and West* (in Japanese). Foreword by Shunsuke Kamei. Tokyo: Nan'un Do Co., 1977.

Auerbach, Erich. *Mimesis: The Representation of Reality in Western Literature.* Trans. Willard R. Trask. Princeton: Princeton Univ. Press, 1953.

Block, Haskell H. *Nouvelles tendances en littérature comparée.* Paris: Nizet, 1970.

Brandt Corstius, Jan. *Introduction to the Comparative Study of Literature.* New York: Random House, 1968.

Cioranescu, Alexandru. *Principios de literatura comparada.* Teneriffa: La Laguna, 1964.

Curtius, Ernst Robert. *Europäische Literatur und lateinisches Mittelalter.* Bern: Francke, 1948.

Deugd, Cornelis de. *De Eenheid van het Comparatisme.* Utrecht: Rijksuniversitet te Utrecht, 1962.

Dima, Alexandru. *Principii de literaturā comparatā.* Bucharest: Ed. Academiei, 1969.

Durisin, Dionyz. *Problemy literarnej komparatistiky.* Bratislava: Vydavatel Stvo Slovenskej Akademie vied, 1967. German version: *Vergleichende Literaturforschung.* Ed. Ludwig Richter. Berlin: Akademie-Verlag, 1972.

Escarpit, Robert. *Sociologie de la littérature.* Paris: Presses Universitaires, 1958.

Étiemble, René. *Comparaison n'est pas raison.* Paris: Gallimard, 1963. English version: *The Crisis in Comparative Literature.* Trans. Georges Joyaux and Herbert Weisinger. East Lansing: Michigan State Univ. Press, 1966.

Farinelli, Arturo. *Aufsätze, Reden und Charakteristiken zur Weltliteratur.* Leipzig: Schroeder, 1925.

Fransen, J. *Iets over vergelijkende literatuurstudie, "perioden" en "invloeden."* Groningen: Wolters, 1936

Friederich, Werner. *The Challenge of Comparative Literature and Other Addresses.* Chapel Hill: Univ. of North Carolina Press, 1970.

Gicovate, Bernardo. *Conceptos fundamentales de literatura comparada.* San Juan: Ediciones Asomante, 1962.

Gifford, Henry. *Comparative Literature.* London: Routledge and Kegan Paul, 1969.

Guyard, Marius-François. *La Littérature comparée.* 3rd ed. Paris: Presses Universitaires, 1969.

Hermand, Jost. *Synthetisches Interpretieren: Zur Methode der Literaturwissenschaft.* Munich: Nymphenburger, 1969.

Hilal, Muhammad. *The Role of Comparative Literature in Contemporary Arabic Literary Studies* (in Arabic). Cairo: Inst. of Advanced Arabic Studies, 1962.

Jameson, Raymond de Loy. *A Comparison of Literatures.* London: Routledge and Kegan Paul, 1935.

Jeune, Simon. *Littérature générale et littérature comparée.* Paris: Les Lettres Modernes, 1968.

Jost, François. *Introduction to Comparative Literature.* Indianapolis: Bobbs-Merrill, 1974.

Kataoka, Jintaro. *An Analytical Approach to Comparative Literature.* Tokyo: Shinozaki Shorin, 1970.

Krauss, Werner. *Probleme der vergleichenden Literaturgeschichte.* Berlin: Akademie-Verlag, 1965.

Levin, Harry. *Refractions: Essays in Comparative Literature.* New York: Oxford Univ. Press, 1966.

Lukács, George. *Theory of the Novel.* Trans. Anna Bostock. Cambridge: MIT Press, 1972.

Mayo, Robert S. *Herder and the Beginnings of Comparative Literature.* Chapel Hill: Univ. of North Carolina Press, 1969.

McNair, Waldo. *Studies in Comparative Literature.* Baton Rouge: Univ. of Louisiana Press, 1962.

Nakajima, Kenzo, and Yoshio Nakano. *Hikaku Bungaku jostesu* (Preface to Comparative Literature). Tokyo: Yajima Shobo, 1951.

Neupokoeva, Irina G. *Problemy vzaimodeistviia sovremennykh literatur.* Moscow: Akademie Nauk, 1963.

Nichols, Stephen G. *Comparatists at Work.* Waltham, Mass.: Ginn, 1968.

Ocvirk, Anton. *Teorija primerjalne literarne zgodovine.* Ljubljana: Znanstveno Društvo, 1936.

Ota, Saburo. *Hikaku Bungaku* (Comparative Literature). Tokyo: Kenkyu-Sha, 1958.

Peyre, Henri. *Les Générations littéraires.* Paris: Boivin, 1948.

Pichois, Claude, and André Rousseau. *La Littérature comparée.* Paris: Armand Colin, 1967.

Porta, Antonio. *La letteratura comparata nella storia e nella critica.* Milan: Marzorati, 1951.

Posnett, Hutcheson Macauley. *Comparative Literature.* 1886; rpt. New York: Johnson Reprints, 1970.

Prawer, S. S. *Comparative Literature Studies: An Introduction.* New York: Barnes and Noble, 1973.

Rudiger, Horst, ed. *Zur Theorie der vergleichenden Literaturwissenschaft.* Berlin: de Gruyter, 1971.

————. *Komparatistik: Aufgaben und Methoden.* Stuttgart: Kohlhammer, 1973.

Silveira, Tasso da. *Literatura Comparada.* Rio de Janeiro: Edições GRD, 1964.

Stallknecht, Newton, and Horst Frenz, eds. *Comparative Literature: Method and Perspective.* Carbondale: Southern Illinois Univ. Press, 1961.

Strelka, Joseph. *Vergleichende Literaturkritik: Drei Essays zur Methodologie der Literaturwissenschaft.* Bern: Francke, 1970.

Strich, Fritz. *Goethe and World Literature.* Trans. C. A. M. Sym. 1949; rpt. Port Washington, N.Y.: Kennikat, 1971.

Texte, Joseph. *Jean-Jacques Rousseau et les origines du cosmopolitisme littéraire.* Paris: Hachette, 1895.

Trousson, Raymond. *Un Problème de littérature comparée: Les Etudes de thèmes.* Paris: Les Lettres Modernes, 1965.

Van Tieghem, Paul. *La Littérature comparée.* Paris: Colin, 1946.

Voisine, Jacques, ed. *Connaissance de l'étranger.* Paris: Didier, 1964.

Wais, Kurt. *Forschungsprobleme der vergleichende Literaturgeschichte.* 2 vols. Vol. I: Tübingen: Universität Tübingen, 1950; Vol. II: Tübingen: Niemayer, 1958.

Wehrli, Max. *Allgemeine Literaturwissenschaft.* Bern: Francke, 1969.

Weisstein, Ulrich. *Einführung in die vergleichende Literaturwissenschaft.* Stuttgart: Kohlhammer, 1968. English version: *Comparative Literature and Literary Theory.* Trans. William Riggan. Bloomington: Indiana Univ. Press, 1973.

Wellek, René, and Austin Warren. *Theory of Literature.* 3rd ed. New York: Harcourt, Brace, 1962.

Wrenn, C. L. *The Idea of Comparative Literature.* Leeds: Modern Humanities Research Assn., 1968.

Yano, Hojin. *Hikaku Bungaku* (Comparative Literature). Tokyo: Nan-Un-Do, 1956.

II. Comparative Literature Journals

1876–77   *La Rivista internazionale brittanica, germanica, slava,* ed. Fanfani e Giusti

1887–88   *Acta comparationis litterarum universarum* (Klausenburg, Hungary)

1886–1910   *Zeitschrift für vergleichende Literaturgeschichte* (Leipzig, Germany), ed. Max Koch

1921–   *Revue de littérature comparée* (Paris: Didier), ed. Baldensperger and Van Tieghem [founders]

1927–   *World Literature Today* (formerly, *Books Abroad*) (Norman, Oklahoma), ed. Ivar Ivask

1942–46   *Comparative Literature Studies* (Liverpool)

1943–   *Orbis Litterarum* (Odense, Denmark)

1948–   *La Rivista di letterature moderne e comparate* (Florence: Sansoni)

1949–   *Comparative Literature* (Eugene, Oregon)

1954–   *Hikaku Bungaku Kenkyu* (Comparative Literature Research) (Tokyo)

1958–   *Hikaku Bungaku* (Comparative Literature) (Tokyo)

1960–   *Yearbook of Comparative and General Literature* (Bloomington, Indiana)

1961–   *Journal of Comparative Literature* (Calcutta: Jadavpur Univ.)

1962–   *Comparative Literature Studies* (Urbana, Illinois), ed. A. Owen Aldridge [founder]

1966–   *Arcadia: Zeitschrift für Vergleichende Literaturwissenschaft* (Berlin), ed. Walter de Gruyter

1966–   *Cahiers algériens de littérature comparée* (Algiers)

1970–   *Tamkang Review: Comparative Studies between Chinese and Foreign Literatures* (Taipei) [biennial]

1972–   *Mosaic: A Journal for the Comparative Study of Literature* (Winnipeg: Univ. of Manitoba)

1972–   *American Comparative Literature Association Newsletter* (Binghamton: State Univ. of New York)

1973–   *Neohelicon: Acta Comparationis Litterarum Universarum* (Budapest: International Comparative Literature Association)

1974–   *Canadian Review of Comparative Literature / Revue canadienne de littérature comparée* (Edmonton: Univ. of Alberta)

1975–   *Synthesis* (Bucharest: National Committee of Comparative Literature, Academy of Sciences)

1977–   *The Comparatist: Annual Journal of the Southern Comparative Literature Association* (Raleigh: North Carolina State Univ.)

III. A Selective Bibliography of Bibliographies, Prepared by George Thompson

A. COMPARATIVE LITERATURE

Baldensperger, Fernand, and Werner P. Friederich. *A Bibliography of Comparative Literature.* Chapel Hill: Univ. of North Carolina Press, 1950.

Betz, L. P. *La Littérature comparée: Essai bibliographique.* Strassbourg: Trübner, 1904. 2nd ed., rev. Fernand Baldensperger.

"Annual Bibliography." *Yearbook of Comparative and General Literature*, 1 (1952) through 19 (1970). [Discontinued.]

"Bibliographie." *Revue de littérature comparée*, 1 (1921) through 34 (1960). [Discontinued; also published separately for 1949 through 1959.]

B. INTERNATIONAL LITERATURE

MLA International Bibliography of Books and Articles on the Modern Languages and Literatures. New York: Modern Language Association, 1921– . [Originally a special issue of *PMLA*. Through 1955 listed work by American scholars only. Now organized in three independent sections.]

Bulletin signalétique, Part 523: Histoire et science de la littérature. Paris: C.N.R.S., 1961– . [Quarterly.]

Humanities Index. New York: H. W. Wilson, 1974– . [Quarterly.]

MLA Abstracts of Articles in Scholarly Journals. New York: Modern Language Association, 1970–75. [Discontinued. Annual, selective.]

The Year's Work in Modern Language Studies. London: Modern Humanities Research Assn., 1931– . [Annual. Evaluative. European literature only. Covers 1929/30 on.]

L'Année philologique: Bibliographie critique et analytique de l'antiquité gréco-latine. Paris: Les Belles Lettres, 1928– . [Annual. Covers 1924 on.]

International Medieval Bibliography. Leeds: Univ. of Leeds, 1968– . [Two issues per year. Covers 1967 on.]

"Bibliographie." *Cahiers de civilisation médiévale: X^e–XIIe siècles*, 1 (1958)– . [Annual from 12 (1969).]

Fisher, John H. *The Medieval Literature of Western Europe: A Review of Research, Mainly 1930–1960.* New York: New York Univ. Press, for the Modern Language Association, 1966.

Bibliographie internationale de l'humanisme et de la renaissance. Geneva: Librairie Droz, 1966– . [Annual. Covers from 1965 on.]

"Litterature of the Renaissance." *Studies in Philology,* 20 (1923) through 66 (1969). [Discontinued. Covered the English Renaissance only through 35 (1938).]

"The Eighteenth Century: A Current Bibliography." *Philological Quarterly,* 50 (1971)– .

"The Romantic Movement: A Selective and Critical Bibliography." *English Language Notes,* 3 (1965–66)– . [From 1937 on had appeared in other journals, see next item.]

The Romantic Movement Bibliography, 1936–1970: A Master Cumulation from ELH, Philological Quarterly, and English Language Notes. 7 vols. Ann Arbor: Pierian Press, 1973.

"Current Bibliography." *Twentieth Century Literature,* 1 (1955)– . [Annotated. In each issue.]

Pownall, D. E. *Articles on Twentieth Century Literature: An Annotated Bibliography, 1954 to 1970.* 5 vols. to date. New York: Kraus-Thomson, 1973– . [A cumulation of the bibliography above, with additions.]

Sader, M. *Comprehensive Index to English-Language Little Magazines, 1890–1970: Series One.* Millwood, N.Y.: Kraus-Thomson, 1976. [100 titles.]

C. LITERATURES OF NATIONS AND CONTINENTS

Annual Bibliography of English Language and Literature. London: Modern Humanities Research Assn., 1921– . [Covers English, American, and Commonwealth literature.]

The Year's Work in English Studies. London: English Assn., 1921– . [Covers from 1919; has included American literature since 1954. Evaluative.]

New Cambridge Bibliography of English Literature. 5 vols. Cambridge: Cambridge Univ. Press, 1969–77.

Literary History of the United States. 4th ed., revised. 2 vols. New York: Macmillan, 1974. [Vol. II: *Bibliography.* Selective and annotated.]

American Literary Scholarship. Durham, N.C.: Duke Univ. Press, 1965– . [Covers from 1963 on. Evaluative.]

"Annual Bibliography of Commonwealth Literature." *Journal of Commonwealth Literature,* 1 (1965)– .

New, W. H. *Critical Writings on Commonwealth Literature: A Selec-*

tive Bibliography to 1970. University Park: Pennsylvania State Univ. Press, 1975.

Bibliographie der französischen Literaturwissenschaft. Frankfurt: Klosterman, 1960– . [Covers from 1956 on.]

Bibliographie de la littérature française du Moyen Âge à nos jours. Paris: Librairie A. Colin, 1967– .

"Bibliographie." *Revue d'histoire littéraire de la France,* 52 (1952)– . [Quarterly. Continues the annual bibliography above.]

Osburn, Charles B. *Research and Reference Guide to French Studies.* Metuchen, N.J.: Scarecrow Press, 1968. Supplementary volume, 1972.

Puppo, M. *Manuale critico-bibliografico per lo studio della letteratura italiana.* 12th ed. Turin: Soc. Editrice Internationale, 1972.

Repertorio bibliografico della storia e della critica della letteratura italiana. [Volumes by various editors and publishers, covers 1902 through 1953.]

Simon Díaz, J. *Manual de bibliografía de la literatura española.* 2nd ed. Madrid. Consejo Superior de Investigaciones Científicas, 1971.

Paci, A. M. *Manual de bibliografía española.* Pisa: Univ. of Pisa, 1970.

Rela, W. *Guía bibliográfica de la literatura hispanoamericana desde el siglo XIX hasta 1970.* Buenos Aires: Casa Pardo, 1970.

Flores, Angel. *Bibliografía de escritores hispanoamericanos / A Bibliography of Spanish American Writers, 1609–1974.* New York: Gordian, 1975.

Bibliographie der deutschen Sprach- und Literaturwissenschaft. Frankfurt: Klostermann, 1957– . [Covers from 1945 on.]

Köttelwesch, C. *Bibliographisches Handbuch der deutschen Literaturwissenschaft, 1945–1969.* 2 vols. Frankfurt: Klostermann, 1971–77.

Handbuch der deutschen Literaturgeschichte: Abteilung Bibliographien. Bern: Francke, 1969– . [12 vols. projected, by various authors; 11 published to date.]

Herdeck, D. E. *African Authors: A Companion to Black African Writing, 1300–1973.* Washington, D.C.: Inscape Corp., 1973.

Jahn, J. *Bibliography of Creative African Writing.* Nendeln: Kraus-Thomson, 1971.

International African Bibliography: Current Books, Articles and Papers in African Studies. London: Mansell, 1971– . [Quarterly.]

Cumulative Bibliography of African Studies: Author Catalogue [and] *Classified Catalogue.* 5 vols. Boston: G. K. Hall, 1973. [Cumulates bibliographies published from 1929 to early 1970s, including the bibliography above.]

Index Islamicus, 1906–1955: A Catalogue of Articles on Islamic Subjects in Periodicals and Other Collective Publications. London: Mansell, 1958. [Continued by supplements through 1975. To be continued by *Quarterly Index Islamicus.*]

"Abstracta Islamica: Bibliographie sélective des études islamiques," a supplement to *Revue des études islamiques*, 1 (1927)– . [Annual.]

Bibliography of Asian Studies. Ann Arbor: Assn. for Asian Studies, 1971– . [Annual. Covers from 1969 on.]

Cumulative Bibliography of Asian Studies, 1941–1965. Author Bibliography. 4 vols. Boston: G. K. Hall, 1969. *Subject Bibliography.* 4 vols. Boston: G. K. Hall, 1970. [Supplements in 6 vols. cover 1966–70.]

D. General Guides to Reference Works

Walford, A. J. *Guide to Reference Material.* 3rd ed. 3 vols. London: Library Assn., 1973–77. [Vol. III covers languages and literatures of the world, the arts, and general sources. Vol. II covers philosophy, religion, and history, among other subjects.]

Sheehy, E. *Guide to Reference Books.* 9th ed. Chicago: American Library Assn., 1976.

Bibliographic Index: A Cumulative Bibliography of Bibliographies. New York: H. W. Wilson, 1945– . [Covers from 1937 on.]

Bibliographische Berichte / Bibliographical Bulletin. Frankfurt: Klostermann, 1959– .

Reynolds, M. M. *A Guide to Theses and Dissertations: An Annotated International Bibliography of Bibliographies.* Detroit: Gale Research, 1975.

Index of Names

Index of Colleges and Universities

341